Worlds

 bot

very

erica

Explorers of New Worlds

John Cabot

and the Rediscovery
of North America

Charles J. Shields

Chelsea House Publishers
Philadelphia

Prepared for Chelsea House Publishers by:
OTTN Publishing, Stockton, N.J.

CHELSEA HOUSE PUBLISHERS
Editor in Chief: Sally Cheney
Associate Editor in Chief: Kim Shinners
Production Manager: Pamela Loos
Art Director: Sara Davis
Director of Photography: Judy L. Hasday
Project Editors: LeeAnne Gelletly, Brian Baughan
Series Designer: Keith Trego

First Printing
1 3 5 7 9 8 6 4 2

Library of Congress Cataloging-in-Publication Data

Shields, Charles J., 1951–
   John Cabot and the rediscovery of North
   America / Charles J. Shields.
     p. cm. – (Explorers of new worlds)
Includes bibliographical references and index.
ISBN 0-7910-6438-7 (hc) – ISBN 0-7910-6439-5 (pbk.)
1. Cabot, John, d. 1498?–Juvenile literature. 2. North
America–Discovery and exploration–English–Juvenile
literature. 3. Explorers–North America–Biography–
Juvenile literature. 4. Explorers–England–Biography–
Juvenile literature. 5. Explorers–Italy–Biography–
Juvenile literature. [1. Cabot, John, d. 1498?
2. Explorers. 3. America–Discovery and exploration–
English.] I. Title. II. Series.

E129.C1 S55 2001
970.01'7–dc21

                          2001028274

Contents

Who Was
John Cabot?

In this painting, John Cabot says farewell to King Henry VII of England. Cabot is preparing to depart from Bristol on a voyage west across the Atlantic Ocean.

I

n December 18, 1497, Raimondo di Soncino wrote a letter to the duke of Milan, a city in what is now Italy. The duke had sent Soncino as an **envoy**, or agent, to live in London. His purpose was to arrange business deals that favored Milan—and to keep an ear open for information. In his letter, Soncino shares news he has heard about a remarkable English sea voyage commanded by a fellow Italian, John Cabot.

In the letter, Soncino calls Cabot by his Italian name, Zoanne Caboto, and describes him as a gentleman who is "very expert in *navigation*." Soncino wrote that in May of 1497, Cabot sailed from Bristol, England, with a crew of 18 men. After stopping in Ireland, his little ship continued westward and slightly north.

After wandering for a long time, Cabot finally returned, claiming incredible discoveries. For instance, Cabot reported sailing into uncharted waters brimming with fish. The crew had only to lower a basket and pull up a big catch! Moreover, Cabot had sighted new lands, waded ashore, and claimed them for England. These new lands, according to Cabot, were excellent places and fairly warm. Perhaps even silk could be found there.

Then Soncino grows excited in his letter. He tells the duke that Cabot's first voyage was only the beginning. Cabot planned to sail even farther west until he reached an island called Cipango (Japan), "where he believes that all the *spices* of the world, as well as the jewels, are found." Cabot might be right, Soncino tells the duke, for provided the world is round and not too large, "the route [for spices] would not cost more than it costs now." The king of

England himself, Henry VII, had already offered to supply ships for Cabot's next voyage.

When he read this letter, the Duke of Milan must have wondered what John Cabot's thrilling discoveries really meant, if the stories were true. What strange places had he found that were not shown on the maps of the day? How did Cabot convince the king of England to put up large sums of money for sailing west and north from England in search of a spice route? After all, had not Christopher Columbus just pointed the way to the Orient by sailing west and south from Spain only five years earlier, in 1492? Was Cabot right in thinking that another route existed over the northwest top of the world?

We know now that Cabot had not reached Asia–just as Columbus had not–but had landed instead somewhere near Newfoundland. He then sailed south, perhaps as far as New England. This does not take away from his achievement. The success of his adventure took years of preparation. And the "new founde lande" he discovered in 1497 was England's first claim in the New World. Other explorers would follow Cabot's course to North America.

Strangely, little is known about John Cabot. Historical records and letters call him Zoanne, Juan, or

Giovanni Caboto. He was a citizen of Venice who moved to the English city of Bristol about 1494. We know more about his deeds as an explorer for England than about his earlier life as a merchant, navigator, and mapmaker. Who was the man who carried England's hopes of discovery on a small ship to North America?

Cabot's interest in new and different lands began early. He was probably born in Genoa–also the birthplace of Christopher Columbus–around 1450, which would make him about the same age as Columbus. One historian has suggested that the two men probably even knew each other.

A merchant like his father, Cabot traded in spices with the ports of the eastern Mediterranean Sea. Rare spices–ones highly prized in preparing food–plus silks and precious stones and metals, arrived in these ports from Asia. Eastern traders brought them either overland, or up the Red Sea.

When he was about 10, Cabot moved with his father to Venice, one of the busiest ports of trade with the Eastern world. Records show that he became a citizen of Venice about 20 years later, in 1471. By about 1482, Cabot was married to a woman from Venice named Mattea, and they had three

Genoa, a port on the northwestern coast of Italy, as it appeared in the late 15th century. Genoa was the birthplace of two great explorers: Columbus and Cabot.

sons—Ludovico, Sebastiano, and Sancto.

To improve his success as a merchant, Cabot learned navigation—steering by charts, maps, instruments, and the stars. Perhaps during these years, he imagined a new route to the Orient, as Asia was generally called. It would be a sea route rather than an overland route. On a business trip to the city of Mecca, where Eastern and Western goods changed hands directly, Cabot, it is said, asked Arabian

Europeans of Cabot's time desired silks, spices, and jewels from Asia. Until a sea route to the East was discovered, these items had been brought by caravans along an overland trail called the "silk road."

merchants where their spices and precious goods came from. No one knew, or would say.

As a trader himself, Cabot would have understood the reasons for secrecy. It cost less to purchase goods directly from their source. Any merchant who knew the source of the spices, silks, and precious stones from the Orient could cut out the traders who brought these goods to the Mediterranean—and could keep for himself the profits these traders normally made.

To his skills as a merchant and navigator, Cabot

added a third—mapmaker. He drew a world map, which mysteriously turned up in Bavaria in 1843. It has four parts that fit together, presenting a view of the known world in the late 1400s. Cabot wrote on the map in Latin, "This figure . . . contains all the lands . . . which have yet been discovered, with their names and the discoverers of them." The care with which the map was made shows that Cabot studied exploration closely. His knowledge of coastlines and *landforms* probably supported his belief that sailing due west from Europe to Asia might make for a shorter route than traveling east—the direction others were taking at the time.

But what of the dangers of long sea voyages west? Did people of 15th-century Europe, including Cabot, think the world was flat and that they might fall off its edge if they sailed too far? Actually, experienced travelers such as Cabot and Columbus strongly suspected that the Earth was round. Even ancient *astronomers*, navigators, and travelers noted that as they journeyed far in any direction, the stars would begin dipping toward the horizon behind them. This could mean only one thing—the surface of the Earth is curved. European explorers believed that with good ships and their skills as navigators, they could sail beyond the horizon and never risk falling off the "edge of the Earth."

After spending nearly 25 years in Venice as a merchant and mapmaker, Cabot finally decided to find a new route to Asia. Around 1490, a Venetian with a name resembling Cabot's appears in the historical records of Valencia, a seaport in Spain.

Cabot, like his fellow countryman Christopher Columbus, may have chosen to move to Spain for a key reason: he wanted to be on the *frontier* of exploration—the Atlantic Ocean. Voyages of discovery were sailing from ports in Spain and Portugal, one after another. Rulers of both countries wanted to find sea routes to Asia. Also, Europeans in the 15th century were very religious, and they wanted to spread Christianity to new lands and new people.

Unfortunately, however, neither Spain nor Portugal showed interest in John Cabot as an explorer. King John II of Portugal supported Bartholomeu Dias. In 1487, Dias led the first of several expeditions that rounded the tip of Africa. The Portuguese eventually reached India. In Spain, King Ferdinand and Queen Isabella rejoiced when their *mariner*-for-hire, Christopher Columbus, returned in 1493. Columbus believed that the islands he had found by

In 1487, the Portuguese navigator Bartholomeu Dias would become the first European to sail around the southernmost tip of Africa and into the Indian Ocean. This route would establish Portugal's right to an eastward sea route to Asia, forcing the sailors of other countries to look to the west.

sailing south and west were also part of Asia.

Cabot must have realized he would need supporters who were willing to think about other routes and new possibilities. So about 1494, he moved again, this time to the English city of Bristol.

He chose England, and probably Bristol in particular, based on his knowledge as a merchant. To start with, England was at the end of the spice trading line. By the time spices passed through various merchants' hands in Europe and reached England, their prices were extremely high. If he could sell the idea of a faster route over the narrow top of the Earth to Asia–England is farther north than

When he reached land after sailing west into the Atlantic Ocean for about a month, Christopher Columbus believed he had found the Orient. Cabot hoped to convince the king of England that a similar route to Asia could be found to the northwest of Columbus's.

Spain and Portugal—success would mean a whole new market for England in spices.

Also, Bristol was England's second-busiest port. Bristol merchants lived on trade, especially from fish caught in the waters off Iceland. From their dealings with Icelanders, Bristol merchants had heard of lands farther west. These coastlines might offer rich fishing grounds. Cabot could interest them in a voyage of discovery from that angle, too.

Finally, Spain and Portugal were rapidly claiming vast areas of newly discovered lands. Perhaps Cabot suspected that King Henry VII of England might welcome an experienced navigator with a bold plan to add a share of these lands to his kingdom.

Cabot must have been a man who could arouse people's excitement. Within two years or so of settling in England, he was on his way to see King Henry VII. His plan was fully backed in Bristol, where the people knew about ships and the sea.

On March 5, 1496, the king granted Cabot and his sons official rights to sail to all parts "of the eastern, western and northern sea" to lands unknown to Christians. (The king did not wish to encourage trespassing on Spanish claims.) Furthermore, one-fifth of any profits coming from the voyage would be paid to the throne.

Ferdinand and Isabella of Spain quickly protested. Columbus had already discovered what there was to discover, they declared. Their complaint came too late. After nearly 10 years of trying to raise interest in a new route to riches, Cabot had the king of England on his side. With the good sailing months of summer coming, he began preparing for his first expedition.

There would be three voyages in all: in 1496, 1497, and 1498. From the final one, however, John Cabot would never return.

The Lands Beyond Iceland

The rocky coast of Newfoundland juts into the Atlantic Ocean. John Cabot was not the first European to reach North America; the Vikings had landed somewhere on the coast (probably Newfoundland) around the year A.D. 1000.

2

There had been rumors about uncharted lands to the west long before Cabot proposed to explore them. Already in the 15th century, Bristol merchants ran a lively trade in the fish caught in waters off Iceland. From their dealings with the Icelanders, the English had heard of faraway places to the west. The Icelanders cherished their own tales about these places, too, especially about a fabled island called Frisland.

Even nearer to England, the people of Ireland proudly told the legend of St. Brendan, born in Ireland about A.D. 489. According to the legend, when Brendan was in his seventies, he and 17 other monks set out on a westward voyage in a *curragh*, a wood- or wicker-framed boat covered in sewn animal hides. The monks sailed about the North Atlantic for seven years. Eventually, they reached "the Land of Promise of the Saints." They explored it and returned home with fruit and precious stones.

Had St. Brendan reached North America? He may have. During the fifth and sixth centuries, Ireland was the northern center of Christian civilization. Irish monks went on sailing missions throughout the North Atlantic to spread Christianity. They reached island groups called the Hebrides and Orkneys (off the coast of Scotland), and the Faeroes (near Denmark). Perhaps Brendan had used these islands as stepping-stones to the area now known as Newfoundland.

In any case, the Irish legends about western lands probably reached the ears of yet another people: the Norse, or Vikings, as they are often called.

From their homes in *Scandinavia*, the Norse started raiding Ireland before the end of the eighth century. Their war galleys, known as longships, were swift and easily steered, perfect for quick hit-and-run raids. Going on such raids was known as going "i-Viking." It was by that name that the Norsemen became feared throughout Europe.

Sometime after 870, the Vikings settled in Iceland. But by 930, good farmland on that island had become scarce. When famine hit in 975, some Norsemen decided to move on. Perhaps the tales of earlier Irish voyages spurred them to sail west. In 982, the Norseman Erik the Red discovered a large island farther west, which he named Greenland. Three years later, a major expedition of several hundred people left Iceland and sailed to Greenland.

The Norse established nearly 300 farms in southeastern Greenland, split into two settlements 160 miles apart. One settlement supported 3,000 to 4,500 people; the other, around 1,500. These Greenland Norse were different from their Viking ancestors. They were merchants, not bloodthirsty sea-raiders. They used **knörrs**, strong ships that were good for carrying cargo. It may have been while sailing in a knörr that a Norse merchant accidentally strayed west to Newfoundland.

According to Norse **sagas**–tales about Viking

heroes that had been written down in the 13th and 14th centuries—a sailor named Bjarni Herjolfsson was making his way from Iceland to Greenland in 986. His ship ran into a severe storm, which blew him far off course. When the storm clouds lifted, he found himself near a strange shore. Instead of the icy mountains he expected, Bjarni saw hilly forests. This meant he was too far south. He sailed north for a week, until at last he reached Greenland.

Bjarni was a merchant, not an explorer. He had no interest in leading a voyage back to the forested shore. But 10 years later, Leif Eriksson, the son of Erik the Red, followed Bjarni's route in reverse.

In a sturdy ship, Leif and his men passed a land of rock and ice, which he called Helluland. This was probably Baffin Island, a large island to the north of Canada. Next, he found a country that was flat and wooded, which he called Markland. This was probably part of southern Labrador on the mainland of North America. Last, he reached a land that the sagas described as a place of grassy meadows, with rivers full of salmon. The area was hospitable enough to stay for the winter. Leif gave this land the name "Vinland." Leif and his men built sod houses and stayed a few months. When they returned to

Around a thousand years ago—some 500 years before Columbus and Cabot—Viking sailors explored North America, which they called "Vinland."

Greenland, they told of their adventures. Their descriptions inspired Leif's brother Thorvald to see Vinland for himself.

Thorvald located Leif's wintering place, but he was killed in a fight with local natives. The Greenlanders called these people Skraelings. They might have been American Indians or Inuit (Eskimos). Repeated attempts to settle in Vinland brought

Timber was scarce in Greenland. In fact, when Leif Eriksson returned from Vinland, he brought long wooden beams. Many of the later Viking visits to the area may have been to gather wood needed by the Greenlanders.

attacks from the Skraelings. Finally, the Greenlanders gave up and Vinland faded from memory.

Where was Vinland? Also, if it was any part of North America, why did the Greenlanders not settle other areas farther south— which were rich with resources—long before European explorers arrived?

For many years, historians believed that Vinland was an imaginary place that existed only in the Norse sagas. But that view began to change in the 1960s with the *excavation* of a Norse settlement at L'Anse aux Meadows in Newfoundland. Vinland, most experts now agree, was in North America.

L'Anse aux Meadows is a small settlement of eight buildings. Probably no more than 75 people— sailors, carpenters, blacksmiths, and perhaps slaves— lived there. Some women probably lived there, too. *Artifacts* uncovered at the site, such as a spindle *whorl*, a bone needle, and a small *whetstone* for sharpening, were often part of a Norse woman's everyday belongings. The purpose of the settlement may have been to repair ships. The site could also have served as a base camp for exploring further south. It isn't hard to imagine Norse settlers going off exploring during the warm summer months.

In fact, given the Norse custom of ranging far and wide, most scholars believe that Vinland probably was not just one place. It may have been a region that included Newfoundland and extended south into the Gulf of St. Lawrence as far as Nova Scotia and coastal New Brunswick. Supporters of this theory point to the discovery that the settlers at L'Anse aux Meadows grew butternut squash. This is a vegetable that normally grows further south.

This still leaves the question of why the Norse didn't move on to friendlier and warmer areas of North America. The answer may be that to the men of Greenland, Vinland was a

Although the Norse were probably the first Europeans to live in North America, their settlement never influenced people of other European countries. The idea of North America as a "New World" would have to wait nearly 500 years, until the time of Christopher Columbus and John Cabot.

These remains at L'Anse aux Meadows, Newfoundland, are probably part of Leif Eriksson's camp, which he established about A.D. 1000. Leif spent the winter here, then returned to Greenland. During the next 10 years, several other attempts to settle in Vinland failed.

distant place. Their sagas describe sailing there as risky and uncertain. Also, the Norse expeditions met with hostile people whose weapons were as advanced as those of the Norse. The small bands of Vikings who tried to gain a foothold in America were no match for their enemies.

More important, at that time in the early 11th century the Greenland Norse settlements were still young. The land was hard to farm and the settlers struggled to survive. They didn't have the material goods to start up again in another land. The situation never improved, either. By the 14th century, hunger stalked the Norse settlements, the thin soil for farming having been stripped away. By Cabot's day in the late 1400s, the Greenland settlements were deserted. Vinland became one of the fabled places known to storytellers but never visited by any living European.

So the Norse exploration of North America, though by far the earliest for which we have definite proof, left only a faint mark in history. On the other hand, the voyages of John Cabot provided England with its first step toward exploring–and eventually settling–a "new founde lande."

A replica of the Matthew *sets sail from Bristol on May 4, 1997, to mark the 500th anniversary of Cabot's voyage to North America.*

Cabot's First Two Voyages 3

When King Henry VII granted Cabot official rights to sail west in March 1496, the best time for such a sea journey from England—April and May—was rapidly approaching. Cabot made his first try that same year. The voyage was a failure. Perhaps he needed more time to prepare.

All that is known about Cabot's first voyage appears in a 1497 letter from John Day, an English explorer and merchant who traded with Spain. The letter, found in 1956, is addressed to a "Lord Admiral"—probably Christopher Columbus. Day writes, "[Cabot] went with one ship, he had a disagreement with the crew, he was short of food and ran into bad weather, and he decided to turn back."

Running short of food may be a sign that Cabot had indeed left too soon. That mistake, added to a second-rate crew, would have been too much bad luck for a wise captain. Cabot headed back to Bristol.

On the other hand, an event during this failed voyage in 1496 may have helped Cabot's second expedition succeed in 1497. An old Icelandic folk tale says someone in a large vessel from Bristol visited Iceland. He was "a Latin man," meaning a person who spoke Spanish, French, or Italian. His fine manners, his great learning, and his ideas about geography impressed the Icelanders who met him. This "Latin man" wished to know about the western lands the Icelanders had discovered, explored, or settled. He was given all possible help. Then he sailed away. The following summer, he returned on a small ship with a small crew.

Could this "Latin man" have been Cabot? If so, perhaps Cabot learned everything he could from the Icelanders in 1496. Then he might have returned the next summer to pick an experienced Icelandic *pilot*, or steersman, to help him sail west.

On May 20, 1497—the summer after his first attempt—Cabot set out from Bristol again.

We don't know whether he had the same ship at his command, but the records show that the *Matthew*, a small two-masted ship, made the second voyage. Cabot's son Sebastian, who was also destined to become a famous explorer, went with his father on this trip.

As a Venetian, Cabot would have recognized a good ship when he saw one. Venice's shipyards worked like assembly plants, with cranes and other machines bringing large parts of a ship together. English shipbuilding was simpler. The builder chose a smooth bank at the water's edge so the finished ship would be easy to slide in for launching. Big wooden blocks set in two lines held the ship upright as it was constructed.

English shipbuilding may have been basic, but the materials used were excellent. The frame and **keel** of a Bristol ship like the *Matthew* would have been made of oak, chosen for its strength. Oak trees

> **Ships were often named for Christian saints or religious figures. Cabot's choice of Matthew followed that tradition. However, it is said that he really named the ship for his wife, Mattea.**

were plentiful in England then. The side planks and deck would be pine, best for flexing under the weight of waves and for shedding water. Iron clamps appeared in a few places, but long wood pegs served as bolts everywhere. Driven into hand-drilled holes, the pegs swelled when wet, holding as tight as metal. The treelike **spars** that held the sails aloft were made of spruce fir that was hundreds of years old so it had the right thickness. The grayish sails were made of flax, a natural fiber, or cut from canvas imported from Europe.

To keep the ship watertight, workmen filled the spaces between the planks with oakum, a hairy cord made from the tough fiber of a plant called **hemp**. Their hammers rang loudly as they drove it deep into cracks. Next, the workmen sealed every inch of oakum and the entire **hull** with black tar or pitch. Then the rigging, or ropes, about the ship were added. Finally, the decks and rails received coats of colorful green, blue, yellow, and red paint.

On the day of launching, a priest would say a prayer and sprinkle holy water on the ship's **bow**. Just for luck, though, the shipbuilder had already made sure a shiny coin rested under the foot of the main mast where it sat on the keel.

This colored woodcut is from an Italian book on shipmaking that was published in 1486. It shows a galley being constructed in a Venetian shipyard. English shipbuilding was not as advanced in Cabot's day, but the English did turn out solid ships, like the Matthew.

From end to end, a ship like the *Matthew* would be from 54 to 60 feet long. It would have two decks: the main deck below for storing supplies, and the spar deck, which was open to the weather. The head room between them was 5 feet or less. The sailors slept wherever they could find a comfortable spot.

A view of the spar deck of the Matthew, *a reconstruction built in the 1990s to commemorate Cabot's voyage. This ship is on display at Cape Bonavista, Newfoundland.*

The only people who had bunks were the officers. These included the captain; the **boatswain**, who gave the captain's orders to the crew and was in charge of the ship's hull; and the ship's carpenter, who kept the ship in good repair.

The mariners supplied their own clothes. The usual outfit consisted of loose trousers, woolen socks, and a kind of long jacket with a hood. The sailors dressed in bright colors such as red or blue. They usually wore the same clothes all the time, causing one writer to complain about the "nasty beastliness" of the smell. They wore shoes, too, but mostly the sailors went barefoot because leather on wet decks is slippery.

With a crew of 18 aboard the *Matthew* (probably a different crew from the one on the unsuccessful first voyage), Cabot began his second voyage of discovery from Bristol on May 20, 1497.

The *Matthew* sailed slowly from Bristol down the Avon River, which leads to the sea. A few churches may have rung their bells in farewell. Bristol tradition says a local pilot went on the voyage with

Supplies were stored on the covered main deck of the Matthew. *Cabot's ship was probably about 54 feet long and carried a crew of 18 sailors.*

Cabot. But it's more likely that he only guided the ship around the dangerous Horseshoe Bend in the river, then went ashore at Avon-mouth. From there, the open ocean lies dead ahead.

Once at sea, discipline was probably the order of the day, every day. Although there are no records to show what life was like on the *Matthew*, historians do know about the practices on other ships during this time. For example, when John's son Sebastian became captain of his own ship, he ordered his crew not to offend God by swearing, telling dirty stories, or gambling. He insisted on morning and evening prayers and hymn singing at dawn.

Punishment on ships was harsh. For instance, a cabin boy who upset the navigation figures by failing to turn the hourglass over every half hour received a whipping from the boatswain. A lazy mariner ran the risk of being pinned to the main mast for hours by a dagger through his hand. Another who argued too much might be held by his ankles and dunked headfirst in the chilly water. Plots to **mutiny**, or take over command–the worst crime aboard a ship–were punishable by keelhauling. Keelhauling meant shoving a mariner over the bow and dragging him by a rope around his waist underwater the entire length of the ship to the **stern**. The hard-shelled barnacles on the belly of the ship cut like razors. Some mutineers did not survive this punishment.

The food on the ship affected the mariners' moods, of course. Most ships allowed each man a pound of biscuit, a quarter pound of butter, a half pound of cheese, a pound of pickled beef or pork, a little honey, and a gallon of beer per day. On Fridays and other Catholic holy days, dried codfish replaced the beef or pork. Mariners could always catch fresh fish as well.

A constant sore point was the biscuit, or hard bread. The mariners needed it for strength, but the dampness of the ship made it moldy. Eggs that insects had laid in the flour hatched and became

> As the sailors hoisted the sails and worked around the ship, they may have sung chants like this one:
> Ho, ho, ho—
> Pull a', pull a'
> bowline a', bowline a',
> darta, darta,
> hard out stiff
> before the wind,
> God send, God send
> Fair weather,
> fair weather,
> Many prizes,
> many prizes
> God fair wind send
> stow, stow
> make fast and belay!

Inedible food was common on long sea journeys. Christopher Columbus's son Ferdinand wrote about the disgusting fare on his father's fourth voyage: "What with the heat and dampness, our ship biscuit had become so wormy that, God help me, I saw many who waited for darkness and to eat the porridge made of it, that they might not see the maggots; and others were so used to eating them that they didn't even trouble to pick them out because they might lose their supper."

wormlike maggots. Warmer weather also brought out cockroaches and rats.

Nothing was heard of Cabot and the *Matthew* after the ship left Dursey Head, Ireland, two days after sailing from Bristol on May 20. Dursey Head was the last dependable point of land west. Beyond that, the ocean turned into a strange, uncharted area. Some mapmakers drew monsters' faces on the large uncharted spots to hide their ignorance of what lay there. For 11 weeks, the families of the *Matthew*'s crew waited.

Then, on the evening of August 5, the *Matthew* appeared quietly again at Avon-mouth, waiting for the tide to carry it on into Bristol. The next morning, August 6, 1497, the ship docked at Bristol Bridge and the crew leaped happily into the arms of friends, family, and sweethearts.

Cabot, hardly waiting to tell his tale, left the same day on horseback for London. He had news that no other man had the right to tell the king of England–that he had succeeded in planting England's flag on a shore unknown to all Europe. Better still, he believed he had found the beginning of a new route to Asia.

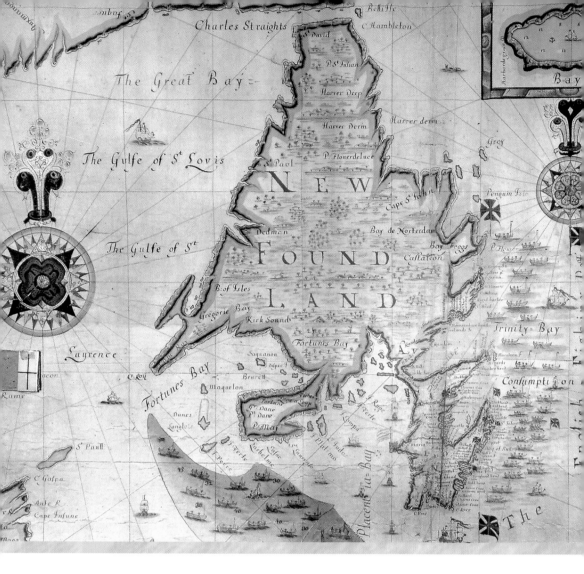

Cabot's "New Founde Lande"

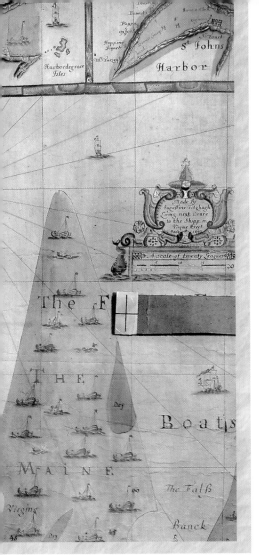

This 1544 map, based on drawings and information by Sebastian Cabot, shows the "New Founde Lande" that John Cabot discovered on his 1497 voyage. Cabot reported that the sea was filled with fish; by the 1530s, both French and English fishermen were sailing to these waters surrounding Newfoundland, which became known as the Grand Banks.

abot arrived in London at the court of King Henry VII on August 10, 1497, just four days after landing safely in Bristol. The distance from Bristol to London is 130 miles, so Cabot must have ridden hard by horseback to arrive that quickly. No doubt he was eager to tell his news and receive a reward. His three sons, mentioned in the king's official letter of permission, may have accompanied their proud father.

The meeting with the king went well. News of it spread throughout the city. Rumors flew that Cabot had discovered a route to the kingdom of the Great Khan in central Asia. This was China, which Marco Polo had written about some 200 years before. A Venetian living in London, Lorenzo Pasqualigo, wrote to his brothers on August 23:

> Our Venetian, who went with a small ship from Bristol to find new islands, has come back. . . . He has been away three months on the voyage. . . . This king has been much pleased. . . . The king has promised for another time, ten armed ships as he desires, and has given him all the prisoners, except such as are confined for high treason, to go with him, as he has requested; and has granted him money to amuse himself till then. Meanwhile, he is with his Venetian wife and his sons at Bristol.

It may seem odd that the king would promise Cabot prisoners as crewmen on a third voyage, or that Cabot would even want them. It must be remembered, however, that finding crews to fill several ships on a dangerous journey would be hard. Prisoners were more likely to volunteer, first to enjoy freedom, and second in the hope that they might come into money somehow.

England had fallen behind other European powers in exploration when King Henry VII gave Cabot permission to seek the northern passage to Asia in 1496.

Lorenzo Pasqualigo says the king awarded Cabot money, but he does not say how much. The royal book of expenses says the amount was £10 (the pound, or £, is the English monetary unit comparable to the American dollar) "to hym that founde the new Isle." This was equivalent to about half a year's average salary. This was not very generous, but the king also promised Cabot an annual *pension* of £20, which would keep him comfortable for life. In January 1498 another note in the king's record book says a "rewarde" of a small amount of money was given "to a Venysian [Venetian]"–probably Sebastian, for accompanying his father on the voyage.

With his sudden fame, Cabot happily plunged into the role of acting like a great man. Pasqualigo says Cabot dressed himself in expensive silk clothes. People began calling him the Great Admiral. He was a celebrity in the streets. When he returned home to Bristol, Cabot rented a house on a street named for St. Nicholas, the patron saint of sailors.

No record exists of what Cabot actually told the king about his voyage (the king himself later began using the phrase "the new founde lande"). Also, neither a map nor a globe made by Cabot exists to show his route to that land. Letter writers of the day have filled in some of the details of what happened to Cabot and the crew of the *Matthew* during their 11-week voyage between May 22 and August 6, 1497. But their "facts" tend to be confusing.

Raimondo di Soncino, the envoy from Milan living in London, wrote to the duke of Milan that Cabot left Bristol, rounded Ireland, and turned northward, finally turning to the west and "leaving the north on his right hand after some days." This rough but clear description means that Cabot headed toward North America. Pasqualigo wrote his brothers that Cabot "says he has discovered mainland 700 leagues away, which is in the country of the

Great Khan." As a measure of distance, a league at sea is a little more than three miles. Therefore, Pasqualigo puts Cabot's sailing distance to a mainland at about 2,100 miles. By contrast, an unsigned letter to the duke of Milan stated that Cabot "has also discovered the Seven Cities, 400 leagues from England." At the Spanish court, Pedro de Ayala told King Ferdinand and Queen Isabella, "I believe the distance is not 400 leagues." Finally, the English merchant John Day wrote to Columbus that "the cape nearest Ireland [in the New World] is 1,800 miles west of Dursey Head." This figure fits better with estimates of 700 leagues or 2,100 miles.

The eastern coast of North America is irregular, so it's impossible to say which estimate is closest to the actual distance Cabot traveled. Likewise, no one can say for sure where Cabot first sighted land.

One person who should have known was Cabot's son, Sebastian. A map, copied from a drawing by Sebastian, carries the date 1544. Next to what is now called the island of Cape Breton appear the words "the first land seen." In the margin there is also a statement in Spanish and Latin saying, "This country was discovered by John Cabot, a Venetian, and Sebastian Cabot, his son."

John Cabot's son Sebastian was also a noted explorer. Under the English flag, he returned to the coast of North America in 1509, sailing into what later became known as Hudson's Bay. After this, he joined the service of Spain, exploring the coast of South America in 1526.

Can the map be trusted? If Sebastian drew the original many years after his father's voyage, he might have been guessing about the *Matthew's* **landfall**. First of all, John Cabot and his crew, gazing from the deck, would have seen nothing familiar to establish where they were. Second, in 1544 Sebastian could have been assisting English claims to North America by choosing a good spot on the map.

Here is how many historians reconstruct John Cabot's voyage to North America. The *Matthew* was a fast, well-made, and seaworthy ship. On May 20, 1497, it departed Bristol with a crew of 18. Like Columbus, Cabot decided to cross the ocean at a specific distance north of the equator. This would make navigating easier. He chose the latitude of Dursey Head, Ireland, and plotted out a north-western course along it. This heading was much farther north than Columbus's route, and well out of the way of Spanish-held territories. Two days later, he rounded Dursey Head and continued westward along this line of latitude, arcing slightly north.

By following this course, Cabot believed he would touch the northeast corner of Asia, maybe the legendary Cathay (China). Then, turning south-east, he would eventually reach Cipango (Japan). From there he would continue south to India. He probably wasn't certain at which latitude he would find Cipango or India, but in terms of longitude, he knew they must be west of the lands Columbus had discovered. Anyone who had read Marco Polo's lush descriptions of his travels in the Orient—which Cabot certainly had—knew that Columbus's landfall of deserted beaches and sparse jungle could not be the realms of the Great Khan.

Perhaps the *Matthew* dropped anchor for a day or two in Iceland to pick up a pilot. Continuing on, Cabot probably showed no interest in Greenland. He knew of it, either from Bristol fisherman or from

Icelanders, if indeed he had visited Iceland during the summer before.

By now, Cabot and his crew had been heading northwest for almost a month. On June 21 or 22, they ran into a storm. In fact, because of the unfavorable weather in the north, Cabot's journey would take him longer than Columbus's, even though the overall distance to landfall was shorter.

About dawn on June 24, a rugged coast poked above the dim horizon, 12 to 15 miles away. American historian Samuel Eliot Morison, an admiral in the United States Navy, argues convincingly that it was Newfoundland and, by coincidence, only five miles away from where Leif Eriksson had stepped ashore on what the Norse called Vinland.

Following his plan, Cabot then turned south, searching for a suitable harbor to drop anchor and claim the land for England. Turning north may not have been possible for a simple reason: ice. As late as June, icebergs and ice floes still drift in the waters where the *Matthew* lay offshore. Their tremendous weight could easily have crushed the *Matthew's* wooden hull.

Once he sighted a harbor, Cabot, being an experienced mariner, would have sent in the small ship's

The Matthew *replica sails within sight of Newfoundland. No one is certain of the exact route Cabot took to reach North America.*

boat to test the holding ground of the harbor's floor. If the bottom was hard stone or slippery, the anchor would fail to grip, and the *Matthew* might drift away. Next, Cabot probably assigned roles for the landing party. Some crewmen would take weapons from their racks–crossbows, cutlasses or broad swords, and pikes, which were sharpened iron poles. The remaining men would carry either an English flag or a cross that could be raised.

From this point, we have John Day's description in his letter to Columbus. Day seems to have talked to a crew member, or perhaps to Cabot himself:

> [H]e landed at only one spot of the mainland, near the place where land was first sighted, and they disembarked there with a crucifix and raised banners with the arms of the Holy Father and those of the King of England, my master; and they found tall trees of the kind masts are made, and other smaller trees and the country is very rich in grass. In that particular spot, as I told your Lordship, they found a trail that went inland, they saw a site where a fire had been made, they saw manure of animals which they thought to be farm animals, and they saw a stick half a yard long pierced at both ends, carved and painted with brazil [reddish purple], and by such signs they believe the land to be inhabited.

Day says that because the men were so few and not heavily armed, they dared not go farther inland. As proof that the land was inhabited, they collected fish nets and snares. Then they climbed back into the ship's boat and rowed back to the *Matthew*. Sailing along the shore, they saw "fields where they thought might also be villages, and they saw a forest whose foliage looked beautiful." They also spotted two figures chasing each other, "but they could not tell if they were human beings or animals."

Cabot continued exploring the coastline, naming

the features he encountered Cape Discovery, Island of St. John, St. George's Cape, the Trinity Islands, and England's Cape. These may be, in order, the present Cape North, St. Paul Island, Cape Ray, St. Pierre and Miquelon, and Cape Race, all in the area of what would many years later be named Cabot Strait. How far south he sailed, no one knows. Perhaps it was as far as New England–but finding the water getting deeper, Cabot believed the land would soon turn to the west so that he could sail to the Orient. The crew hauled up plenty of fish too. Cabot was pleased. He knew that he could tell the king that England would no longer have to depend on Iceland for fishing grounds.

But with the season of good sailing weather growing short, and food no doubt running low, Cabot turned for home about July 20. Only one small mishap occurred on the speedy return voyage. The *Matthew* sailed to the coast of France, instead of England. After two more days of sailing almost straight north, Cabot's crew arrived at the mouth of the Avon River, which carried them triumphantly into Bristol.

It was August 6, 1497.

Lost at Sea Forever

A memorial to John Cabot looks out over the Atlantic Ocean near Cape Bonavista, Newfoundland. Although it would be nearly a century before England followed up on Cabot's discovery by attempting to settle Newfoundland, his voyages mark the start of England's development into a seafaring power and the master of a colonial empire.

5

Although Henry VII received Cabot warmly in London, some fisherman in Bristol grumbled that the foreigner from Venice had found nothing. They said they already knew about his "new founde lande."

But none of this dampened the enthusiasm of the king. Despite the fact that Cabot had produced no jewels, gold, or spices from his voyage—just fish nets and a humble painted stick—on February 3, 1498, Henry granted new letters of permission "to our well beloved John Kaboto, Venician" to undertake a third voyage. This time the expedition Cabot assembled was impressive. The king financed one ship, and Bristol merchants paid for another four, which were stocked with trade goods they hoped would appeal to strangers: caps, lace, cloth, and "other trifles." Three hundred men signed on to crew the ships.

At the beginning of May 1498 the little *flotilla* sailed away. Sebastian was not on board.

They first went north. Cabot probably wanted to make certain that there wasn't a passage lying farther above where he had sighted land on the previous trip. Not long after departing, one of the five ships returned to Ireland, badly beaten by the weather. The other ships never returned.

It is believed that Cabot reached Greenland in June. He then sailed northward along the coast. The crew may have mutinied because of the severe cold, forcing Cabot to turn south. He may then have cruised along the coast of North America to Chesapeake Bay or Cape Hatteras. If by then the ships had not somehow resupplied with food, it would have been time to turn homeward again. If so, then perhaps a storm sank all four ships in the open ocean.

On the other hand, a storm may have dashed Cabot, his men, and his ships against a rockbound coast even earlier in the expedition. In 1501, the Portuguese explorer Gaspar Corte-Real found an Italian gilt sword and Venetian earrings in the possession of a Beothuk Indian in Newfoundland. It's rather sad to think of the body of John Cabot washing ashore on the land he proclaimed was the doorstep to a new world. One historian of the day wrote sneeringly that Cabot "found his new lands only in the ocean's bottom, to which he and his ships are thought to have sunk, since, after that voyage, he was never heard of more."

Whatever happened to the doomed expedition, no stampede of nations followed Cabot in other ships. Between 1498 and 1500, a few Portuguese explorers—Miguel and Gaspar Corte-Real being the most famous—visited Greenland, Labrador, and Newfoundland. Between 1501 and 1505, five English traders working as a group made voyages to Newfoundland. By 1504, French, Spanish, Portuguese, and English fishermen were crossing the ocean to catch fish on the Newfoundland banks.

But Cabot's voyages did not immediately inspire the founding of colonies in North America. In fact,

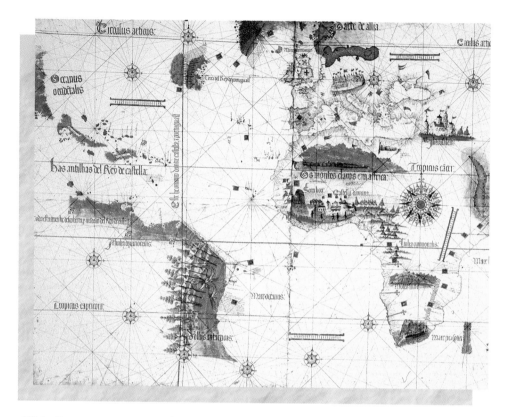

This Portuguese map of 1501 shows only the vague eastern coastline of South America and the islands of the Caribbean. John Cabot's voyages would help place North America on European maps, and would eventually lead to English colonization of the New World.

none would take hold for almost another century. What, then, is John Cabot's place in history?

Until Cabot started out in the *Matthew* in 1497, it seemed as though Spain and Portugal would take possession of the unknown lands of the New World unchallenged by any other nation. When Cabot planted the English flag on the North American continent, England took its first step in the Age of Discovery. The timid fishing expeditions that followed Cabot to Newfoundland led much later to English settlements in Virginia and New England. Likewise, the throne used Cabot's expeditions to lay claim to Canada.

Cabot also assisted a revolution in exploration and mapmaking. It gradually became clear to Europeans that Cabot had not found the lands Marco Polo had described, no more than had Christopher Columbus. Asia must lie beyond this huge, mysterious landmass to the west. Finding a way around or through it–a route later referred to as the Northwest Passage–became the goal. Over the next two centuries, such English explorers as Martin Frobisher, John Davis, and Henry Hudson would undertake the search.

Because of the Venetian merchant sailor John Cabot, fewer monster faces and other fanciful decorations appeared in the empty places on European maps. In their place, additional coastlines of an expanded world came into focus.

Chronology

500s According to legend, St. Brendan, an Irish monk, sets sail with 17 other monks on a westward voyage to spread Christianity; during their seven-year journey, they reach "the Land of Promise of the Saints," which may have been Newfoundland.

870s The Norse settle in Iceland.

982 Erik the Red, a Norseman, discovers Greenland.

985 The Norse organize a major expedition in Iceland, sail to Greenland, and establish 300 farmsteads spread throughout southeastern Greenland.

1000s The Norse build a small settlement at L'Anse aux Meadows in Newfoundland; it may have been used as a place for Norse ships to restock and be repaired.

1450s John Cabot is born in Genoa, Italy.

1471 Becomes a citizen of Venice.

1482 Marries a Venetian woman, Mattea, with whom he has three sons.

1490 Moves with his family to Valencia in Spain, perhaps because he wants to be part of Spanish plans to find a sea route to Asia.

1493 Christopher Columbus announces he has made the westward trip across the Atlantic Ocean to Asia.

1494– Cabot settles his family in England; builds support among
1495 Bristol merchants and King Henry VII to find a shorter, northern route to Asia.

1496 On March 5, King Henry VII grants official permission for Cabot and his sons to explore any lands unknown to Christians in any area except where the Spanish have claims; Cabot sets out from Bristol on his first trip, but the ship runs short of food and the weather turns bad, forcing an early return to Bristol.

1497 With a crew of 18 men, Cabot sails again from Bristol on the *Matthew* on May 20; on June 24, after a rough voyage, Cabot reaches either southern Labrador, Newfoundland, or Cape Breton Island. He explores the coastline for a month; on August 6, he sails triumphantly into Bristol.

1498 On February 3, King Henry VII grants new letters of permission for a third Cabot expedition; Cabot's third expedition, consisting of five ships and 300 men, leaves Bristol in May.

1499 Only one of Cabot's ships returns to Ireland, damaged by weather. The others never return, and Cabot is never heard from again.

Glossary

artifact—a handmade tool or ornament from a particular period or culture, or any product of human activity.

astronomer—a person who studies the stars, planets, and other objects in the sky.

boatswain—the member of a ship's crew who is responsible for taking care of the ship's hull.

bow—the front or forward part of a ship.

curragh—a wood- or wicker-framed boat covered in sewn animal hides used by medieval Irish and British sailors.

envoy—a person who represents a government or leader in dealings with another government or leader.

excavation—the process of digging to uncover something buried.

flotilla—a fleet of ships.

frontier—the farthest limits of knowledge, exploration, or settlement.

hemp—a plant with tough fibers, from which ropes can be woven.

hull—the outer frame or body of a ship.

keel—a timber on the bottom of a ship's hull that extends the entire length of the hull.

knörr—a sturdy sailing ship used especially by the Norse, or Vikings, to carry cargo.

landfall—the land first sighted on a voyage.

landform—a natural surface feature of an area of land.

mariner—a sailor.

mutiny–to rebel against the authority of a captain or commanding officer.

navigation–the science of directing the course of a seagoing vessel, and of determining its position.

pension–a fixed amount of money paid regularly to a person, usually as a reward for a period of employment or for outstanding service rendered.

pilot–a skilled sailor who is qualified to take over a ship.

saga–a heroic tale, about historic or legendary figures, that was recorded in Iceland during the 12th or 13th century; or another story that resembles the Icelandic sagas.

Scandinavia–a region of northern Europe that includes the present-day countries of Denmark, Finland, Norway, and Sweden.

spars–wooden pieces on a sailing ship, such as masts and booms, that hold sails aloft.

spices–any of various aromatic vegetable products, such as pepper or nutmeg, used to season or flavor foods. In the 15th and 16th centuries, spices were rare and highly valued by the people of Europe.

stern–the rear or back end of a ship.

whetstone–a stone used to sharpen tools or weapons.

whorl–a drum-shaped part of a spindle (which is used for spinning or weaving cloth) that helps turn the spindle.

Further Reading

Boorstin, Daniel J. *The Discoverers.* New York: Random House, 1983.

Faber, Harold. *The Discoverers of America.* New York: Scribner, 1992.

Fritz, Jean. *Around the World in a Hundred Years: From Henry the Navigator to Magellan.* New York: Putnam, 1994.

Gallagher, Jim. *The Viking Explorers.* Philadelphia: Chelsea House, 2001.

Kemp, Peter, ed. *The Oxford Companion to Ships and the Sea.* London: Oxford University Press, 1976.

Lauber, Patricia. *Who Discovered America? Mysteries and Puzzles of the New World.* New York: HarperCollins, 1992.

Martin, Steve, and Colin Sanger. *Matthew: A Voyage from the Past into the Future.* Cornwall, England: Godrevy Publications, 1996.

Morison, Samuel Eliot. *The European Discovery of America: The Northern Voyages, 500-1600 AD.* New York: Oxford University Press, 1971.

Sheaves, D. Pamela. *A Merchant's Tale: The Life and Times of John Cabot.* Newfoundland, Canada: Tuckamore Books, 1997.

Wilson, Ian. *The Columbus Myth: Did Men of Bristol Reach America Before Columbus?* Toronto: Simon & Schuster, 1991.

Picture Credits

CHARLES J. SHIELDS lives in Homewood, a suburb of Chicago, with his wife Guadalupe, an elementary school principal. He has a degree in history from the University of Illinois in Urbana-Champaign, and was chairman of the English department and the guidance department at Homewood-Flossmoor High School in Flossmoor, Illinois.

Specialist Training in
GYNAECOLOGY

Edited by

Margaret Rees MA DPhil FRCOG

Reader in Reproductive Medicine
Honorary Consultant Medical Gynaecologist
Nuffield Department of Obstetrics and Gynaecology
Women's Centre
John Radcliffe Hospital
Oxford, UK

Sally Hope FRCGP DRCOG

General Practitioner
Honorary Research Fellow Women's Health
Department of Primary Health Care
University of Oxford
Oxford, UK

ELSEVIER
MOSBY

Edinburgh London New York Oxford Philadelphia St Louis Sydney Toronto 2005

ELSEVIER
MOSBY

An imprint of Elsevier Limited

First published 2005

ISBN 0723432449

British Library Cataloguing in Publication Data
A catalogue record for this book is available from the British Library

Library of Congress Cataloging in Publication Data
A catalog record for this book is available from the Library of Congress

Notice
Medical knowledge is constantly changing. Standard safety precautions must be followed, but as new research and clinical experience broaden our knowledge, changes in treatment and drug therapy may become necessary or appropriate. Readers are advised to check the most current product information provided by the manufacturer of each drug to be administered to verify the recommended dose, the method and duration of administration, and contraindications. It is the responsibility of the practitioner, relying on experience and knowledge of the patient, to determine dosages and the best treatment for each individual patient. Neither the Publisher nor the editors assume any liability for any injury and/or damage to persons or property arising from this publication.
The Publisher

 your source for books, journals and multimedia in the health sciences

www.elsevierhealth.com

The publisher's policy is to use **paper manufactured from sustainable forests**

Printed in China

Contributors

Adam Balen MB BS MD FRCOG
Professor of Reproductive Medicine
and Surgery
Assisted Conception Unit
Department of Obstetrics and
Gynaecology
Leeds General Infirmary
Leeds, UK

Fiona Blake MBChB MRCGP MRCPsych
Consultant Psychiatrist
Cambridgeshire and Peterborough
Mental Health Partnership Trust
Addenbrooke's Hospital
Cambridge, UK

Annabelle Glasier MD FRCOG MFFP
Consultant/Director
Family Planning Services
Lothian Primary Care NHS Trust
Family Planning and Well Women Services
Edinburgh, UK

Cynthia Harper MB ChB MFFP
Staff Grade Colposcopy
Women's Centre
John Radcliffe Hospital
Oxford, UK
Senior Clinical Medical Officer
Family Planning
Alec Turnbull Clinic
Radcliffe Infirmary
Oxford, UK

Sally Hope FRCGP DRCOG
General Practitioner
Honorary Research Fellow Women's
Health
Department of Primary Health Care
University of Oxford
Oxford, UK

Gillian Lockwood MA DPhil MRCOG
Medical Director
Midland Fertility Services
Aldridge, UK

Ian MacKenzie MA MD FRCOG DSc
Consultant Obstetrician
and Gynaecologist
Nuffield Department of Obstetrics
and Gynaecology
John Radcliffe Maternity Hospital
Oxford, UK

Jane Moore MRCOG
Honorary Consultant Gynaecologist
Nuffield Department of Obstetrics
and Gynaecology
John Radcliffe Hospital
Oxford, UK

Margaret Rees MA DPhil FRCOG
Reader in Reproductive Medicine
Honorary Consultant Medical
Gynaecologist
Nuffield Department of Obstetrics and
Gynaecology
Women's Centre
John Radcliffe Hospital
Oxford, UK

Karina Reynolds MD FRCS MRCOG
Consultant Gynaecological Oncologist
St Bartholomew's Hospital
London, UK

Alison Scott MBChB MRCOG MFFP
Consultant Gynaecologist
Lothian Primary Care NHS Trust
Family Planning and Well Women Services
Edinburgh, UK

Partha Sengupta MBBS MD MRCOG
Specialist Registrar in Gynaecological
Oncology
Academic Unit of Obstetrics and
Gynaecology
University of Manchester
St Mary's Hospital
Manchester, UK

Jackie Sherrard MB BS DFFP FRCP
Consultant GUM Physician
Department of Genitourinary Medicine
Radcliffe Infirmary
Oxford, UK

Brett Winter-Roach MRCOG FRCS(Ed)
Clinical Lecturer
Academic Unit of Obstetrics and
Gynaecology
University of Manchester
St Mary's Hospital
Manchester, UK

Contents

Menorrhagia and dysmenorrhoea

1

Margaret Rees

> **THIS CHAPTER** Menorrhagia and dysmenorrhoea are two common gynaecological conditions. This chapter covers their aetiology, investigation and treatment.

Background

Menstruation is a periodic discharge of sanguinous fluid and a sloughing of the uterine lining. It is an event characteristic of the reproductive cycle in humans and most subhuman primates such as the rhesus monkey. Its function is unknown. Regular monthly menstruation has become part of a woman's life only relatively recently. This is because previously women were either pregnant or lactating almost continuously. With the advent of modern contraception, the number of menstruations that a woman can have has increased from fewer than 10 to several hundred. It is thus not surprising that menstrual complaints have correspondingly increased.

Occurrence

Women will each experience about 400 menstruations between the menarche and the menopause. Two clinical problems of menstruation are common:

- Menorrhagia (excessive bleeding).
- Dysmenorrhoea (painful periods).

In a national community survey undertaken by MORI in 1990, 31% of women reported heavy periods and 38% reported painful periods. Of these, one-third had consulted a doctor within the past 4 months. The Fourth National Morbidity Survey in General Practice (1991–1992) showed that, for women aged 25–44 years, the respective consultation rates for menorrhagia and dysmenorrhoea were 65 and 40 per 1000 person-years at risk; 5% of women aged 30–49 years consult their general practitioner for menorrhagia in a year.

Menorrhagia is the main presenting complaint in women referred to gynaecologists.

MENORRHAGIA

Definition

Menorrhagia has been defined as a subjective complaint of heavy cyclical menstrual blood loss (MBL) over several consecutive cycles without any intermenstrual or postcoital bleeding.

In objective terms, it is a blood loss of greater than 80 mL per period. In population studies, MBL shows a skewed distribution, with a mean of about 35 mL and 90th centile of 80 mL. In hospital practice, only about 40% of women complaining of excessive bleeding have objective menorrhagia. Intolerance of the volume of their bleeding is not a key feature among women attending clinics for bleeding problems. A survey of hospital referrals has shown that broad menstrual complaints tend to be reframed as excessive bleeding. Lack of awareness of this may result in women receiving inappropriate care.

MBL measurement

Although not routinely available, objective MBL measurement is a valuable tool. It can be measured using the non-invasive alkaline haematin method, in which sanitary devices are soaked in 5% sodium hydroxide to convert the blood to alkaline haematin whose optical density is then measured.

Various pictorial representations of blood-loss charts have been developed in order to obtain a semi-quantitative measurement of MBL. However, the results of studies correlating scores and measured MBL are conflicting.

Aetiology

Although various pathologies have been implicated in menorrhagia (see Box 1.1), in 50% of cases of objective menorrhagia no pathology is found at hysterectomy. In most cases of objective menorrhagia, the cycles are ovular, with anovular cycles mainly occurring soon after the menarche or near to the menopause.

Menorrhagia may be due to systemic or pelvic pathology, or iatrogenic causes, but there is a paucity of confirmatory data with objective MBL measurement.

Box 1.1: Proposed causes of menorrhagia

Systemic
- Disorders of haemostasis
- Thyroid dysfunction

Pelvic
- Fibroids
- Endometriosis
- Pelvic inflammatory disease
- Endometrial polyps

Iatrogenic
- Inert contraceptive devices
- Anticoagulants

Systemic causes

Disorders of haemostasis, such as von Willebrand disease, deficiencies of factors V, VII, X and XI and idiopathic thrombocytopenic purpura are thought to increase menstrual loss, but MBL has only rarely been measured. In the few studies where it was estimated, menorrhagia since menarche was noted in a higher proportion of women with von Willebrand disease and factor XI deficiency than in those without a bleeding disorder.

Pelvic causes

Fibroids (leiomyomas), endometriosis, pelvic inflammatory disease and endometrial polyps are thought to cause menorrhagia, but studies with MBL measurement show an association with objective menorrhagia in only about one-half to two-thirds of cases.

Iatrogenic causes

Although iatrogenic causes such as inert intrauterine contraceptive devices (IUCDs) have been shown objectively to increase MBL, data for anticoagulants are very limited.

Tubal sterilization does not increase the risk of menstrual abnormalities.

Investigation of menorrhagia

A flowchart that outlines the investigation and management of menorrhagia is given in Fig. 1.1. The investigations are summarized in Box 1.2.

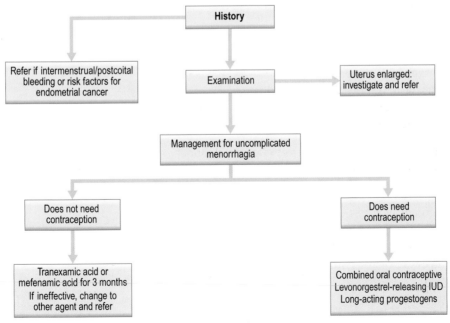

Figure 1.1
Flowchart for the management of menorrhagia (adapted from RCOG guidelines 1 and 5).

> **Box 1.2: History, examination and investigation of menorrhagia**
>
> **History**
> - Duration of the problem
> - Have periods changed suddenly?
> - Duration of menstruation
> - Menstrual cycle length
> - Intermenstrual/postcoital bleeding
>
> **Examination**
> - General
> - Speculum
> - Bimanual
>
> **Blood tests**
> - Haemoglobin
>
> **Endometrial/uterine assessment**
> - Transvaginal ultrasound
> - Biopsy
> - Hysteroscopy

History and examination

The time over which the woman has had the problem, whether it was a gradual or a sudden change in menstrual bleeding, needs to be ascertained. Duration of periods, menstrual cycle and any intermenstrual or postcoital bleeding should be documented. The method of contraception should also be noted. A general examination, including bimanual and pelvic examination, should be performed. A cervical smear should be obtained if it is due.

Blood tests

A full blood count should be performed as routine in all women since menorrhagia is a common cause of anaemia. Ferritin estimation is not recommended. Testing for inherited bleeding disorders and thyroid dysfunction should only be undertaken if clinically indicated. No other endocrine investigations are warranted.

Uterine/endometrial assessment

The main methods of assessment are:

- Transvaginal ultrasound.
- Endometrial biopsy.
- Hysteroscopy.

There is insufficient evidence to indicate an arbitrary age cut-off for further investigation if pelvic examination is normal. Rather, the risk factors for endometrial neoplasia should be ascertained, such as:

- Bleeding severity.
- Lack of response to treatment.
- Association with intermenstrual bleeding.
- Polycystic ovary syndrome.
- Obesity.
- Tamoxifen use.

Following endometrial resection or ablation, assessment of the endometrium may be difficult since the endometrial cavity may be partially obliterated.

Women with menorrhagia who have not responded to initial medical management, whatever their age, are more likely to have intrauterine pathology such as endometrial polyps or submucosal fibroids. Whether transvaginal ultrasound or hysteroscopy is used in a particular case depends on the local facilities.

Transvaginal ultrasound

The RCOG guideline 5 states that, where possible, transvaginal ultrasound should be used to select the women with a normal cavity who do not require hysteroscopy. Transvaginal ultrasound can rule out any co-existing pelvic pathology, such as ovarian cysts and fibroids, but does not give a histological diagnosis.

Endometrial thickness varies during the menstrual cycle from 4–8 mm in the proliferative phase to 8–16 mm during the secretory phase. Thus, transvaginal ultrasound should ideally be performed after menstruation in the proliferative phase. A thickened endometrium or a cavity filled with fluid is suggestive of malignancy or other pathology (hyperplasia, polyps). An endometrial thickness of 10–12 mm in the proliferative phase should be used as the cut-off point for endometrial hyperplasia and carcinoma.

Ultrasound can sometimes miss small polyps, particularly when performed in the late secretory phase. The instillation of a contrast medium such as saline may improve the diagnosis of polyps, submucous fibroids and focal thickening of the endometrium.

Endometrial biopsy

Dilation and curettage

The classic method of obtaining endometrium is by dilation and curettage (D&C), which was first described by the French gynaecologist Recamier in 1843. It was considered to be the 'gold standard', but it does not sample all the endometrium. Furthermore, since D&C is essentially a blind procedure, it can miss lesions such as polyps, submucous fibroids, hyperplasia and carcinoma. D&C is being increasingly replaced by outpatient procedures that avoid general anaesthesia and are associated with fewer complications such as uterine perforation, haemorrhage, cervical laceration and even death.

For many years D&C was erroneously thought to be a therapeutic procedure. However, objective MBL measurement has shown that, although the first period after D&C is lighter than previous ones, subsequent ones are no different.

Vacuum or aspiration curettage

Vacuum or aspiration curettage, introduced in the 1970s, avoids general anaesthesia and has fewer complications than D&C. The first instrument was a 3-mm diameter stainless steel cannula with a curved tip and a wide slit on the concave surface attached to a plastic aspiration chamber and a vacuum (Vabra). A variety of instruments are available with either 3- or 4-mm cannulae, suction being generated mechanically or electrically with a pump or internal piston (Rockett, Pipelle) (Fig. 1.2).

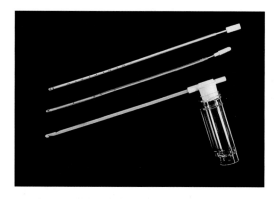

Figure 1.2
Various aspiration biopsy samplers.

There have been many comparative studies of the different methods that support the use of outpatient aspiration curettage. Comparisons of Vabra, Pipelle and D&C show equal accuracy despite the Pipelle sampling significantly less of the endometrial surface than the Vabra. Conversely, Pipelle is less painful than Vabra curettage, but discomfort is usually mild and lasts only for about 10–15 sec as the cannula is passed and the biopsy taken.

Hysteroscopy

The hysteroscope, which was introduced over a century ago, provides direct visualization of the endometrial cavity. Flexible and rigid hysteroscopes are available.

Hysteroscopy is indicated if the original transvaginal sound scan was abnormal. It also allows the opportunity for directed endometrial biopsy to be undertaken at the same time. It should be noted, however, that hysteroscopy is not 100% accurate and, albeit rarely, adenocarcinomas are missed.

Hysteroscopy can be undertaken as an outpatient or an inpatient procedure. Some women require a paracervical block or intrauterine instillation of local anaesthetic for pain relief.

Treatment of menorrhagia

The aims of therapy are to reduce blood loss, reduce the risk of anaemia and improve quality of life. The first line of therapy should be medical in the absence of pelvic pathology and when the woman wishes to retain her fertility. Each year about £7 million is spent on primary care prescribing for menorrhagia in the UK; 822 000 prescriptions were issued to 345 225 women for this condition in 1993. Since menorrhagia is a common cause of iron-deficiency anaemia, iron therapy is often indicated.

Drug therapy

The poor correlation between subjective and objective assessment of MBL means that clinical trials of drug therapies need objective assessment of efficacy as a primary end-point.

Drug treatments for menorrhagia can be divided into two main classes:

- Non-hormonal: e.g. non-steroidal anti-inflammatory drugs (NSAIDs) and antifibrinolytics.
- Hormonal: e.g. progestogens, combined oral contraceptives, hormone replacement therapy, danazol, gestrinone and GnRH (gonadotrophin-releasing hormone) analogues.

Non-hormonal treatments

Non-hormonal treatment, using either mefenamic acid or tranexamic acid, taken during menstruation itself should be the first line. Both drugs can be used together, but there are no good studies of the effect of the combination. Referral should be considered if neither inhibitors of prostaglandin synthesis nor antifibrinolytic agents are effective after 3 months of therapy. Box 1.3 summarizes the current drug therapies that are available for menorrhagia.

Non-steroidal anti-inflammatory drugs

Mefenamic acid is the most studied NSAID for menorrhagia. NSAIDs will also alleviate menstrual pain. Mefenamic acid reduces MBL by 29% (range: 19–47%; 95% confidence interval [CI]: 27.9–30.2). Mefenamic acid is given in a dose of 1.5 g/day during menstruation. Duration of menstruation is reduced in some, but not all, studies. Follow-up at 12–15 months after commencing treatment shows continuing effectiveness.

Reductions in menstrual loss have also been documented for other NSAIDs such as:

- Naproxen.
- Ibuprofen.
- Diclofenac sodium.
- Flurbiprofen.

Box 1.3: Drug therapy for menorrhagia

Non-hormonal

- Non-steroidal anti-inflammatory drugs
  - Mefenamic acid
  - Meclofenamic acid
  - Naproxen
  - Ibuprofen
  - Flurbiprofen
  - Diclofenac
- Antifibrinolytics
  - Tranexamic acid
  - ε-Aminocaproic acid
- Other
  - Etamsylate

Hormonal

- Progestogens
  - Norethisterone
  - Medroxyprogesterone acetate
  - Dydrogesterone
- Intrauterine progestogens
  - Levonorgestrel IUCD
  - Progestasert IUCD (licensed outside the UK)
- Combined oestrogen–progestogens
  - Oral contraceptives
  - Hormone replacement therapy
- Other
  - Danazol
  - Gestrinone
  - GnRH analogues

The reduction in blood loss varies from 25% to 47%, depending on the agent and dose used. NSAIDs are also effective in women with a copper or non-hormonal IUCD. Naproxen and ibuprofen have been reported to be ineffective in women with leiomyomas. In general, NSAIDs are contraindicated in women with peptic ulceration, but otherwise have few side-effects if taken for only a few days each cycle.

Antifibrinolytics

Tranexamic acid reduces MBL by 46.7% (range: 35–56%; 95% CI: 45–46.7). The recommended dose is 3 g/day. Symptoms of dysmenorrhoea were improved in some, but not all, studies. The duration of menstruation is not reduced. Tranexamic acid is also effective in women with a copper or non-hormonal IUCD.

Side-effects experienced during treatment are: nausea, vomiting, diarrhoea, headache, dizziness, weight gain and leg cramp in up to 60–80% of women. The main reported adverse event is thromboembolism. However, large studies undertaken in Scandinavia showed no increase of thrombotic events over and above that of the general population of the same age.

Etamsylate

Studies with objective MBL measurement using the currently recommended doses show that etamsylate is ineffective.

Hormone treatments

Oral progestogens

These are a common prescription for menorrhagia. Studies with objective MBL measurement have shown that short-term low-dose luteal use (7 days of oral norethisterone 5 mg twice daily, given during the secretory phase of the cycle) is ineffective. However, oral norethisterone 5 mg three times daily from day 5 to day 26 reduces blood loss by 87%.

Intrauterine levonorgestrel

This is more effective than oral progestogens in reducing menstrual loss and is effective for 5 years. The levonorgestrel IUCD reduced MBL by 88% and 96% after 6 months and 12 months, respectively. Its mode of action probably involves induction of endometrial atrophy. While it provides very effective contraception, fertility is preserved.

Intrauterine levonorgestrel can be considered to be an alternative to the surgical management of menorrhagia and may be more cost-effective. Women need to be counselled about irregular bleeding, which can occur in the first few months after insertion. The levonorgestrel IUCD can be fitted in a fibroid uterus but may be less effective or may be expelled, especially if the lesions are submucous, but more data are required.

Long-acting progestogens

Continued use of long-acting progestogens renders most women amenorrhoeic and therefore these agents could be considered for use in menorrhagia.

Medroxyprogesterone acetate and norethisterone enanthate are available as depot injections for contraception. They may cause unpredictable, irregular spotting and bleeding in the first few months of use. However, with repeated administration, amenorrhoea becomes common.

Subdermal implants that release etonogestrel or levonorgestrel over several years are another way of administering long-acting progestogens for contraceptive purposes. Their efficacy needs to be assessed as a treatment for objective menorrhagia.

Combined oestrogen–progestogen

Combined oral contraception is often used clinically to reduce MBL. Its mode of action is unclear but probably involves induction of endometrial atrophy. Many of the original studies used a higher dose than the 30–35-μg ethinylestradiol preparations that are currently employed. It is unclear, therefore, whether low-dose preparations are as effective in reducing MBL as the higher-dosage preparations, and whether any particular progestogen dose or type makes any difference.

Monthly sequential oestrogen–progestogen hormone replacement therapy is also used clinically to treat menorrhagia in perimenopausal women. However, there are no randomized controlled trials in women with objective menorrhagia.

Danazol/gestrinone/GnRH analogues

These are all effective treatments, which usually render women amenorrhoeic, but their side-effects generally limit their use to 6 months. Danazol and gestrinone have androgenic side-effects. Women must be advised to use barrier methods of contraception because of potential virilization of a female fetus if pregnancy occurs during treatment.

The effects of the hypo-oestrogenic state induced by GnRH analogues can be prevented by add-back oestrogen combined with progestogen or tibolone. This treatment combination is expensive and should not be used as a first line.

Surgical treatment

Surgery is indicated when:

- Medical treatment has failed.
- There are pelvic abnormalities: e.g. polyps, fibroids, chronic pelvic inflammatory disease or endometriotic masses.

Operations should be as conservative as possible in women who wish to retain their fertility.

Table 1.1 (p. 10) provides details of three surgical procedures for menorrhagia undertaken in NHS hospitals in England during 2000–2001. Menorrhagia accounts for two-thirds of all hysterectomies and nearly all endoscopic endometrial destructive surgery.

Table 1.1: Surgical procedures for menorrhagia undertaken in NHS hospitals in England, 2000–2001 (source: OPCS Hospital Episode Statistics)

Procedure (ICD code)	Number	Mean length of stay (days)
Abdominal excision of the uterus (Q07)	38 348	6.5
Vaginal excision of the uterus (Q08)	8 704	4.7
Therapeutic endoscopic operations on the uterus (Q17)	17 298	1.4

Hysterectomy

Hysterectomy can be performed:

- Abdominally.
- Vaginally.
- Laparoscopically.

In the UK, 20% of women will have undergone hysterectomy by the age of 55 years. In the VALUE study of 37 298 hysterectomies undertaken in 1994 and 1995, the median age was 45 years, and the most common indication for surgery was dysfunctional uterine bleeding (46%) (Maresh et al 2002). The proportions of women having abdominal, vaginal or laparoscopically assisted hysterectomy were 67%, 30% and 3%, respectively. Forty-three per cent of women had no ovaries conserved after surgery. The overall operative complication rate was 3.5% and was highest for the laparoscopic techniques. The overall postoperative complication rate was 9%. One per cent of these was regarded as severe, with the highest rate for severe occurring in the laparoscopic group (2%). There were no operative deaths. Fourteen deaths were reported within the 6-week postoperative period: a crude mortality rate soon after surgery of 0.38 per thousand (95% CI: 0.25–0.64).

There is concern about the long-term sequelae of hysterectomy, which may include:

- Premature onset of ovarian failure, even when the ovaries are conserved.
- Psychosexual dysfunction.
- Urinary tract symptoms.
- Bowel symptoms.

Subtotal hysterectomy does not seem to be less likely than total hysterectomy to impair sexual function. Cervical smears should be continued after subtotal hysterectomy.

Endometrial destructive techniques

The aim of the various methods is to remove or destroy all of the endometrium, as well as myometrium up to 3 mm thick, to prevent regeneration. The methods include:

- Resection.
- Ablation by laser, rollerball diathermy, radiofrequency, cryoablation, microwaves, thermal balloons and hysteroscopic instillation of hot saline.

Like hysterectomy, these treatments should only be offered to women who desire no further children. However, although the risk of pregnancy is minimal, patients cannot be assured that it is a sterilization procedure. Higher rates of amenorrhoea are achieved in older women.

Preoperative medical therapy with progestogens, danazol and GnRH analogues, to render the endometrium atrophic in order to simplify surgery and thus maximize the possibility of complete resection, is usually offered.

The most common complications are:

- Haemorrhage.
- Perforation.
- Need for emergency surgery.
- Absorption of distending medium (NB: radiofrequency-induced thermal ablation, microwaves and thermal balloons do not use a distending medium).

Perioperative complications occur in about 4–5% of women and mortality is 2–3 per 10 000. There is no difference in terms of perforation between the three most widely used techniques (0.7–2.5% with combined resection and rollerball, resection alone or laser ablation). However, the need for emergency surgery is greater for resection alone (2.4%) compared with resection and rollerball (1.4%) or laser ablation (0.3%).

Whether endometrial destruction hinders the diagnosis of endometrial cancer is unknown.

Treatment of fibroids

Uterine fibroids are smooth muscle tumours that arise in the myometrium. They are the most common form of pathology in women, being present in about 30% of those over the age of 35 years. Fibroids are frequently asymptomatic, but may present with menorrhagia, pelvic pain or pressure symptoms.

Management depends on:

- Size.
- Associated symptoms.
- Age.
- Reproductive plans.

Management options

Small asymptomatic fibroids rarely require treatment. However, they do need to be monitored regularly, with annual ultrasound for example, because of the small risk (less than 0.2%) of sarcomatous change.

Women with fibroids and menorrhagia are usually treated by hysterectomy. For those wishing to conserve their fertility, myomectomy may be offered. Endoscopic techniques allow removal of subserous and intramural fibroids by laparoscopy and of submucous fibroids by hysteroscopy. Local destruction by laser or electrocoagulation are techniques currently being evaluated.

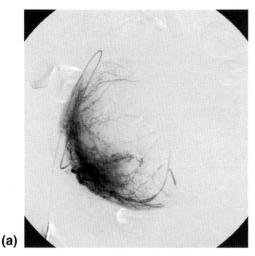
(a)

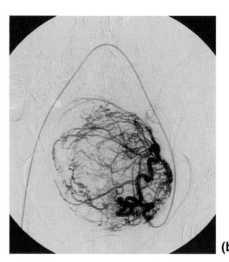
(b)

Figure 1.3
Fibroid embolization.

Alternatives to surgery

There is considerable demand for an alternative to surgery in the management of fibroids. GnRH analogues induce fibroid shrinkage, but this is rarely complete and not sustained after cessation of therapy. Another concern is the bone mineral loss associated with a prolonged hypo-oestrogenic state, which limits the use of GnRH analogues to 6 months.

GnRH analogues are especially useful prior to hysterectomy as the operation becomes technically easier and operative blood loss is reduced. The combination of the GnRH analogue goserelin and endometrial resection as an alternative to hysterectomy for fibroids is extremely encouraging.

Embolization

Uterine embolization involves selectively cannulating both uterine arteries and injecting them, usually with polyvinyl alcohol particles, to the point of complete or near-total occlusion (see Fig. 1.3). No attempt is made to embolize only the fibroids as opposed to the rest of the uterus. Following the procedure, pain and discharge (sometimes fragments of fibroids may be passed) are common. The most significant complication is infection and some deaths have been reported. Data are limited and protocols need to be established and randomized controlled trials undertaken.

DYSMENORRHOEA

Dysmenorrhoea can be classified into two types:

- Primary dysmenorrhoea.
- Secondary dysmenorrhoea.

In primary dysmenorrhoea there is no pelvic pathology, whereas secondary dysmenorrhoea implies underlying pathology that leads to painful menstruation.

Primary dysmenorrhoea

In general, primary dysmenorrhoea appears 6–12 months after the menarche when ovulatory cycles have become established. The early cycles after the menarche are usually anovular and tend to be painless. The pain usually consists of lower abdominal cramps and backache and there may be associated gastrointestinal disturbances such as diarrhoea and vomiting. Symptoms occur predominantly during the first 2 days of menstruation. Primary dysmenorrhoea tends not to be associated with excessive menstrual bleeding and it is rare for women to have both dysmenorrhoea and menorrhagia.

Primary dysmenorrhoea is associated with uterine hypercontractility. During contractions endometrial blood flow is reduced, favouring the concept that ischaemia due to hypercontractility causes primary dysmenorrhoea. Increased levels of prostaglandins, leukotrienes and vasopressin have been found in primary dysmenorrhoea.

Secondary dysmenorrhoea

Secondary dysmenorrhoea is associated with pelvic pathology such as:

- Endometriosis.
- Adenomyosis.
- Pelvic inflammatory disease.
- Submucous leiomyomas.
- Endometrial polyps.

The use of a non-hormonal IUCD may also lead to dysmenorrhoea. Secondary dysmenorrhoea tends to appear several years after the menarche and the patient may complain of a change in the intensity and timing of her pain. The pain may last for the whole of the menstrual period and may be associated with discomfort before the onset of menstruation.

Investigation of dysmenorrhoea

The investigations for dysmenorrhoea are outlined in Box 1.4.

Box 1.4: History, examination and investigation of dysmenorrhoea

History	Examination	Investigation
▪ Duration of problem	▪ General	▪ Transvaginal ultrasound
▪ Onset of dysmenorrhoea and its relation to menstruation	▪ Speculum	▪ Magnetic resonance imaging
▪ Presence of an IUCD	▪ Bimanual	▪ Hysteroscopy
▪ History of infertility		▪ Laparoscopy

Treatment of dysmenorrhoea

Primary dysmenorrhoea

The first line of treatment is either a prostaglandin synthetase inhibitor or the combined oral contraceptive pill. Vasopressin antagonists are under development.

Non-steroidal anti-inflammatory drugs (NSAIDs)

The clear involvement of prostaglandins in primary dysmenorrhoea has led to their use. Meta-analysis shows that they are all effective and that ibuprofen is the preferred analgesic because of its favourable efficacy and safety profiles.

Commencing treatment before the onset of menstruation appears to have no demonstrable advantage over starting treatment when bleeding starts. This observation is compatible with the short plasma half-life of prostaglandin synthetase inhibitors. The advantage of starting treatment at the onset of menstruation is that it prevents the patient treating herself when she is unknowingly pregnant, which would only become apparent when a period is missed.

Cyclo-oxygenase (COX), the major enzyme in the prostaglandin synthetic pathway, exists in at least two isoforms: COX-1, which is constitutive; and COX-2, which is inducible. One highly selective COX-2 inhibitor, rofecoxib, is licensed for the treatment of dysmenorrhoea.

Combined oestrogen–progestogen oral contraception

This is a useful tool, especially when control of fertility is required. The 'pill' is clinically effective in about 80–90% of women and probably acts by reducing the capacity of the endometrium to produce prostaglandins. Most of the evidence is based on preparations with a high oestrogen dose.

Other

Vasopressin antagonists have been examined, but are not available for routine use at present. The use of orally acting antagonists has recently been described. Transdermal glyceryl trinitrate is being evaluated.

Secondary dysmenorrhoea

Effective treatment of secondary dysmenorrhoea must be based on a correct diagnosis since different pathologies require different therapies. In addition, the type of treatment offered must take into account:

- The patient's age.
- Her desire for conception.
- The severity of the symptoms.
- The extent of the disease.

FUTURE DIRECTIONS Menorrhagia and dysmenorrhoea are common conditions seen in primary and secondary care. The past few years have seen significant changes, mainly in the management of menorrhagia and fibroids. There has been more use of effective medical treatments such as antifibrinolytic agents, non-steroidal anti-inflammatory agents and intrauterine progestogens. Women have been seeking alternative interventions to hysterectomy. The further refinement of endometrial destructive techniques and fibroid embolization has increased the options available.

Selected References and Further Reading

Anonymous. Which operation for menorrhagia? Drug Ther Bull 2000; 38:77–80.

Anonymous. Levonorgestrel intra-uterine system for menorrhagia. Drug Ther Bull 2001; 39:85–87.

Kennedy AD, Sculpher MJ, Coulter A, et al. Effects of decision aids for menorrhagia on treatment choices, health outcomes, and costs: a randomized controlled trial. JAMA 2002; 288:2701–2708.

Maresh MJ, Metcalfe MA, McPherson K, et al. The VALUE national hysterectomy study: description of the patients and the surgery. BJOG 2002; 109: 302–312.

O'Brien PMS, Cameron I, Maclean A, eds. Disorders of the menstrual cycle. London: RCOG Press, 2000.

Oehler MJ and Rees MCP. Menorrhagia: an update. Acta Obstet Gynecol Scand 2003; 82:405–422.

OPCS Hospital Episode Statistics 2000–2001. http://www.doh.gov.uk/hes/free/data; accessed 23 May 2003.

Proctor ML, Roberts H, Farquhar CM. Combined oral contraceptive pill (OCP) as treatment for primary dysmenorrhoea [Cochrane review]. Cochrane Database Syst Rev 2001; 4:CD002120.

Royal College of Obstetricians and Gynaecologists. The initial management of menorrhagia. Evidence-based guideline 1. London: RCOG, 1998.

Royal College of Obstetricians and Gynaecologists. The management of menorrhagia in secondary care. Evidence-based guideline 5. London: RCOG, 1999.

Shankar M, Lee CA, Sabin CA, Economides DL, Kadir RA. von Willebrand disease in women with menorrhagia: a systematic review. BJOG. 2004 Jul; 111(7):734–740.

Thakar R, Ayers S, Clarkson P, Stanton S, Manyonda I. Outcomes after total versus subtotal abdominal hysterectomy. N Engl J Med. 2002 Oct 24; 347(17):1318–1325.

Zhang WY, Li Wan Po A. Efficacy of minor analgesics in primary dysmenorrhoea: a systematic review. BJOG 1998; 105:780–789.

Oligomenorrhoea and amenorrhoea

2

Adam Balen

> **THIS CHAPTER** Oligo- and amenorrhoea are defined, classified and discussed in terms of their causes, investigation and treatment.

Definitions

Oligomenorrhoea

Oligomenorrhoea can be defined as menses occurring less frequently than every 35 days.

Amenorrhoea

Amenorrhoea is the absence of menstruation, which may be temporary or permanent, of more than 6 months' duration. Two types of amenorrhoea are recognized:

- Primary amenorrhoea.
- Secondary amenorrhoea.

Classification of amenorrhoea

Amenorrhoea is best classified according to its aetiology or site of origin and can be subdivided into:

- Disorders of the hypothalamic–pituitary–ovarian–uterine axis.
- Generalized systemic disease.

Primary amenorrhoea

The failure to menstruate by the age of 16 years in the presence of normal secondary sexual development, or 14 years in the absence of secondary sexual characteristics, warrants investigation. This distinction helps to differentiate reproductive tract anomalies from gonadal quiescence and gonadal failure.

Primary amenorrhoea may be the result of congenital abnormalities in the development of ovaries, genital tract or external genitalia, or of a disturbance of the normal endocrinological events of puberty (Box 2.1). Delayed puberty is often constitutional, but it is important to exclude primary ovarian failure or hypothalamic/pituitary dysfunction.

Box 2.1: Classification of primary amenorrhoea

Uterine causes	■ Müllerian agenesis (e.g. Rokitansky syndrome)
Ovarian causes	■ Polycystic ovary syndrome ■ Premature ovarian failure (usually genetic, e.g. Turner's syndrome)
Hypothalamic causes **(hypogonadotrophic hypogonadism)**	■ Weight loss ■ Intense exercise (e.g. ballerinas) ■ Idiopathic
Delayed puberty	■ Constitutional delay or secondary (see text)
Pituitary causes	■ Hyperprolactinaemia ■ Hypopituitarism
Causes of hypothalamic/pituitary **damage (hypogonadism)**	■ Tumours (craniopharyngiomas, gliomas, germinomas, dermoid cysts) ■ Cranial irradiation, head injuries (rare in young girls)
Systemic causes	■ Chronic debilitating illness ■ Weight loss ■ Endocrine disorders (thyroid disease, Cushing's syndrome etc.)

Overall it is estimated that endocrine disorders account for approximately 40% of the causes of primary amenorrhoea, the remaining 60% having developmental abnormalities.

A detailed description of congenital anomalies of the genital tract and of puberty is beyond the scope of this chapter.

Secondary amenorrhoea

The principal causes of secondary amenorrhoea are outlined in Box 2.2.

EXAMINATION AND INVESTIGATION OF AMENORRHOEA

A summary of investigations to be considered is given in Box 2.3.

Physical examination

First, it is always important to exclude pregnancy.

A bimanual examination is inappropriate in a young woman who has never been sexually active. Examination of the external genitalia of an adolescent should be undertaken in the presence of the patient's mother. A transabdominal ultrasound examination of the pelvis is an excellent non-invasive method of obtaining valuable information in these patients. An examination under anaesthesia is sometimes indicated for cases of intersex with primary amenorrhoea; it is rarely required in cases of secondary amenorrhoea.

Box 2.2: Classification of secondary amenorrhoea

Uterine causes	■ Asherman's syndrome ■ Cervical stenosis
Ovarian causes	■ Polycystic ovary syndrome ■ Premature ovarian failure (genetic, autoimmune, infective, radio/chemotherapy)
Hypothalamic causes (hypogonadotrophic hypogonadism)	■ Weight loss ■ Exercise ■ Chronic illness ■ Psychological distress ■ Idiopathic
Pituitary causes	■ Hyperprolactinaemia ■ Hypopituitarism ■ Sheehan's syndrome
Causes of hypothalamic/pituitary damage (hypogonadism)	■ Tumours (e.g. craniopharyngiomas) ■ Cranial irradiation ■ Head injuries ■ Sarcoidosis ■ Tuberculosis
Systemic causes	■ Chronic debilitating illness ■ Weight loss ■ Endocrine disorders (thyroid disease, Cushing's syndrome, etc.)

Box 2.3: Investigation of amenorrhoea

Physical examination	■ Note body mass index, pubertal development, stigmata of PCOS and other endocrine disease
Endocrine assessment	■ Pregnancy test if suspected ■ FSH, LH ■ Prolactin ■ Thyroid function tests ■ Testosterone (if stigmata of PCOS) ■ Further endocrinology only if above do not provide diagnosis
Pelvic imaging	■ Ultrasound: morphology of ovaries and endometrial thickness (for oestrogenization) ■ MRI if suggestion of complex developmental problem
Pituitary/hypothalamic imaging	■ MRI if indicated
Bone mineral densitometry	■ If at risk of osteoporosis
Karyotype	■ If premature ovarian failure

FSH, follicle-stimulating hormone; LH, luteinizing hormone; PCOS, polycystic ovary syndrome; MRI, magnetic resonance imaging.

Endocrinology

Physical signs

Signs of hyperandrogenism (acne, hirsutism, alopecia) are suggestive of the polycystic ovary syndrome (PCOS). Women with PCOS have hyperandrogenism and not virilization, which is additionally associated with high circulating androgen levels and causes deepening of the voice, increase in muscle bulk and cliteromegaly.

Acanthosis nigricans is a sign of profound insulin resistance and is usually visible as hyperpigmented thickening of the skin folds of the axilla and neck; it is associated with PCOS and obesity.

Baseline endocrine status

A baseline assessment of the endocrine status should include measurement of serum prolactin and gonadotrophin concentrations and an assessment of thyroid function. Elevated gonadotrophin (follicle-stimulating hormone [FSH] and luteinizing hormone [LH]) concentrations indicate ovarian failure; suppressed levels suggest hypogonadotrophic hypogonadism.

Prolactin levels

Prolactin concentrations may be elevated in response to a number of conditions, including stress, a recent breast or physical examination, or even having a blood test. The elevation, however, is moderate and transient. A more permanent, but still moderate elevation (greater than 700 mIU/L), is associated with hypothyroidism. An elevated serum prolactin is also a common finding in women with PCOS, where concentrations of up to 2500 mIU/L have been reported.

A serum prolactin concentration greater than 1000 mIU/L warrants further investigation (see section on imaging below). Serum prolactin concentrations greater than 5000 mIU/L are usually associated with a macroprolactinoma.

Progestogen challenge

Amenorrhoea in women with PCOS is secondary to acyclical ovarian activity and continuous oestrogen production. A positive response to a progestogen challenge test, which induces a withdrawal bleed, will distinguish patients with PCOS-related hyperprolactinaemia from those with polycystic ovaries and unrelated hyperprolactinaemia, because the latter causes oestrogen deficiency and therefore failure to respond to the progestogen challenge.

Endometrial biopsy

Amenorrhoea may also have long-term metabolic and physical consequences. In women with PCOS and prolonged amenorrhoea, there is a risk of endometrial hyperplasia and adenocarcinoma. If, on resumption of menstruation, there is a history of persistent

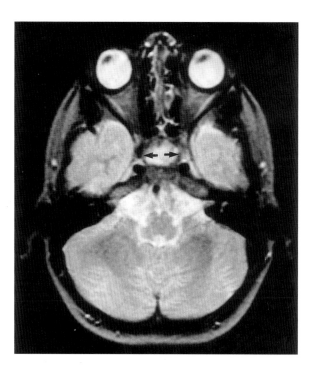

Figure 2.1
Magnetic resonance imaging of a prolactinoma. Reproduced, with permission, from Balen AH, Jacobs HS. Infertility in practice. Edinburgh: Churchill Livingstone; 2003.

intermenstrual bleeding or on ultrasound there is a postmenstrual endometrial thickness of greater than 10 mm, then an endometrial biopsy is indicated.

Imaging

Computed tomography (CT) or magnetic resonance imaging (MRI) of the pituitary fossa may be used to exclude a hypothalamic tumour, a non-functioning pituitary tumour compressing the hypothalamus or a prolactinoma (Fig. 2.1). A macroprolactinoma is, by definition, greater than 1 cm in diameter.

Chromosomal abnormalities

Women with premature ovarian failure (under the age of 40 years) may have a chromosomal abnormality, such as Turner's syndrome (45,X or 46,XX/45,X mosaic) or other sex chromosome mosaicisms.

Autoimmune disease

An autoantibody screen should also be undertaken in women with a premature menopause, although it can be difficult to detect anti-ovarian antibodies.

Bone mineral density

Measurement of bone mineral density is indicated in amenorrhoeic women who are oestrogen-deficient. The vertebral bone is more sensitive to oestrogen deficiency and vertebral fractures tend to occur in a younger age group (50–60 years) than fractures at the femoral neck (70+ years).

UTERINE CAUSES OF SECONDARY AMENORRHOEA

Asherman's syndrome

Asherman's syndrome is a condition in which intrauterine adhesions prevent normal growth of the endometrium. This may be the result of too vigorous an endometrial curettage affecting the basal layer of the endometrium, or adhesions may follow an episode of endometritis. Oestrogen deficiency may increase the risk of adhesion formation in breastfeeding women who require a curettage for retained placental tissue. Typically, amenorrhoea is not absolute, and it may be possible to induce a withdrawal bleed using a combined oestrogen–progestagen preparation. Intrauterine adhesions may be seen on a hysterosalpingogram. Alternatively, hysteroscopic inspection of the uterine cavity will confirm the diagnosis and enable treatment by adhesiolysis. Following surgery, a 3-month course of cyclical progesterone/oestrogen should be given. The insertion of a non-hormonal intrauterine contraceptive device for 2–3 months may prevent the recurrence of adhesions.

OVARIAN CAUSES OF SECONDARY AMENORRHOEA

Premature ovarian failure

Premature ovarian failure occurs in approximately 1% of women and is defined as the cessation of ovarian function under the age of 40 years. The function of the ovary depends upon the total number of oocytes contained within primordial follicles. Primordial follicles and oocytes are derived during fetal life and the oogonial stem cell line is lost before birth. The maximum number of germs cells is approximately 7 million and this is achieved at 20 weeks' gestation; by birth this is reduced to between 1 and 2 million. The size of the follicle store is not directly related to the rate of ovulation but to the daily fraction recruited, which changes with age. Recruitment of primordial follicles occurs throughout life and is initially independent of FSH. Menopause occurs when there are only about 1000 follicles left in the ovary.

Incidence

The exact incidence of premature ovarian failure is unknown as many cases go unrecognized, but estimates vary between 1% and 5% of the female population. In a study of 1858 women, the incidence of premature ovarian failure was 1 in 1000 by age 30 years and 1 in 100 by age 40 years. Studies of amenorrhoeic women report the incidence of premature ovarian failure to be between 10% and 36%.

Resistant ovary syndrome

Prior to the absolute cessation of periods of true premature ovarian failure, some women experience an intermittent return to menses, interspersed between variable periods of amenorrhoea. Gonadotrophin levels usually remain moderately elevated during these spontaneous cycles, with plasma FSH concentrations of 15–20 IU/L. This occult/incipient ovarian failure, or 'resistant ovary syndrome', is associated with the presence of primordial follicles on ovarian biopsy. Ovarian biopsy is no longer recommended in the assessment of these cases because a single sample is not reliably representative and will not help with management. Occasionally pregnancies occur spontaneously in patients with resistant ovary syndrome. Ovulation induction therapy is of no benefit as the ovaries are usually as resistant to exogenous gonadotrophins as they are to endogenous hormones.

Ability to conceive

If a patient with resistant ovary syndrome and symptoms of oestrogen deficiency wishes to conceive, she should be advised to take a hormone replacement preparation, which will not inhibit ovulation (or adversely affect a pregnancy). On the other hand, if a pregnancy would be unwanted, it is important to advise the use of either an oral contraceptive preparation or contraception together with hormone replacement therapy.

Definitive diagnosis

If a woman has amenorrhoea and an elevated serum FSH concentration (>20 IU/L) on more than two occasions, it is likely that she has premature ovarian failure. The longer the period of amenorrhoea and the higher the FSH level, the greater the likelihood that the ovarian failure is permanent. A single elevated FSH level, even if greater than 40 IU/L, should be treated with caution as spontaneous ovulation and pregnancy have still been observed.

Additional investigations

Once the diagnosis of premature ovarian failure has been made, further specific endocrinological tests are unnecessary. Additional investigations include:

- Karyotype.
- Screening for autoantibodies and associated autoimmune disease if relevant.
- A baseline assessment of bone mineral densitometry.

As always, a detailed history is important, with particular attention to a family history of premature ovarian failure or autoimmune disease.

Causes of premature ovarian failure

In approximately two-thirds of cases, the cause of ovarian failure cannot be identified. It is unknown whether these cases are truly 'idiopathic' or due to as yet undiscovered

> **Box 2.4: Causes of premature ovarian failure**
>
> - Idiopathic
> - Genetic
>   - Commonly, Turner's syndrome
>   - Familial
> - Autoimmune
> - Pelvic surgery
> - Pelvic irradiation
> - Chemotherapy
> - Viral/bacterial infection
> - Galactosaemia

genetic, immunological or environmental factors. In a series of 323 women with premature ovarian failure attending an endocrinology clinic in London, 23% were identified with Turner's syndrome, 6% after chemotherapy, 4% with familial premature ovarian failure and 2% each who had pelvic surgery, pelvic irradiation, galactosaemia and 46,XY gonadal dysgenesis (see Box 2.4).

Infection

Viral and bacterial infection may also lead to ovarian failure. Thus infections such as mumps, cytomegalovirus or HIV in adult life can adversely affect long-term ovarian function, as can severe pelvic inflammatory disease.

In younger patients

Ovarian failure occurring before puberty is usually due to a chromosomal abnormality, or a childhood malignancy that required chemotherapy or radiotherapy. The likelihood of developing ovarian failure after therapy for cancer is difficult to predict, but the age of the patient is a significant factor: the younger the patient, the greater the follicle pool and the better her chances of retaining ovarian function.

Toxins

Environmental toxins might be a factor in causing premature ovarian failure. The most well-known toxin is of course smoking, which has been shown to lower the age of the menopause.

Genetic causes of premature ovarian failure

Adolescents who lose ovarian function soon after menarche are often found to have a Turner's mosaic (46,XX/45,X) or an X chromosome trisomy (47,XXX). There are many genes on the X chromosome that are essential for normal ovarian function. It would appear that two active X chromosomes are required during fetal life in order to lay down a normal store of follicles. In fetuses with Turner's syndrome, normal numbers of oocytes appear on the genital ridge, but accelerated atresia takes place during late fetal life. Thus streak gonads occur and it is only the mosaic form of Turner's syndrome that permits any possibility of ovarian function. X mosaicisms are the most common chromosomal abnormality in reported series of premature ovarian failure, ranging from 5% to 40%.

Turner's syndrome Turner's syndrome is the most common cause of gonadal dysgenesis. In its most severe form, the 45,X genotype is associated with the classic Turner's features, including:

- Short stature.
- Webbing of the neck.
- Cubitus valgus.
- Widely spaced nipples.
- Cardiac and renal abnormalities.
- Often autoimmune hypothyroidism.

Spontaneous menstruation may occur, particularly when there is mosaicism, but premature ovarian failure usually ensues. Management includes low-dose oestrogen therapy to promote breast development without further disturbing linear growth; cyclical oestrogen plus progestogen may be used as maintenance therapy.

Fragile X syndrome Fragile X syndrome is the most common inherited cause of learning disability, with a prevalence of 1 in 4000 males and 1 in 8000 females. It is characterized by a heterogeneous mixture of physical, behavioural and cognitive features. Most published information refers to fragile X syndrome in males, of whom about 80% are moderately to severely mentally retarded. Females usually display a milder phenotype, with a borderline IQ of 70–85.

Fragile X syndrome is an X-linked dominant disorder with reduced penetrance. Unaffected carriers in a family have an increased risk of transmitting the disorder with successive generations. The disorder is due to a mutation in a gene on the long arm of the X chromosome, known as 'fragile X mental retardation-1' (*FMR-1*, Xq27.3), which transcribes a cytoplasmic protein that is found in all cells, but in higher concentrations in ovary, brain and testis. It is the absence of the protein that results in the fragile X syndrome phenotype. Affected families have mutations in *FMR-1*, leading to hereditary instability.

The mutations can be of variable size. The largest result in a 'full mutation'; the smaller mutations are known as 'premutations'. As somatic cells in females have a randomly inactivated X chromosome, only half of females with the full mutation have a fragile X phenotype. Women with a premutation are phenotypically normal but appear to have a significantly increased risk of premature ovarian failure. The largest series of 395 premutation carriers found 16% with premature ovarian failure compared with 0.4% of a control population.

Familial premature ovarian failure There is evidence for strong genetic factors determining the age of the menopause. Interest has recently turned to specific familial forms of premature ovarian failure in which abnormalities are present in the critical region of the long arm of the X chromosome from Xq13 to Xq26. At least two genetic variants have been identified: *POF1* (Xq21.3–q27) and *POF2* (Xq13.3–q21.1). There are also a number of rare syndromes that are associated with premature ovarian failure (e.g. galactosaemia).

Autoimmune causes of premature ovarian failure

Ovarian autoantibodies can be measured and have been found in up to 69% of cases of premature ovarian failure. However, the assays are expensive and not readily available in most units. It is also important to consider other autoimmune disorders and screen for autoantibodies to the thyroid gland, gastric mucosa parietal cells and adrenal gland if there is any clinical indication.

There are a number of potential ovarian antigens, and the potential for autoantibody formation has long been recognized. The clinical significance of anti-ovarian antibodies is uncertain, particularly as their concentrations fluctuate and do not always relate to the severity of disease. It is also uncertain whether anti-ovarian antibodies are pathogenic or secondary to antigen release after ovarian damage.

Management of premature ovarian failure

Living with premature ovarian failure

The diagnosis and consequences of premature ovarian failure require careful counselling of the patient. It may be particularly difficult for a young women to accept the need to take oestrogen preparations that are clearly labelled as being intended for older postmenopausal women, while at the same time having to come to terms with the inability to conceive naturally. The short- and long-term consequences of ovarian failure and oestrogen deficiency are similar to those occurring in the fifth and sixth decades. However, the duration of the problem is much longer, and hormone replacement therapy is advisable to reduce the consequences of oestrogen deficiency in the long term (see below).

Risk of osteoporosis

Younger women with premature loss of ovarian function have an increased risk of osteoporosis. A study of 200 amenorrhoeic women between the ages of 16 and 40 years demonstrated a mean reduction in bone mineral density of 15% compared with a control group and after correction for body weight, smoking and exercise. The degree of bone loss was correlated with the duration of the amenorrhoea and the severity of the oestrogen deficiency rather than the underlying diagnosis, and was worse in patients with primary amenorrhoea than in those with secondary amenorrhoea. A return to normal oestrogen status may improve bone mass density, but bone mineral density is unlikely to improve more than 5–10% and it probably does not return to its normal value. However, it is not certain if the radiological improvement seen will actually reduce the risk of fracture, as remineralization is not equivalent to the restrengthening of bone. Early diagnosis and early correction of oestrogen status is therefore important.

Cardiovascular disease

Women with premature ovarian failure have an increased risk of cardiovascular disease. Oestrogens have been shown to have beneficial effects on cardiovascular status in women.

They increase the levels of cardioprotective high-density lipoprotein as well as total triglyceride levels, whilst decreasing total cholesterol and low-density lipoprotein levels. The overall effect is of cardiovascular protection.

Hormone replacement

Women with hypo-oestrogenic amenorrhoea require hormone replacement. Oestrogen combined with a progestogen is required for patients with a uterus in order to reduce the risk of endometrial neoplasia.

The hormone replacement preparations prescribed for menopausal women are also preferred for young women, as even modern low-dose combined oral contraceptive preparations contain at least twice the amount of oestrogen that is recommended for hormone replacement therapy. Such preparations also contain 'natural' oestrogens rather than the synthetic ethinyloestradiol that is found in most oral contraceptives.

Risk of breast cancer

The beneficial effects of hormone replacement therapy in reducing osteoporosis and cardiovascular mortality are thought to outweigh the risk of breast cancer, particularly in women with premature ovarian failure.

It is now thought necessary only to perform annual breast examination in women considered to be at high risk, such as those with a family history of breast cancer. Mammography in normal women with active glandular breasts is difficult to interpret; thus the role of mammography as a screening procedure in young women taking hormone replacement therapy is not recommended. It is the lifetime exposure to oestrogen that is important; thus young women with premature ovarian failure should be reassured that the use of hormone replacement therapy will not put them at increased risk of breast cancer at least until they reach the average age of menopause (i.e. 51 years), and only then if they continue the hormone therapy for a further 5 years or more.

Follow-up

Follow-up of patients with premature ovarian failure should be at least on an annual basis to monitor hormone replacement therapy, detect the development of associated diseases and provide appropriate support and counselling.

Oocyte donation

Oocyte donation can be used to treat women with premature ovarian failure, of whatever cause. The implantation rates for the recipient are those appropriate to the age of the oocyte donor and usually about 30–40% per treatment cycle. However, uterine effects are apparent when one examines the aetiology of the ovarian failure, as the best pregnancy rates are achieved in women with premature ovarian failure who have an anatomically normal uterus.

Women with Turner's syndrome who have not had a spontaneous puberty and women who have received radiotherapy to the pelvis have reduced uterine blood flow and suboptimal endometrial development in response to exogenous oestrogen therapy (sometimes radiotherapy destroys any subsequent endometrial function). These patients therefore do less well when undergoing oocyte donation. Furthermore, it would seem inadvisable to use the oocytes donated by a sister of a woman with premature ovarian failure as they appear to do less well than those of anonymous fertile donors.

Cryopreservation of ovarian tissue

Experimental work in animals has succeeded in transplanting primordial follicles into irradiated ovaries, with subsequent ovulation and normal pregnancy. An extension of this work has resulted in successful cryopreservation of human ovarian tissue and re-implantation of the thawed tissue with resultant follicular growth, after stimulation with exogenous FSH. The methods employed were devised for the preservation of fertility and ovarian function in young women prior to sterilizing chemotherapy or radiotherapy (see section on iatrogenic causes of amenorrhoea).

The potential exists for the cryopreservation of ovarian tissue for women destined to undergo ovarian failure – an event that might be predictable from genetic or family studies. Whether the cryopreserved ovarian tissue is genetically competent would, of course, be uncertain, but it is easy to foresee the day when women with fragile X premutations or Turner's mosaicism might be asking for ovarian cryopreservation during their adolescent years. At the present time, however, appropriate advice would be for these women to aim for pregnancy using healthy donated oocytes.

Polycystic ovary syndrome

Polycystic ovary syndrome (PCOS) is the most common endocrine disturbance to affect women. The presence of enlarged ovaries with multiple small cysts (2–9 mm) and a hypervascularized, androgen-secreting stroma is associated with signs of androgen excess (hirsutism, alopecia, acne), obesity and menstrual cycle disturbance (oligomenorrhoea or amenorrhoea). The pathophysiology of PCOS thus appears to be multifactorial and polygenic.

Definition of PCOS

The definition of PCOS has been much debated. Key features include:

- Menstrual cycle disturbance.
- Hyperandrogenism.
- Obesity.

Although there are many extra-ovarian aspects to the pathophysiology of PCOS, ovarian dysfunction is central. At a recent joint ASRM/ESHRE consensus meeting, a refined definition of PCOS was agreed: namely, the presence of two out of the following three criteria, with the exclusion of other aetiologies:

- Oligo- and/or anovulation.
- Hyperandrogenism (clinical and/or biochemical).

- Polycystic ovaries. The morphology of the polycystic ovary has been redefined as an ovary with 12 or more follicles measuring 2–9 mm in diameter and/or increased ovarian volume (>10 cm^3).

Signs and symptoms

There is considerable heterogeneity of symptoms and signs amongst women with PCOS (see Box 2.5); for an individual, these may change over time, as may her needs (e.g. cycle control versus fertility). Furthermore, polycystic ovaries can exist without clinical signs of the syndrome, which may then become expressed over time.

Ovarian dysfunction leads to the main signs and symptoms of PCOS. Moreover, the ovary is influenced by external factors, in particular the gonadotrophins and insulin, which are themselves dependent upon both genetic and environmental influences; for example, symptoms are exacerbated by obesity.

Approximately 20–33% of women of reproductive age will have polycystic ovaries on ultrasound scan (see Fig. 2.2), and perhaps 75–80% of these will have symptoms consistent with the diagnosis of PCOS.

Long-term risks

There are long-term risks of developing diabetes and cardiovascular disease. The long-term risk of endometrial hyperplasia and endometrial carcinoma due to chronic anovulation

---

Box 2.5: The spectrum of clinical manifestations of polycystic ovary syndrome

Signs and symptoms (% patients affected)	▪ Obesity (38%)
	▪ Menstrual disturbance (66%)
	– Oligomenorrhoea (47%)
	– Amenorrhoea (19%)
	– Regular cycle (30%)
	▪ Hyperandrogenism (48%)
	▪ Infertility (73% of anovulatory infertility)
	▪ Asymptomatic (20% of those with polycystic ovaries)
Endocrine disturbances	▪ ↑ Insulin
	▪ ↓ Sex hormone binding globulin
	▪ ↑ Androgens (testosterone and androstenedione)
	▪ ↑ Luteinizing hormone
	▪ ↑ Prolactin
Possible late sequelae	▪ Dyslipidaemia
	▪ ↑ LDL, ↓ HDL
	▪ ↑ Triglycerides
	▪ Diabetes mellitus
	▪ Cardiovascular disease
	▪ Hypertension
	▪ Endometrial carcinoma

LDL, low-density lipoprotein; HDL, high-density lipoprotein.

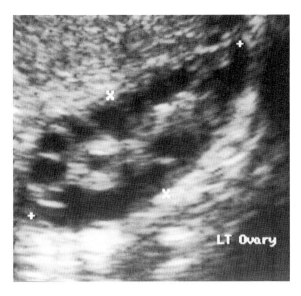

Figure 2.2
Ultrasound scan of an ovary from a woman
with polycystic ovary syndrome.

and unopposed oestrogen has long been recognized. Similarly, there may be an increased
risk of breast carcinoma, but the evidence is conflicting.

Prevention of endometrial hyperplasia

For women with PCOS who experience amenorrhoea or oligomenorrhoea, it is advisable
to induce artificial withdrawal bleeds to prevent endometrial hyperplasia. Indeed, women
with PCOS should shed their endometrium at least every 3 months. For those with
oligomenorrhoea/amenorrhoea who do not wish to use cyclical hormone therapy, an
ultrasound scan to measure endometrial thickness and morphology every 6–12 months is
recommended (depending upon menstrual history). An endometrial thickness greater than
10 mm in an amenorrhoeic woman warrants an artificially induced bleed, which should
be followed by a repeat ultrasound scan and endometrial biopsy if the endometrium has
not been shed.

Management of PCOS

The management of PCOS is symptom-orientated. With respect to menstrual cycle
control, this depends upon whether fertility is desired. Patients with PCOS are not
oestrogen-deficient, and those with amenorrhoea are at risk not of osteoporosis but
rather of endometrial hyperplasia or adenocarcinoma.

Cycle control and regular withdrawal bleeding is achieved with the oral contraceptive pill,
which has the additional beneficial effect of suppressing serum testosterone concentrations
and hence improving hirsutism and acne. A combined oral contraceptive containing the
anti-androgen cyproterone acetate is usually recommended. An alternative is a progestogen

(e.g. medroxyprogesterone acetate or dydrogesterone) for 12 days every 1–3 months to induce a withdrawal bleed. Whereas obesity worsens the symptoms, weight loss improves the endocrine profile and the likelihood of ovulation and a healthy pregnancy.

The role of non-pharmacological interventions for hirsutism, such as waxing, electrolysis and laser, must not be forgotten.

Induction of ovulation for the management of anovulatory PCOS and the management of hyperandrogenism are beyond the scope of this chapter. Similarly, the use of insulin-lowering drugs such as metformin are showing initial promise and have been reviewed elsewhere.

Genetics of PCOS

Genetic studies have demonstrated the familial nature of PCOS, with approximately 50% of first-degree female relatives being affected. Hyperinsulinaemia is thought to be key in the pathophysiology of PCOS and many studies have suggested a link between PCOS and the genetic dysregulation of insulin secretion and action.

PITUITARY CAUSES OF SECONDARY AMENORRHOEA

Hyperprolactinaemia is the most common pituitary cause of amenorrhoea. There are many causes of a mildly elevated serum prolactin concentration, including stress and a recent physical or breast examination. If the prolactin concentration is found to be greater than 1000 mIU/L, the measurement should be repeated. If it is still elevated, it is necessary to image the pituitary fossa (CT or MRI scan).

Causes of hyperprolactinaemia

Hyperprolactinaemia may result from a prolactin-secreting pituitary adenoma or from a non-functioning 'disconnection' tumour in the region of the hypothalamus or pituitary, which disrupts the inhibitory influence of dopamine on prolactin secretion.

Other causes include:

- Stress.
- Hypothyroidism.
- PCOS.
- Many drugs: e.g. the dopamine antagonist phenothiazines, domperidone and metoclopramide.

Additional symptoms

In women with amenorrhoea associated with hyperprolactinaemia, the main symptoms are usually those of oestrogen deficiency. Galactorrhoea may be found in up to a third of hyperprolactinaemic patients, although its occurrence is not correlated with prolactin levels or with the presence of a tumour. Approximately 5% of patients present with visual field defects.

Management of hyperprolactinaemia

Drug therapy

The management of hyperprolactinaemia centres around the use of a dopamine agonist, of which bromocriptine is the most widely used. Most patients show a fall in prolactin levels within a few days of commencing bromocriptine therapy and a reduction of tumour volume within 6 weeks. Longer-acting preparations (e.g. quinagolide, twice-weekly cabergoline) may be prescribed to those patients who develop unacceptable side-effects.

Surgery

Surgery, in the form of a trans-sphenoidal adenectomy, is reserved for cases of drug resistance and failure to shrink a macroadenoma, or if there are intolerable side-effects of the drugs (the most common indication).

Elevated prolactin in the presence of a regular cycle

If the serum prolactin is found to be elevated and the patient has a regular menstrual cycle, no treatment is necessary unless the cycle is anovulatory and fertility is desired. Amenorrhoea is the 'bioassay' of prolactin excess and should be corrected for its sequelae, rather than for the serum level of prolactin.

HYPOTHALAMIC CAUSES OF SECONDARY AMENORRHOEA

Hypothalamic causes of amenorrhoea (hypogonadotrophic hypogonadism) may be either primary or secondary.

Primary causes

Primary hypothalamic lesions include:

- Craniopharyngiomas.
- Germinomas.
- Gliomas.
- Dermoid cysts.

These lesions either disrupt the normal pathway of prolactin inhibitory factor (dopamine), thus causing hyperprolactinaemia, or compress and/or destroy hypothalamic and pituitary tissue. Treatment is usually surgical, with additional radiotherapy if required.

Secondary causes

Secondary hypogonadotrophic hypogonadism may result from systemic conditions, including:

- Sarcoidosis.
- Tuberculosis.
- Following head injury or cranial irradiation.

Hormone replacement therapy is required to mimic ovarian function, and, if the pituitary gland is damaged either by the lesion or by the treatment, replacement thyroid and adrenal hormones are required. Ovulation may be induced with pulsatile subcutaneous gonadotrophin-releasing hormone (GnRH) or human menopausal gonadotrophins.

SYSTEMIC DISORDERS CAUSING SECONDARY AMENORRHOEA

Chronic disease may result in menstrual disorders as a consequence of:

- The general disease state.
- Weight loss.
- Effect of the disease process on the hypothalamic–pituitary axis.

Management should concentrate on the underlying systemic problem and on preventing complications of oestrogen deficiency. If fertility is required, it is desirable to achieve maximal health and, where possible, to discontinue teratogenic drugs.

Studies have failed to demonstrate a link between stressful life events and amenorrhoea of greater than 2 months.

WEIGHT-RELATED AMENORRHOEA

Weight and eating disorders are common in women.

Weight loss may be due to a number of causes, including:

- Self-induced abstinence.
- Starvation.
- Illness.
- Exercise.

Even very mild dieting, with restriction of fat intake, can interfere with gonadotrophin secretion.

The clinical presentation depends upon the severity of the nutritional insult and the age of onset. To cause amenorrhoea the loss must be 10–15% of the women's normal weight for height.

Endocrinology and metabolism

Weight can have profound effects on gonadotrophin regulation and release. A regular menstrual cycle will not occur if the body mass index is less than 19 kg/m^2. Fat appears to be critical to a normally functioning hypothalamic–pituitary–gonadal axis. It is estimated that at least 22% of body weight should be fat in order to maintain ovulatory cycles. This level enables the extra-ovarian aromatization of androgens to oestrogens, and maintains appropriate feedback control of the hypothalamic–pituitary–ovarian axis.

The role of leptin

Leptin is a 167 amino acid peptide that is secreted by fat cells in response to insulin and glucocorticoids. Leptin decreases the intake of food and stimulates thermogenesis. Leptin also appears to inhibit the hypothalamic peptide neuropeptide Y, which is an inhibitor of GnRH pulsatility. Leptin appears to serve as a signal from the body fat to the brain about the adequacy of fat stores for reproduction. Thus menstruation will only occur if fat stores are adequate.

Anorexia nervosa

Anorexia nervosa is at the extreme end of a spectrum of eating disorders and is invariably accompanied by menstrual disturbance; indeed, it may account for 15–35% of patients with amenorrhoea. Women with anorexia nervosa should be managed in collaboration with a psychiatrist, and it is essential to encourage weight gain as the main therapy.

An artificial menstrual cycle may be induced with the combined oral contraceptive. However, this may corroborate in the denial of weight loss being the underlying problem. Similarly, while it is possible to induce ovulation with GnRH or exogenous gonadotrophins, treatment of infertility in the significantly underweight patient is associated with a significant increase in intrauterine growth retardation and neonatal problems.

Worldwide, involuntary starvation is the most common cause of reduced reproductive ability, resulting in delayed pubertal growth and menarche in adolescents and infertility in adults. The chronic malnutrition that is common in developing countries has less profound effects on fertility, but is associated with small and premature babies.

EXERCISE-INDUCED AMENORRHOEA

Menstrual disturbance is common in women undergoing intensive exercise and training. Studies have reported rates of oligomenorrhoea/amenorrhoea of:

- 16–79% in dancers.
- 47% in gymnasts.
- 24–30% in runners.
- 12% in swimmers and cyclists.

Amenorrhoea is more common in athletes under 30 years of age and is particularly common in women involved in endurance events (e.g. long-distance running). Up to 50% of competitive runners training 80 miles per week may be amenorrhoeic.

Risk of osteoporosis and other injuries

Athletes

Exercise-induced amenorrhoea has the potential to cause severe long-term morbidity, particularly with regard to osteoporosis. Young athletes may be placing themselves at risk at an age when the attainment of peak bone mass is important for long-term skeletal strength.

Dancers

Studies on young ballet dancers have shown that the amount of exercise undertaken by these dancers does not compensate for osteoporotic changes. Oestrogen is also important in the formation of collagen, and soft tissue injuries are common in dancers.

Psychological considerations

It is sometimes difficult to unravel the interaction between desire to exercise and an eating disorder, as under-eating and over-exercising are considered to be mutually reinforcing and self-perpetuating behaviours. The psyche of the young athlete is affected by pressure not only to compete against peers but also from parents and coaches. Stresses – mental as well as physical – can be immense, and some athletes are found to be abusing 'performance-enhancing drugs' at a young age.

Management

Appropriate advice should be given, particularly with regard to improving the diet, and use of vitamin, calcium and iron supplements. Use of a cyclical oestrogen–progestogen preparation should also be considered.

If possible, the amount of exercise itself should be reduced, for which the support of parents and trainers is essential.

IATROGENIC CAUSES OF AMENORRHOEA

There are many iatrogenic causes of amenorrhoea, which may be either temporary or permanent. Such causes include malignant conditions that require radiation to the abdomen/pelvis or chemotherapy. Both these treatments may result in permanent gonadal damage, the amount of damage being directly related to the age of the patient, the cumulative dose and the patient's prior menstrual status.

It is estimated that 1 in 1000 adults are now survivors of childhood malignancy and, for these women, the cryopreservation of gonadal tissue (see section on cryopreservation above) prior to treatment might soon offer a real chance of restoring fertility (and, possibly, without the need for exogenous hormone replacement therapy).

Gynaecological procedures such as oophorectomy, hysterectomy and endometrial resection inevitably result in amenorrhoea. Hormone replacement should be prescribed for these patients where appropriate. Hormone therapy itself can be used to deliberately disrupt the menstrual cycle. However, iatrogenic causes of ovarian quiescence have the same consequences of oestrogen deficiency as any other aetiology.

FUTURE DIRECTIONS Amenorrhoea is a disorder with a spectrum of aetiologies. In future years research is likely to be directed towards improving our understanding of the genetic origins of conditions such as premature ovarian failure and PCOS. More work is also required in ascertaining optimal regimens of hormone replacement therapy, particularly for young women with premature ovarian failure.

Selected References and Further Reading

Balen AH. The pathogenesis of polycystic ovary syndrome: the enigma unravels [editorial]. Lancet 1999; 354:966–967.

Balen AH, Conway GS, Kaltsas G, et al. Polycystic ovary syndrome: the spectrum of the disorder in 1741 patients. Hum Reprod 1995; 10:2107–2111.

Conway GS. Premature ovarian failure. Curr Opin Obstet Gynecol 1997; 9:202–206.

Cumming DC, Rebar RW. Exercise and reproductive function in women. Am J Indust Med 1983; 4:113–125.

Davies MC, Hall M, Davies HS. Bone mineral density in young women with amenorrhoea. BMJ 1990; 301:790–793.

Frisch RE. Fatness of girls from menarche to age 18 years, with a nomogram. Hum Biol 1976; 48:353–359.

Garner DM, Rosen LW, Barry D. Eating disorders among athletes. Research and recommendations. Child Adolesc Psychiatr Clin N Am 1998; 7:839–857.

Michelmore KF, Balen AH, Dunger DB, et al. Polycystic ovaries and associated clinical and biochemical features in young women. Clin Endocrinol 1999; 51:779–786.

Rajkowha M, Glass MR, Rutherford AJ, et al. Polycystic ovary syndrome: a risk factor for cardiovascular disease? BJOG 2000; 107:11–18.

Robinson TL, Snow-Harter C, Taaffe DR, et al. Gymnasts exhibit higher bone mass than runners despite similar prevalence of amenorrhoea and oligomenorrhoea. J Bone Miner Res 1995; 10:26–35.

Soule SG, Jacobs HS. Prolactinomas: present day management. BJOG 1995; 102:178–181.

Sexually transmitted infections

3

Jackie Sherrard

> **THIS CHAPTER** This chapter outlines the principles behind management of sexually transmitted infections (STIs), including risk assessment, sexual history-taking and examination. It discusses the importance of confidentiality in the context of STIs. The presentation, diagnosis and management of the common clinical syndromes caused by STIs in women are described, together with the effects of STIs on pregnancy.

Background

Sexually transmitted infections (STIs) are a major public health burden, both globally and nationally. The World Health Organization estimates that, in 1999, 340 million new cases of treatable STIs occurred in the world, of which there were:

- 92 million cases of chlamydia.
- 62 million cases of gonorrhoea.
- 12 million cases of syphilis.
- 174 million cases of trichomoniasis.

Overall, the number, of all new episodes seen each year in genitourinary medicine clinics in the UK has more than doubled since 1990, and this rise continued between 2001 and 2002 to 1.63 million new episodes. Large increases in many acute STIs have contributed to the overall increase in all new diagnoses. Diagnoses of chlamydia, gonorrhoea and infectious syphilis have all more than doubled since 1995 (Fig. 3.1). By the end of the second quarter of 2003, 57 763 HIV-infected individuals had been reported to the UK HIV dataset, which began in 1982. The total number of reports received for 2002 was 5542, the highest for any year since reporting began.

The long-term health consequences of STIs are considerable (Box 3.1), and include:

- Chronic pelvic pain.
- Infertility.
- Ectopic pregnancy.
- Pregnancy-related complications.
- Neonatal infection.
- Genital tract cancers.

Globally, HIV infection is a major cause of lost productive years. The presence of any STI increases the risk of an individual acquiring HIV infection. HIV-infected individuals who

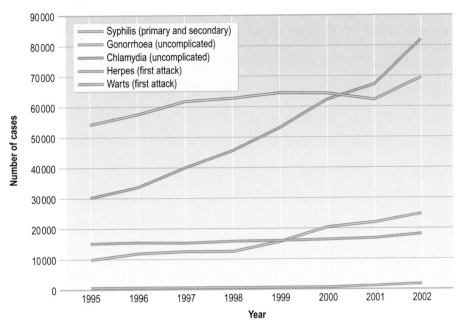

Figure 3.1
New diagnoses of selected STIs in genitourinary medicine clinics in England, 1995–2002.

Box 3.1: Consequences of poor sexual health

- Pelvic inflammatory disease, leading to ectopic pregnancies and infertility
- HIV infection, leading to immunosuppression, AIDS and death
- Enhanced HIV transmission
- Cervical and other anogenital cancers
- Hepatitis, chronic liver disease and liver cancer
- Adverse pregnancy outcomes and neonatal morbidity
- Unintended pregnancies and abortions

---

are infected with other STIs have increased shedding of HIV and are more likely to transmit the infection to others sexually.

WHAT ARE STIs?

A number of different organisms can be transmitted sexually (Table 3.1). Bacterial and viral STIs can be asymptomatic in both men and women. Viral STIs in particular exhibit latency, and the recent diagnosis of an STI does not necessarily equate to recent acquisition of infection. This is of great importance when counselling the patient as to the possible source of infection.

Table 3.1: Sexually transmitted organisms and infections

	Causative organism	Infection
Bacteria	Chlamydia trachomatis (serovars D–K)	Chlamydia
	Neisseria gonorrhoeae	Gonorrhoea
	Treponema pallidum	Syphilis
	Chlamydia trachomatis (serovars L1–L3)	Lymphogranuloma venereum
	Haemophilus ducreyi	Chancroid
	Calymmatobacterium granulomatis	Granuloma inguinale
Virus	Herpes simplex virus (types 1 and 2) (HSV)	Anogenital herpes
	Human papilloma virus (HPV)	Anogenital warts
	Human immunodeficiency virus (HIV)	HIV infection and AIDS
	Pox virus	Molluscum contagiosum
Protozoa	*Trichomonas vaginalis*	Trichomoniasis
Ectoparasites	*Phthirus pubis*	Pubic lice
	Sarcoptes scabiei	Scabies

SEXUALLY ASSOCIATED INFECTIONS

Bacterial vaginosis (a syndrome characterized by a depletion of the normal vaginal lactobacilli and overgrowth of vaginal anaerobes) and candidiasis are included in the differential diagnosis of many STIs, although they are not considered as sexually transmitted infections. Both occur in the absence of sexual activity, although the presence of bacterial vaginosis is associated with sexual activity.

RISK GROUPS AND RISK FACTORS

There are identifiable factors that make an individual more likely to have an STI (Box 3.2). Those at greatest risk of infection are:

- The young.
- The single.
- Those using non-barrier contraception.

Concurrent sexual partners or rapid rates of partner change increase the risk of acquisition of STIs.

The risk factors are not exclusive and many people diagnosed with an STI do not fall into identified risk groups, so the possibility of an STI should always be considered. The women at greatest risk of infection, those aged less than 20 years, are not in the national cervical screening programme and may attend health services erratically. Healthcare

Box 3.2: Risk factors for STIs

- Young age (less than 25 years, but particularly females younger than 20 years)
- Single
- Non-use of barrier contraception
- Residence in an urban centre
- Other STIs
- Symptoms, or diagnosis of infection, in partner
- Two or more sexual partners in the preceding 6 months, or a new partner

professionals seeing these young women in any context should always consider the possibility of STIs.

The recent increasing rates of STIs have also been seen, albeit to a lesser extent, among older people. These individuals may have seen long-term relationships break down and are entering new relationships with little awareness of the personal risks of STIs. Often they do not need contraception and fail to consider the use of condoms for protection against infection.

Co-infection

The risk factors that put an individual at risk of one STI put them at risk of others. Consequently, individuals with one STI are more likely to have another. For example, 30–50% of women with gonorrhoea will also have chlamydia, although fewer women with chlamydia will have gonorrhoea as it is less prevalent. This potential for co-infections needs to be considered when managing an individual with any STI.

CLINICAL ASPECTS

The majority of infections (at least 50%) in women are asymptomatic. This can make the diagnosis difficult unless there is a high index of suspicion and/or facilities for screening. The symptoms that do occur are frequently non-specific for any condition and are often due to complications arising from untreated infection, such as deep dyspareunia or altered menses due to pelvic infection.

CONFIDENTIALITY

In England, all patients with STIs are subject to the NHS Trusts and Primary Care Trusts (Sexually Transmitted Diseases) Directions 2000. These state that:

> Every NHS Trust and Primary Care Trust shall take all necessary steps to secure that any
> information capable of identifying an individual obtained by any of their members or

employees with respect to persons examined or treated for any sexually transmitted disease shall not be disclosed except:

(a) for the purpose of communicating that information to a medical practitioner, or to a person employed under the direction of a medical practitioner in connection with the treatment of persons suffering from such disease or the prevention of the spread thereof; and

(b) for the purpose of such treatment or prevention.

All healthcare professionals managing patients with STIs should have a clear policy on confidentiality.

TAKING A SEXUAL HISTORY

A sexual history enables the healthcare professional to establish an individual's risk of infection. Clear direct questions should be asked in a non-judgemental way. A doctor who feels comfortable asking the relevant questions goes a long way to putting the patient at ease. Explaining why the questions are being asked reduces the patient's embarrassment. Likewise, the assurance of privacy (both by stating this and taking the history in a room where the conversation will not be overheard) is much more likely to encourage a patient to answer questions. Conversely, trying to take a sexual history behind curtains on an open ward is unlikely to be very productive.

A general history should be taken first and include:

• Physical symptoms.
• The duration and nature of the physical symptoms.
• A menstrual and contraceptive history.

A sexual history should then be taken (see Box 3.3). If necessary, more detailed questions can then be asked. These may include:

• Relevant past medical history.
• Past history of an STI.
• Symptoms or known infection in a partner.
• Any current medication, especially antimicrobials.

The more often these questions are asked and a routine developed, the easier it becomes for both the doctor and the patient.

Box 3.3: Some key questions in a sexual history

- When did you last have sex?
- Was that with a regular or casual partner, male or female?
- Did he use a condom?
- How long have you been together?
- When did you last have sex with anyone else?

EXAMINATION AND INVESTIGATION

Informed consent should be obtained before examination, investigation and management. Box 3.4 lists the main indications for carrying out an examination for STIs.

The examination should include:

- Inspection of the whole anogenital area and the superficial inguinal glands.
- Speculum examination (ideally with a plastic speculum, which offers better visibility of the vaginal walls).
- Bimanual pelvic examination for cervical motion tenderness (cervical excitation) and adnexal tenderness.

Why perform investigations?

The decisions as to which investigations to perform will depend upon the local epidemiology and clinical setting. An accurate diagnosis is important for several reasons, some of which are listed in Box 3.5.

The samples to be obtained depend upon the tests that can be performed locally, thus liaison with the local genitourinary medicine and microbiology services is required. Newer DNA-based tests are becoming available. Many of the tests require specific sampling kits

---

Box 3.4: Indications for carrying out examination and screening for STIs

- Diagnosis of any STI
- Risk behaviour for STI acquisition, especially unprotected sexual intercourse with a new or casual partner
- Signs or symptoms suggestive of an STI, which in females include:
  - Alteration in normal vaginal discharge
  - Genital lumps
  - Genital ulcers
  - Symptoms of upper genital tract infection, including pelvic pain, deep dyspareunia, altered menses (intermenstrual/postcoital bleeding)
- Sexual contact with a person with symptoms of an STI (in males: urethral discharge and/or dysuria, genital lumps or ulcers, testicular pain)
- Diagnosis of an STI in a sexual partner
- Prior to instrumentation of the cervix, in particular in those at risk of STIs: i.e. termination of pregnancy and insertion of an intrauterine device for postcoital contraception

---

Box 3.5: Why perform investigations?

- Asymptomatic infections are common and can only be excluded by appropriate investigation
- An accurate diagnosis is important, as infections may have serious health implications for patients and partners
- An accurate diagnosis allows more appropriate treatment
- Allows decisions as to whether follow-up and tests of cure are necessary
- Facilitates partner notification
- Allows collection of epidemiological data to improve planning of interventions

or swabs, but reduce the need for invasive sampling. Nevertheless, a speculum examination is always advised in symptomatic patients.

As a minimum, a screen for infection should include samples for chlamydia and gonorrhoea. Serology should be obtained for syphilis. As indicated by symptoms, history and examination, further tests may need to be taken from the vagina for bacterial vaginosis, candida and trichomoniasis, and, if genital ulcers are present, for herpes simplex. Serology for hepatitis B and HIV antibodies may be indicated.

CLINICAL SYNDROMES

Although many women with STIs have no symptoms, there are several typical syndromes that are associated with the presence of an STI.

Vaginal discharge

Three common infections are associated with vaginal discharge:

- Bacterial vaginosis (Fig. 3.2).
- Candidiasis (Fig. 3.3).
- Trichomoniasis.

Altered vaginal discharge may be associated with a number of other physiological and pathological conditions which need to be considered, especially if specific tests for infections are negative. These include pregnancy, allergic vaginitis, vaginal douching, retained foreign body (e.g. tampon or condom), cervical ectropium and cervical carcinoma. Cervical infections such as gonorrhoea and chlamydia uncommonly present with altered discharge, often due to the presence of a co-existent vaginal infection. This should be borne in mind in the investigation of a woman with vaginal discharge and these infections tested for if the woman has risk factors for infection.

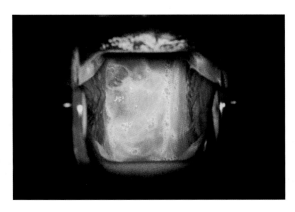

Figure 3.2
Typical discharge of bacterial vaginosis.
Reproduced, with permission of Health Press
Limited, from Edwards A, Sherrard J,
Zenilman J. Fast facts. Sexually transmitted
infections. 2nd edn. Oxford: Health Press; 2001.

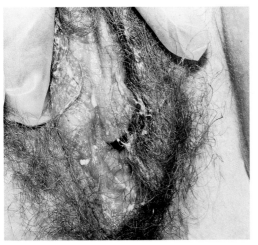

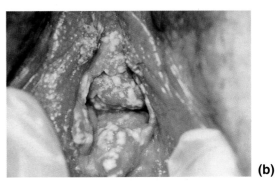

(a)

(b)

Figure 3.3
(a) Vulvitis and discharge in patient with vaginal candidiasis. (b) Candida vulvovaginitis. Reproduced, with permission of Health Press Limited, from Edwards A, Sherrard J, Zenilman J. Fast facts. Sexually transmitted infections. 2nd edn. Oxford: Health Press; 2001.

Table 3.2: Symptoms associated with vaginal infections

	Bacterial vaginosis	Trichomoniasis	Candidiasis
No symptoms	Approximately 50%	10–50%	10–20%
Vulval itching	No	Yes	Yes
Vaginal discharge	Offensive	Offensive	Non-offensive
Others		Dysuria Rarely, low abdominal discomfort	Superficial dyspareunia

Symptoms are not specific for any infection, although some symptoms are more characteristic of one infection than another (Table 3.2). Characteristic physical findings are associated with each infection (Table 3.3), but atypical presentations are common. The definitive diagnosis for each infection is based upon laboratory tests of samples of the discharge from the vaginal wall (see Boxes 3.6–3.8). This is important when symptoms have failed to respond to empirical treatment or recurred shortly following treatment.

If *Trichomonas vaginalis* infection is suspected, an accurate diagnosis is important as this is an STI and treatment of the partner is necessary. A sample of the discharge is taken from the vaginal wall with a swab. Direct microscopy can be done immediately if facilities are available. In the absence of direct microscopy, measurement of the pH of the vaginal secretions with narrow-band pH paper is helpful (see p. 45, Figs 3.4, 3.5).

Table 3.3: Signs associated with vaginal infections

	Bacterial vaginosis	Trichomoniasis	Candidiasis
Anogenital skin			Satellite skin lesions
Vulva		Erythema	Erythema Fissuring Oedema
Vagina	Thin white homogeneous discharge, coating walls of vagina and vestibule	Vaginitis Discharge in up to 70%, frothy and yellow in 10–30%	Discharge, may be curdy
Cervix		Approx. 2% 'strawberry' cervix to the naked eye	
No abnormal signs	Yes	Yes	Yes

Box 3.6: Diagnosis of bacterial vaginosis

- Amsel's criteria (the presence of three of the following criteria is required):
  - Thin white-grey homogeneous discharge (sometimes frothy)
  - Vaginal fluid pH >4.5
  - Release of fishy odour on adding alkali (10% potassium hydroxide) ('whiff test')
- Clue cells present on direct microscopy
- Nugent's criteria, based on a Gram-stained vaginal smear. The relative proportions of bacterial morphotypes are estimated to give a score: 0–4, normal; 4–6, intermediate; 6–10, indicative of bacterial vaginosis

Box 3.7: Diagnosis of Trichomonas vaginalis infection

- Direct observation of the organism by a wet smear (normal saline) or acridine orange stained slide from the posterior vaginal fornix (will diagnose 40–80% of cases)
- Trichomonads are sometimes reported on cervical cytology, where the sensitivity is approximately 60%. However, there is a high false-positive rate and it is prudent to confirm the diagnosis by a vaginal swab
- Culture media are available and will diagnose up to 95% of cases

Box 3.8: Diagnosis of vaginal candidiasis

- Vaginal pH of 4–4.5
- Absence of smell (in 'whiff test' on speculum and in amine odour test on slide)
- Yeasts or pseudohyphae seen on wet preparation and/or Gram stain (40–60% positive) of vaginal discharge
- Vaginal or vulval culture positive for a yeast species

Figure 3.4
Narrow-range pH paper (colour develops in
30 seconds).

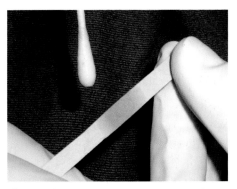

Figure 3.5
Vaginal secretions on pH paper (patient with
bacterial vaginosis).

Figure 3.6
Vulval herpes. Reproduced, with permission
of Health Press Limited, from Edwards A,
Sherrard J, Zenilman J. Fast facts. Sexually
transmitted infections. 2nd edn. Oxford:
Health Press; 2001.

Genital ulcers

In the UK, genital ulcers are most commonly due to herpes simplex virus (HSV) infection
(Fig. 3.6). The diagnosis is mainly clinically based, but should be confirmed if possible by
laboratory tests. Tissue culture of fluid from a vesicle remains the method of choice.

The primary genital infection has an incubation period of 2–14 days, and an untreated
attack may last up to 4 weeks. There may be a systemic viraemic prodrome, followed by
the development of multiple genital vesicles that ulcerate and finally heal by forming scabs.
There is often bilateral painful inguinal lymphadenopathy. Cervical lesions may cause a
watery vaginal discharge. Associated symptoms include external dysuria, headache and
myalgia. Labial adhesions may develop if extensive ulceration is present. Women with a
primary attack of herpes should be treated promptly with oral antiherpetic medication.
Symptomatic treatment with saline bathing, regular analgesics and locally applied ice-packs
is usually helpful.

HSV establishes latency in the sensory nervous system and reactivates from time to time.
Viral shedding may occur from genital surfaces in the absence of symptoms or signs.

Symptomatic recurrent episodes are usually milder and shorter than first episodes, with fewer systemic symptoms. Patients with mild or infrequent recurrences require only symptomatic therapy. Those with more frequent episodes may be managed with antiviral suppressive therapy.

The differential diagnosis of genital herpes in the UK includes:

- Pyogenic lesions.
- Folliculitis or a ruptured furuncle.
- Aphthous ulceration.
- Trauma.
- Fixed drug eruptions.
- Malignant lesions.
- Syphilis.

Patients with genital ulcers and a history of sex in endemic areas may require additional diagnostic tests for:

- Chancroid.
- Lymphogranuloma venereum.
- Granuloma inguinale.

These tests are highly specialized and such patients should be referred to a genitourinary medicine clinic for appropriate investigations.

Genital lumps

Genital warts may be noticed during routine genital examination. Alternatively, the woman may notice lumps in the genital area and present for diagnosis and management. The areas most commonly affected are the fourchette and labia, but the perianal area, vagina and cervix may all be involved (Fig. 3.7). Genital warts rarely cause any symptoms, although some patients complain of itching. Many cases of infection are subclinical. There are a number of strains of human papilloma virus (HPV) that infect the genital mucosa, the most common being HPV-6 and HPV-11.

The incubation period is long, commonly 3 months and possibly extending up to 18 months. The diagnosis is clinical, although in cases of atypical lesions or older patients biopsy should be considered, as the differential diagnosis includes premalignant and malignant diseases of the genitals. The main differential diagnoses are:

- Molluscum contagiosum.
- Normal anatomical variants: e.g. fibroepithelial papillae of the inner surface of the labia minora, sebaceous cysts and glands.

Treatment modalities are all aimed at clearance of the macroscopic wart. No treatment reliably clears wart virus from the skin and recurrence following treatment is common. Eventually, however, most patients will clear the virus. Treatment modalities include:

- Local destruction: e.g. cryotherapy, diathermy, scissor excision, trichloroacetic acid.
- Antimitotic agents: e.g. podophyllin and podophyllotoxin.

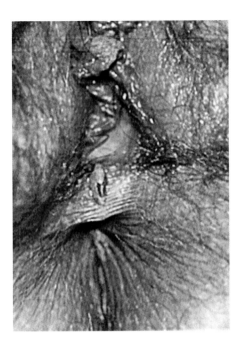

Figure 3.7
Solitary genital wart.

The latter agents are contraindicated in pregnancy. More recently, immunomodulators have become commercially available. These are expensive and have a slow clearance rate, but they probably have a lower recurrence rate.

Cervical and vaginal warts should be assessed with a colposcope and, if intraepithelial neoplasia has been excluded, can be treated using cryotherapy, electrosurgery or podophyllin.

Pelvic pain/dyspareunia

In a young, sexually active woman complaining of pelvic pain or associated symptoms, there should be a low threshold for considering the possibility of pelvic inflammatory disease. As a result of increased concern about silent pelvic inflammatory disease, recommendations for diagnosis have moved to a syndromic approach based on the history and clinical findings. This may result in unnecessary treatment, but it has been shown that delayed treatment increases the risk of long-term sequelae, which include chronic pelvic pain, ectopic pregnancy and tubal infertility.

Chlamydia and gonorrhoea are endocervical infections in the female. Uncomplicated infection is often asymptomatic, but the resulting cervicitis may present as intermenstrual or postcoital bleeding and, less commonly, as altered vaginal discharge. On speculum examination the cervix may appear inflamed with a purulent discharge. Contact bleeding commonly occurs.

If untreated, 10–30% of women with chlamydial and/or gonococcal cervicitis will develop pelvic inflammatory disease. The clinical spectrum ranges from asymptomatic or subclinical endometritis to symptomatic salpingitis, pyosalpinx, tubo-ovarian abscess, pelvic peritonitis

> **Box 3.9: Signs and symptoms suggestive of pelvic inflammatory disease**
>
> **Symptoms**
>
> - Pelvic pain
> - Deep dyspareunia
> - Altered menses
> - Intermenstrual/postcoital bleeding
> - Altered vaginal discharge
>
> **Signs**
>
> - Cervical excitation (cervical motion tenderness)
> - Adnexal tenderness
> - Pyrexia (unusual in chronic infection)

and occasionally perihepatitis (see Box 3.9). Symptoms may be intermittent and chronic, or acute.

A screen for infections, including appropriate tests for gonorrhoea and chlamydia, should be undertaken, but it should be noted that negative microbiological tests do not exclude a diagnosis of pelvic inflammatory disease; in at least 50% cases no specific organisms are identified. Urinalysis, a pregnancy test and a mid-stream urine specimen may assist in the differential diagnosis.

The differential diagnosis of pelvic inflammatory disease includes:

- Ectopic pregnancy.
- Irritable bowel syndrome.
- Endometriosis.
- Appendicitis.
- Ovarian cysts.
- Urinary tract infection.

Current sexual partners should be contacted and screened for infection, or referred to the local genitourinary medicine department, even if no organism is isolated in the woman (see below).

MANAGEMENT PRINCIPLES

All patients diagnosed with an STI should be recommended to have a screen for co-existent infections. When any sexually transmitted organism or syndrome is diagnosed, it is recommended that partners should be screened for infections and treatment if necessary (see below). Sexual abstinence should be advised until treatment of all partners is completed to prevent re-infection.

TREATMENT

Recommended treatments for the common infections are given in Table 3.4.

Table 3.4: Recommended treatments for common infections (adapted from UK national guidelines)

Infection	First-line treatment	Pregnancy
Chlamydia: uncomplicated	Doxycycline 100 mg bd for 7 days Azithromycin 1 g as single dose	Erythromycin 500 bd for 14 days Erythromycin 500 qds for 7 days
Gonorrhoea: uncomplicated	Ciprofloxacin 500 mg stat Ceftriaxone 250 mg i.m. stat Ampicillin 2 g or 3 g plus probenecid 1 g as a single dose, depending on regional prevalence of penicillin-resistant infection	Ampicillin 2 g or 3 g plus probenecid 1 g as a single dose, depending on regional prevalence of penicillin-resistant infection Spectinomycin 2 g i.m. as a single dose Cefotaxime 500 mg i.m. as a single dose Ceftriaxone 250 mg i.m. as a single dose
Bacterial vaginosis	Metronidazole 400–500 mg bd for 5–7 days	Metronidazole 400–500 mg bd for 5–7 days
Trichomonas vaginalis	Metronidazole 400–500 mg bd for 5–7 days	Metronidazole 400–500 mg bd for 5–7 days
Candida	Pessaries are as effective as oral antifungals	Avoid oral preparations
First episode of genital herpes	Aciclovir 200 mg five times a day Famciclovir 250 mg tds Valaciclovir 500 mg bd (all for 5 days)	

STIs AND PREGNANCY

STIs can affect all stages of conception, pregnancy and birth, including:

- Infertility.
- Ectopic pregnancy.
- Spontaneous abortion.
- Intrauterine death.
- Preterm labour.
- Intrapartum and postpartum maternal infection.
- Perinatal infection.
- Congenital abnormalities.

Chlamydia

Chlamydia may cause tubal damage, resulting in ectopic pregnancy or tubal infertility. Infection during pregnancy can lead to chorioamnionitis, resulting in postpartum endometritis. Perinatal transmission may occur at the time of delivery, resulting in ophthalmia neonatorum or pneumonitis (20–50% and 10–20%, respectively, of babies born to infected mothers).

Gonorrhoea

Gonorrhoea may cause tubal damage, resulting in ectopic pregnancy or tubal infertility. Infection during pregnancy has been associated with prelabour rupture of membranes and preterm delivery. Postpartum endometritis and severe pelvic sepsis may occur. Perinatal transmission may occur at the time of delivery, resulting in ophthalmia neonatorum (30–47% of babies born to infected mothers). Occasionally, disseminated gonococcal infection develops in the neonate.

Trichomoniasis

Trichomoniasis has until recently been thought not to affect pregnancy, but a recent observational study has suggested association with preterm delivery and low birth weight.

Bacterial vaginosis

Bacterial vaginosis is associated with an increased risk of preterm birth, especially in women with a history of previous preterm birth.

Syphilis

Syphilis may result in stillbirth, neonatal death or congenital syphilis in neonates that survive. Intrauterine or perinatal transmission will occur in two-thirds of mothers with untreated infection.

Herpes

Primary herpes in early pregnancy may cause spontaneous abortion in up to 25% of cases. Infection later in pregnancy may result in premature delivery and/or disseminated neonatal HSV infection. Recurrent herpes in pregnancy is not usually associated with an adverse outcome. Guidelines for the management of herpes infection are available.

Warts

Wart virus may be transmitted perinatally and result in laryngeal papillomas in the neonate or perianal area. The risk of developing macroscopic lesions appears low, and warts may occur in babies born to mothers with no history of wart virus infection, due to the subclinical nature of many infections.

HIV

HIV can be transmitted to the baby *in utero*, during delivery and via breast milk. The risk of perinatal transmission can be markedly reduced by the use of antiretroviral therapy in pregnancy, elective caesarean section and avoidance of breastfeeding. Recent emphasis has been on the identification of infected women during pregnancy so that interventions to reduce transmission can be planned.

The neonate

Whenever an STI is diagnosed in a neonate it is important that the mother and her sexual partner(s) are screened and treated as contacts (see below).

PARTNER NOTIFICATION

By definition, whenever an individual is identified as having an STI, there is at least one other infected individual and often more. Partner notification is the process by which the recent sexual contacts of a patient (index case) are informed that they are at risk of an infection, invited for screening and offered treatment if found to be infected.

This is a method of targeted case finding that leads to early diagnosis and treatment of infection, reduces the risk of re-infection and complications in both the index case and their contacts, reduces onward transmission of STIs in the community and offers an opportunity to discuss safer sex.

FUTURE DIRECTIONS Changing sexual attitudes and lifestyles resulting in changing pattern of STIs and the advent of HIV/AIDS have led to recognition of importance of sexual health. The sexual health and HIV strategy was published by the Department of Health in England in 2001 with the following aims:

- Reduce transmission HIV and STIs.
- Reduce prevalence of undiagnosed STIs and HIV.
- Reduce unintended pregnancy rates.
- Improve health and social care for those living with HIV.
- Reduce the stigma associated with STIs and HIV.

It sets out a widened role for primary care with closer working between primary and secondary care and service standards at each level. It aims to improve access to genitourinary medicine services and see the establishment of managed clinical networks for HIV and other services, which are likely to include obstetrics and gynaecology.

Targeted chlamydia screening began in 2002 and this will roll out over the next few years, accompanied by a switch to nucleic acid diagnostic tests, allowing non-invasive sampling. This should eventually lead to a reduction in the long-term sequelae of pelvic inflammatory disease, ectopic pregnancies and tubal infertility.

Selected References and Further Reading

Adler M. ABC of sexually transmitted diseases. London: BMJ Books; 1999.

Anonymous. Sexually transmitted diseases. Lancet 1998; 351(suppl 3).

Anonymous. Sexually transmitted infections. Medicine 2001; 29:1–84.

Barton SE, Hay PE. Handbook of genitourinary medicine. London: Arnold; 1999.

Clinical Effectiveness Group. UK guidelines for management of STIs, 2001. www.mssvd.org.uk/CEG/ceguidelines.htm.

Department of Health. The NHS trusts and primary care trusts (sexually transmitted diseases) directions 2000. London: HMSO; 2000.

Department of Health. The national strategy for sexual health and HIV. London: Department of Health; 2001.

Dimian CO, Bingham JS. Sexually transmitted diseases and pregnancy. J Eur Acad Dermatol Venereol 1996; 6:1–10.

Edwards A, Sherrard J, Zenilman J. Fast facts. Sexually transmitted infections. Oxford: Health Press; 2001.

Holmes KK, Sparling PF, Mardh P-A, et al, eds. Sexually transmitted diseases. 3rd edn. New York: McGraw-Hill; 1999.

Public Health Laboratory Service. www.phls.co.uk/facts/STI/sti_uk_data.htm.

Wisdom A, Hawkins DA. Sexually transmitted diseases: diagnosis in colour. 2nd edn. St Louis: Mosby; 1997.

Gynaecological emergencies

4

Ian MacKenzie

THIS CHAPTER This chapter deals with emergencies that may confront the general practitioner or gynaecological resident when patients present from the community, rather than while they are inpatients on a gynaecological ward following surgery. Emergencies are considered according to symptomatology, in the way that they present, rather than using the final diagnosis. The likely causes for the presentations are given, together with appropriate examination and investigations and the initial first-aid management.

Background

The need to manage women presenting with acute gynaecological symptoms or signs has always existed. The traditional approach in the UK was for women in whom a gynaecological emergency was diagnosed to be sent to the gynaecological ward for admission and assessment by the admitting senior house officer. When an operation was required, this would often be performed out-of-hours when an operating theatre became available. During the past 10 years, the management of gynaecological emergencies involving women in whom pregnancy is suspected has changed dramatically, with the introduction of daily early pregnancy assessment, or bleeding-in-pregnancy clinics, provided by a gynaecologist, or in some units a specialist nurse, with a sonographer processing the patient quickly. This approach to care has not included all types of gynaecological emergencies in some units, and patients with other acute problems may wait for attention if other staff are not available to deal with them urgently.

Symptomatology

Four categories of symptoms presenting as emergencies are recognized:

- Abnormal vaginal bleeding.
- Acute pelvic pain.
- Acute pelvic mass.
- Acute vulvovaginal symptoms.

Initial investigation

Since gynaecological emergencies frequently involve women during their menstrual years, the possibility of pregnancy should always be considered and diagnosed or eliminated (see below). The result will often significantly influence the management of the presenting symptoms or signs.

In all cases, an appropriate history should be obtained, supported by the relevant clinical examinations. A vaginal examination should usually be performed, since valuable information can be gathered which will aid in reaching the correct diagnosis.

Although ultrasound examinations can be very helpful, the findings should always be interpreted in conjunction with the clinical findings, and not acted upon in isolation.

Diagnosis of pregnancy

Some disorders only occur during pregnancy, but many occur in both pregnant and non-pregnant women. The diagnosis of pregnancy is thus a very important aspect of emergency gynaecology and should be addressed in a number of ways, as illustrated in Box 4.1.

Women who are pregnant and are believed to be 16 weeks' gestation or more will not be considered here. Most units manage these patients in the antenatal clinic or delivery unit rather than in the gynaecological department.

When to refer

See section on referral.

VAGINAL BLEEDING

Of the four categories of symptom presentation, this is the most common, and frequently requires pregnancy to be diagnosed or excluded. Management is influenced by any relationship to pregnancy and recent surgery, as outlined in Figure 4.1.

Box 4.1: Diagnosis of pregnancy during the first 8 weeks of gestation

At risk	■ Has woman been having coitus? ■ Was contraception being used? ■ Has she had any amenorrhoea?
Symptoms	■ Nausea and vomiting ■ Breast symptoms, including tenderness, enlargement, tingling ■ Urinary frequency ■ Changes in appetite (pica), including aversions to tea, coffee, alcohol and smoking
Clinical signs	■ Breast signs, including: marbling (venous dilatation), Montgomery's tubercles, darkening of areola, tenderness ■ Vaginal and cervical blueness ■ Uterine enlargement and softness (Hegar's sign)
Investigations	■ Urinary pregnancy test: positive within 7–10 days of conception; remains positive for up to 3 weeks after abortion ■ Ultrasound scan: identifies intrauterine pregnancy reliably after 5 weeks of conception

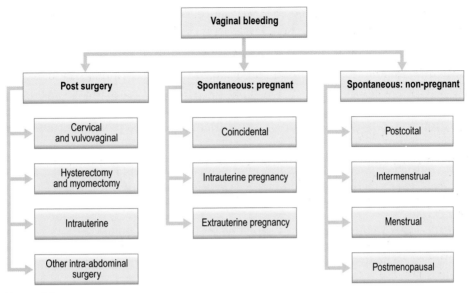

Figure 4.1
Types of vaginal bleeding by origin and preceding features.

Box 4.2: Causes of vaginal bleeding in the non-pregnant woman

Menorrhagia	**Intermenstrual**	**Postcoital**	**Postmenopausal**
■ Dysfunctional uterine bleeding	■ Endometrial polyp	■ Cervical polyp	■ Endometrial carcinoma
■ Fibroids	■ Cervicitis	■ Cervicitis	■ Hormone therapy
■ Endometrial polyp	■ Cervical carcinoma	■ Cervical carcinoma	■ Cervical carcinoma
■ Endometrial carcinoma	■ Endometrial carcinoma	■ Cervical ectropion	■ Cervical polyp
■ Intrauterine contraceptive device	■ Hormone therapy	■ Coital 'trauma'	■ Endometrial polyp
	■ Vaginitis	■ Vaginitis	■ Vaginitis
	■ Cervical polyp		

Vaginal bleeding in the non-pregnant woman

Emergency advice is sought usually because:

- The bleeding is heavy.
- The bleeding is prolonged.
- There is associated discomfort.

It is necessary to identify the relationship with the menstrual cycle. It is also necessary to determine whether the blood loss is from the genital tract, as opposed to haematuria or rectal bleeding.

Causes

Box 4.2 lists the common causes of vaginal bleeding in relation to menstruation.
Figure 4.2 shows an endometrial polyp, a common cause of bleeding.

Acute menorrhagia   Occasionally this can be severe, likened to 'turning a tap on', and emergency management is needed. Dysfunctional uterine bleeding is the most common reason for emergency treatment for acute menorrhagia.

Postcoital bleeding   Bleeding or bloodstained discharge is a relatively rare emergency presentation, but can be very worrying to the patient. Trauma to the vagina or cervix as a consequence of normal or enforced coitus is generally the explanation, although it also may follow self-mutilation or an assault with a foreign body, but reported by the patient as the result of coitus.

Intermenstrual bleeding   Usually, intermenstrual bleeding is not heavy and only rarely presents as an emergency. When it is heavy, it is difficult to differentiate from a heavy menstrual loss, and demands similar considerations to menorrhagia.

Postmenopausal bleeding   Occasionally, postmenopausal bleeding can be very heavy and require emergency attention. Whatever the volume, considerable anxiety is often generated. Many women who complain of postmenopausal bleeding are using hormone replacement therapy or tamoxifen. The likelihood of a malignancy being responsible for the bleeding is now around 1%, compared with the 10% previously associated with this symptom.

Investigations

In all cases where pregnancy has been excluded, careful abdominal, vaginal and speculum examinations are necessary to help identify the source of the bleeding. Pelvic imaging may be helpful if a pelvic mass is felt.

A haemoglobin check and serum taken for grouping and possibly cross-matching should be organized if the blood loss is especially severe. If there are reasons for contemplating a bleeding diathesis, a clotting screen should be requested.

If trauma is responsible for the bleeding and deeper structures might be involved, an examination under anaesthetic might be necessary. A cystoscopy or urethroscopy should be considered if the anterior vaginal wall has been damaged, and a proctoscopy or sigmoidoscopy if the posterior wall is involved. A laparoscopy should be considered if the vaginal vault is lacerated in case there has been full-thickness penetration and trauma to adjacent bowel.

Management

If the bleeding is from a traumatized cervical polyp or cervical ectropion, the former might be removed with forceps, while the latter might need treatment by cautery with silver nitrate, styptic, cryocautery or diathermy.

If a 'small' prolapsed fibroid is diagnosed (Fig. 4.3), this might be avulsed in the clinic setting. If the fibroid is large with a broad base, hysterectomy may prove necessary, and the patient should be advised of this possibility.

If a cervical carcinoma is suspected, initial vaginal packing should help control the bleeding if heavy, with urgent referral for specialist management.

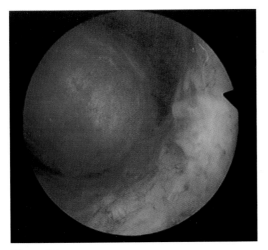

Figure 4.2
Hysteroscopic appearance of an endometrial polyp.

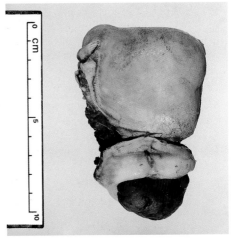

Figure 4.3
Intraluminal fibroid prolapsed through the cervix, causing acute pain and bleeding.

Box 4.3: Options for managing acute dysfunctional uterine haemorrhage

1. Confirm no lower genital tract cause for the bleeding

2. Try high-dose progestogens: e.g. norethisterone 10 mg 6-hourly

If not effective:
3. Try an antifibrinolytic: e.g. tranexamic acid 1 g 6–8-hourly

If not effective:
4. Try a prostaglandin synthase inhibitor: e.g. mefenamic acid 500 mg 6-hourly

If not effective:
5. Examination under general anaesthetic with hysteroscopy and curettage

If no pathology found and still bleeding, consider:
6. A balloon catheter for uterine tamponade

Some foreign bodies will need to be removed under anaesthesia, because of the discomfort experienced and likely vaginismus leading to a risk of more damage.

Box 4.3 lists management options for dysfunctional uterine bleeding if it is thought to be the explanation for acute menorrhagia.

Vaginal bleeding in the pregnant woman

Causes

Once pregnancy is diagnosed, the gestation should be determined from the menstrual history, the opportunities when conception could have occurred and whether quickening has been experienced. Vaginal bleeding during the early weeks of pregnancy suggests that the patient is experiencing some form of abortion, as outlined in Box 4.4.

Box 4.4: Vaginal bleeding in pregnant women

Threatened abortion	Inevitable abortion: incomplete	Inevitable abortion: complete	Missed abortion	Ectopic pregnancy
Symptoms of pregnancy	Symptoms of pregnancy	Symptoms of pregnancy	No pregnancy symptoms	Symptoms of pregnancy
Usually light bleeding	Variable volume of bleeding	Variable bleeding, which may have subsided	Often no history of bleeding	Classically small volume of dark 'prune juice' discharge
Often no pain	Usually colicky pains	Usually colicky pains	No pain	Usually significant pain
Pregnancy positive	Pregnancy positive	Pregnancy positive	Pregnancy often positive	Pregnancy positive
Uterus = dates	Uterus = dates	Uterus < dates	Uterus = dates	Uterus < dates
Cervix closed	Cervix open	Cervix open	Cervix closed	Cervix closed
Ultrasound: intrauterine sac with FH seen	Ultrasound: disrupted sac, no FH seen	Ultrasound: uterus empty	Ultrasound: intrauterine sac with no FH seen	Ultrasound: no gestation sac in uterus

FH, fetal heart pulsations.

It is possible that the bleeding has originated from the lower genital tract from pathologies described above for non-pregnant women.

The history should determine the relationship of the pain to the bleeding. A bimanual pelvic examination is necessary to determine if the cervix is dilated and if there are products of conception in the cervix or vagina; tenderness or cervical excitation should be noted.

An ultrasound scan should demonstrate an intrauterine gestational sac (Fig. 4.4) if present, but often only with confidence 5 weeks after conception (7 weeks after the

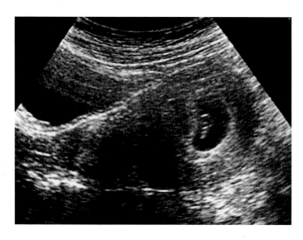

Figure 4.4
Ultrasound image of an early intrauterine gestation sac with fetal echoes.

previous period). The ultrasonographer should not be asked to diagnose or exclude an ectopic pregnancy. If a gestational sac containing a fetal heart is reliably seen outside the endometrial cavity, this is convincing evidence for an ectopic pregnancy. However, the endometrial cavity without a fetal echo within does not mean that there is not a pregnancy elsewhere; nor does an intrauterine gestation sac exclude the possibility of a co-existing ectopic pregnancy.

Management

Figure 4.5 provides a flowchart for the diagnosis and management of vaginal bleeding in women thought to be pregnant.

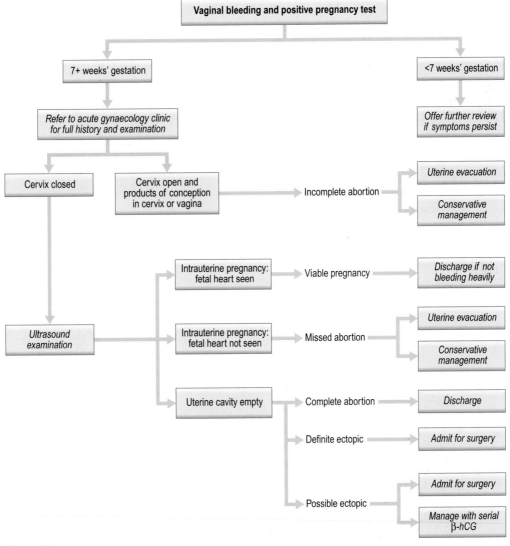

Figure 4.5
Flowchart for the investigation and management of vaginal bleeding during early pregnancy. β-hCG, human chorionic gonadotrophin β-subunit.

When an inevitable abortion has been diagnosed with an open cervix, ultrasound assessment for the presence and volume of retained products of conception can be misleading.

Management is determined by the amount of bleeding and discomfort, and the size of the uterus.

Vaginal bleeding following surgery

Causes

The cause of vaginal bleeding following gynaecological surgery will depend upon the nature of the operation. Significant vaginal bleeding associated with secondary infection can follow major surgery, such as:

- Hysterectomy.
- Myomectomy.
- Endometrial resection.
- Vaginal repairs.

The possibility of a haematoma discharging from the vaginal vault or wall, or from the uterine wall following myomectomy, should be considered.

If fibroid embolization has been performed, necrotic fibroid tissue may be passed with bleeding; these patients should have been forewarned of this possibility.

Occasionally, vaginal granulation tissue forms following a hysterectomy or repair surgery, and can lead to heavy bleeding.

Management

If secondary infection is suspected, a broad-spectrum antibiotic should be given (after appropriate specimens for microbiological culture have been collected), combined with a period of increased rest.

Bleeding following cervical cautery or biopsy is thought to be due to secondary infection and should be managed with antibiotics and, if necessary, vaginal packing for 24 h. If a specific bleeding focus is found, cautery under anaesthesia may be necessary.

Granulation tissue bleeding will usually cease spontaneously, or with silver nitrate cautery and a short period of local pressure. Admission for observation, or even examination under anaesthesia, with attention to any specific bleeding points if evident, followed by vaginal packing, may be necessary.

Vault haematomas usually discharge spontaneously and settle, although discharge may continue for some weeks. Occasionally active drainage of a haematoma is required.

Bleeding after termination of pregnancy or evacuation of incomplete or missed abortions may indicate retained products of conception; the cervix will be open with a tender enlarged uterus and uterine curettage will be indicated. If the bleeding is light, the patient afebrile with no tachycardia, a non-tender uterus and a closed cervix, conservative management anticipating spontaneous resolution is appropriate. Figure 4.6 illustrates the delay in return to a negative pregnancy test after abortion.

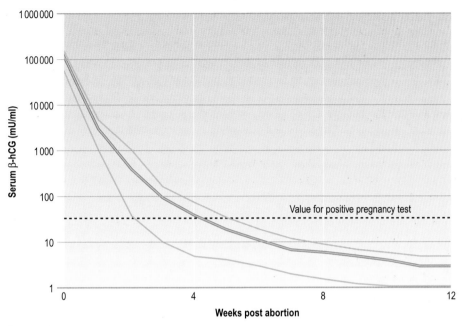

Figure 4.6
Return to a negative pregnancy test after therapeutic abortion. β-hCG, human chorionic gonadotrophin β-subunit.

PELVIC PAIN

Pain in the lower abdomen or in the vagina or vulva may be due to a variety of reasons. Figure 4.7 provides a schedule for considering the causes of pain.

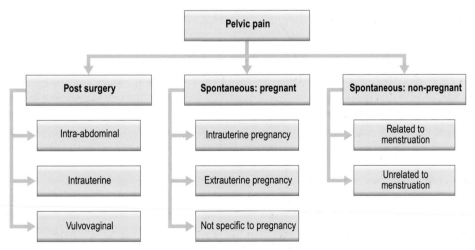

Figure 4.7
Schedule for addressing the cause of acute pelvic pain.

Acute pelvic pain following surgery

As with bleeding, the relationship to any recent previous surgery should be established and the issue of pregnancy should be addressed.

Vulvovaginal surgery

Causes

Pain is usually associated with haematoma formation.

Investigation

Bimanual examination should identify a mass beneath the vaginal wall or at the vaginal vault. An ultrasound examination may confirm the diagnosis.

Management

If the haematoma is not large or tender, it is probably best left to resolve spontaneously. If there is tenderness, an antibiotic should be given and the patient admitted, with arrangements for drainage by opening the suture line, with or without a general anaesthetic.

Intra-abdominal surgery

Causes

Possible causes are:

- Abdominal wall bruising and haematomas related to the incision for laparotomy/laparoscopy.
- Reactive intra-abdominal bleeding, including vaginal vault haematomas.
- Urinary leakage from bladder or ureteric damage.
- Acute peritonitis from bowel damage.
- Loin discomfort from ureteric obstruction.
- Acute urinary retention.

Investigation

Specific diagnoses suspected on clinical examination will often need to be confirmed using various imaging techniques, including radiology and ultrasound.

The findings of tachycardia, pyrexia and acute abdominal signs will usually indicate that there is a serious complication.

Management

Admission should be arranged as an emergency for urgent treatment of the suspected complication.

Intrauterine surgery

Causes

Following transcervical endometrial or fibroid resection and pregnancy termination or evacuation, uterine perforation with broad ligament haematoma formation or damage to other hollow viscera might be the explanation.

Retained products of conception following uterine evacuation should be considered.

Investigation

This is as described for bleeding after pregnancy termination or uterine evacuation.

Abdominal tenderness with rebound and other signs of peritoneal irritation suggests the possibility of uterine perforation.

Management

Retained products of conception require evacuation with antibiotic cover.

A perforated uterus could possibly be managed conservatively unless active bleeding is present or other organ repair is necessary.

Pain in the non-pregnant woman

Causes

Box 4.5 summarizes the possible causes of pelvic pain both related and unrelated to the menstrual cycle.

Investigation

History with abdominal and vaginal examinations will identify prolapsed polyps and fibroids and the presence of blood clots in the cervix.

Imaging should identify intraluminal polyps and fibroids, acute retention, other pelvic masses and ascites.

Box 4.5: Causes of pelvic pain related and unrelated to menstruation

Pain related to the menstrual cycle	Pain unrelated to the menstrual cycle
■ Severe dysmenorrhoea	■ Acute urinary retention
■ Cervical pain due to blood clots	■ Ovarian cyst torsion
■ Prolapsed intraluminal fibroid or polyp	■ Ovarian cyst rupture or haemorrhage
■ Ruptured corpus luteum cyst	■ Acute ascites
■ Ovarian hyperstimulation syndrome	■ Constipation
■ Mittelschmerz	■ Acute bowel disease

Management

Hospitalization will be necessary to manage the underlying cause of the pain in many instances. Simple analgesia may help, but if the pain is due to a prolapsed fibroid, an emergency examination under anaesthesia may be necessary to remove the polyp.

If menorrhagia with the passage of clots is the explanation, attention to the heavy losses will be required. Mid-cycle pain (mittelschmerz) is managed by analgesia, followed by the combined contraceptive pill in many cases. Pain associated with a delay in menstruation is probably due to a ruptured functional ovarian cyst. Analgesia is required for this, although occasionally it is associated with significant bleeding and warrants hospitalization and surgical control.

Ovarian hyperstimulation requires urgent admission and careful attention to fluid balance by physicians experienced in treating the condition.

Pain in the pregnant woman

Pregnancy-specific

Causes

These include the various types of intrauterine abortion, as described earlier. Bleeding commonly precedes the colicky pain.

In ectopic pregnancies, the pain commonly precedes the loss of a 'prune-juice' discharge, and is usually continuous in one or other iliac fossa, with guarding, rebound tenderness and cervical excitation on vaginal examination. A history of shoulder-tip pain is classically elicited if there has been significant intraperitoneal bleeding.

Investigation

The presenting history and clinical examination findings will often provide a pointer to the diagnosis. Further investigation is as described for bleeding in the pregnant woman (see Fig. 4.5).

Management

This depends on the diagnosis, as outlined earlier. In those cases where an ectopic pregnancy is a diagnostic probability, admission with a view to laparoscopy must be considered.

Ovarian

Causes

Ovarian accidents, including a ruptured corpus luteum cyst and ovarian torsion, usually present with acute central pelvic pain localizing to one or other iliac fossa. The pain is often colicky and associated with a tachycardia, pyrexia and nausea.

Investigation

A pelvic mass may be felt if guarding and rebound are not too protective; an ultrasound should confirm the diagnosis of a pelvic mass if torsion is the diagnosis. No specific features are seen with luteal cyst rupture unless there is significant blood loss, when free fluid should be evident.

Management

Admission for observation is indicated if an ovarian accident is suspected. If symptoms and physical signs persist, a laparoscopy or laparotomy may be required urgently to control persistent bleeding and conserve a torsioned ovary before infarction occurs.

PELVIC MASS

A woman may become alarmed when she discovers that her abdomen is distended and her clothing has become tight. Such distension may occur acutely or develop insidiously, only to be recognized suddenly by the patient. In some women the recognition of the swelling coincides with the development of menstrual, gastrointestinal or urinary tract symptoms. For women still menstruating, pregnancy must always be considered. Acute anxiety may therefore be generated, prompting a request for an emergency consultation.

Pelvic mass in the non-pregnant woman

A list of diagnoses for the unexpected finding of a pelvic mass is given in Table 4.1.

Table 4.1: Differential diagnosis for a pelvic mass

Anatomical site	Condition
Vagina	Haematocolpos Paravaginal tumour
Uterus	Pregnancy Fibroid
Fallopian tube	Hydrosalpinx/pyosalpinx
Ovary	Primary tumour, benign or malignant Metastatic tumour
Other	Urinary retention Ascites Pseudocyesis Bowel tumour Retroperitoneal tumour Visceroptosis

Haematocolpos

This presents in a teenager who has not started menstruating. A previous history of cyclical pains for 2–3 days every few weeks will usually be obtained. Apart from a non-tender mass arising from the pelvis, a blue-coloured membrane will be seen within the introitus, representing the intact vaginal membrane. Referral for surgery is indicated, but this is not an emergency.

Pseudocyesis

It is easy to mistakenly 'feel' a pelvic mass in a woman who claims to be pregnant, especially if she is overweight. Symptomatic enquiry is not likely to be helpful and an ultrasound examination will be needed to exclude pregnancy and reach the correct diagnosis. This is not an emergency, but managing the patient requires considerable sensitivity.

Ovarian tumour

Ovarian tumours are often symptomless, but may cause pressure symptoms on the bladder and bowel when palpable *per abdomen*. Vaginal examination and subsequent ultrasound examination may help differentiate an ovarian tumour from a fibroid. If pain is associated with the tumour this suggests possible ovarian torsion that will require emergency surgery. Otherwise urgent referral for further investigation is required.

Uterine fibroid

This is usually symptomless but, like ovarian tumours, may have been present for some months or years. It will not necessarily have been identified at the time of previous cervical cytology screening if a bimanual examination was not performed as a routine. Pressure symptoms on the bowel or bladder may be present and the diagnosis should be suspected if there is a history of increasing menstrual losses. Referral in the near future for further investigations is advisable.

Ascites

Although not strictly a pelvic mass, ascites may present this way. Clinical examination should differentiate this from pelvic masses. Since ascites could represent a malignant process, an urgent referral for investigation is indicated.

Urinary retention

This should be considered in at-risk groups, including those with a neuromuscular disease, the elderly and patients who have recently undergone abdominal or vaginal surgery or delivered a baby. If suspected, catheterization will confirm the diagnosis and subsequent care and advice should be sought for the individual patient.

Acute urinary retention will occur with an incarcerated retroverted gravid uterus, usually at 14–16 weeks' gestation. The diagnosis is usually obvious, and management is by immediate catheterization and admission for continued bladder drainage in the expectation of spontaneous reversion within a day or so.

Non-gynaecological tumours

These include bowel and retroperitoneal tumours. Systematic enquiry might assist in reaching the correct diagnosis, but referral for further investigation is urgently required.

Unsuspected pregnancy

This must be considered in women during their menstrual years, particularly teenage girls and women approaching the menopause. Inquiry about the possibility of pregnancy, relevant symptoms and physical examination will increase the suspicion of pregnancy, which must be confirmed urgently by an ultrasound examination if necessary.

Pelvic mass following gynaecological surgery

The explanation for a pelvic mass identified after abdominal or intrauterine surgery will depend upon the nature of the previous surgery.

After abdominal operations

Causes

A mass arising from the pelvis is most probably:

- A vault haematoma if a hysterectomy has been performed.
- A pelvic haematocoele (haematoma in the pouch of Douglas) or abscess.
- A distended urinary bladder.

Vault haematomas usually present within 4–5 days of surgery and thus might present following hospital discharge. Acute urinary retention is uncommon after a period of a few days of satisfactory spontaneous voiding.

Investigation

Vaginal examination should differentiate between bladder distension and other diagnoses, with bladder catheterization providing confirmation.

With a vault haematoma, some offensive stale bloodstained discharge might be evident and vaginal examination usually causes marked discomfort. Haematomas or abscesses of clinical significance are usually obvious and require no further investigation.

Management

Admission for drainage of a haematoma or abscess by colpotomy with or without a general anaesthetic is required, often with antibiotic cover. Resolution of symptoms is rapid.

Acute urinary retention should be managed by indwelling catheterization and admission.

After intrauterine surgery

Causes

A pelvic haematocoele or abscess is a possible diagnosis, especially if uterine perforation had complicated the operation.

A continuing pregnancy must always be considered if the mass has no inflammatory features.

Investigation

Clinical examination should lead to the diagnosis of haematocoele or abscess, as described above.

Inquiry about persisting pregnancy symptoms and the re-establishment of menstruation should be made if more than 4 weeks post termination. Breast signs and an enlarged soft uterus will be present. An urgent ultrasound examination is then required.

Management

An haematocoele or abscess is managed as described above.

The management of a continuing pregnancy needs urgent discussion with the patient and the gynaecologist involved in the previous termination procedure.

VULVOVAGINAL SYMPTOMS

These may take the form of:

- Trauma.
- Swelling.
- Pain with acute inflammation and discharge.

Figure 4.8 provides a schedule of aetiologies.

Vulval trauma

Causes

Trauma may occur as a result of:

- Falling astride a bicycle, or onto furniture (Fig. 4.9) or rough object.
- A road traffic accident.
- Self-mutilation.
- Criminal assault.

Investigation

A thorough vulval and vaginal examination is necessary to assess the extent of any damage. In the young girl, a vaginal examination, if indicated, should be performed under anaesthesia.

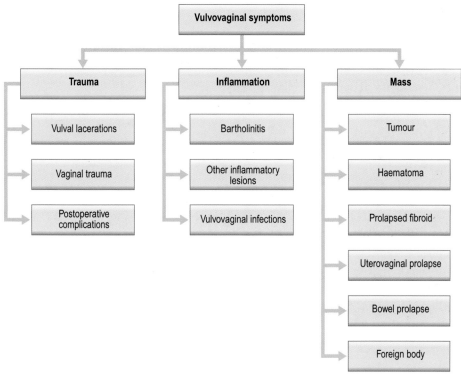

Figure 4.8
Types of vulvovaginal pathology that present as an emergency.

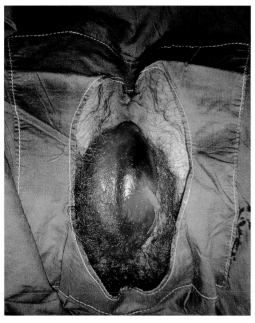

Figure 4.9
A left vulval haematoma sustained following a fall onto furniture.

Management

This is as described earlier.

Vulval pain, inflammation and discharge

Causes

Pain presenting with gradual onset and increasingly throbbing is most commonly due to:

- Bartholinitis.
- Bartholin's abscess.
- Other vulval abscesses.

Other less common causes for vulval pain or discomfort are:

- Vulval herpes.
- Behçet's syndrome.
- Vulvadynia.
- Allergic vulvitis.
- Insect bites.

Vaginal discharge could be due to:

- Infection with monilia, trichomonas.
- Bacterial vaginosis.
- Cervical polyp.
- Ectropion.
- Carcinoma.
- A foreign body (foreign bodies retrieved during the 24-month period referred to in Table 4.3 include a tampon, a small bottle, razor blades, broken glass and a candle).

Investigation

For bartholinitis or vulval abscess, clinical examination of the vulva reveals a swelling with redness and tenderness. Small discrete ulcers may be seen for the other infections and insect bites. See Ch. 3 for a full discussion on STDs.

A generally reddened vulva will be seen with non-infective vulvitis. The appearances will be unremarkable with vulvadynia.

A thorough vaginal examination is necessary to identify vaginal causes for discharge.

Management

Acute vulval inflammation should be managed with a broad-spectrum antibiotic to try and promote resolution. If suppuration has occurred, incision using some local anaesthetic spray could be tried, but more usually admission for surgical treatment under general anaesthesia is necessary.

The various vaginal causes should be treated as described earlier. (See also Ch. 3.)

Vulval mass

The patient may complain that a mass has appeared at her vulva or she has passed something that has been retained for inspection.

Causes

A 'specimen' presented by the patient could be:

- A blood clot, products of conception (which will generally be accompanied by significant bleeding).
- A large polyp or fibroid, especially one shed after fibroid embolization, associated with some bleeding.
- A swab retained after surgery or childbirth.

Possible diagnoses for swellings still attached include:

- A placental polyp if recently post partum.
- A large cervical polyp.
- A prolapsed intraluminal fibroid.
- Acute vaginal wall prolapse.
- Bowel prolapsed through a ruptured vaginal vault.
- Rectal prolapse.
- Prolapse of a rectal tumour.

Investigation

Any tissue specimen passed must be sent for histological examination. Vulvovaginal examination should identify which of the possible diagnoses is responsible.

Management

If the patient is now symptomless, no further action is required. All the other situations require urgent referral for inpatient attention.

Ruptured vaginal vault is a very rare entity requiring very urgent attention.

REFERRAL

When to admit/refer

The decision when to admit or to refer to the next emergency gynaecology clinic is important. Table 4.2 provides some guidance.

A pregnancy test should be performed before referral, since a negative result will often avoid the need for referral.

Table 4.2: Indications for emergency admission or referral to the emergency gynaecology clinic

Symptom	Clinical condition
Emergency admissions	
Severe vaginal bleeding	Spontaneous abortion
	Postoperative complication
	Menorrhagia
	Unrecognized cause
Severe hyperemesis	With dehydration
Acute abdominal pain	Possible ectopic pregnancy
	Ovarian accident
	Severe pelvic infection
	Postoperative complication
	Acute urinary retention
Acute vulval trauma or infection	Vulval trauma
	Vulval abscess
Urgent clinic referrals	
Vaginal bleeding in early pregnancy	If more than 7 weeks' gestation and woman is concerned
Subacute pain in early pregnancy	Uncertain origin
Subacute vulval infection	Non-suppurative
Subacute postoperative complications	Wound sepsis
	Moderate vaginal bleeding
Hyperemesis	Symptomatic distress

Table 4.3: Indications for emergency referral to the acute gynaecology clinic at a large district teaching hospital over a period of 2 years

Nature of referral	1999	2000	Total
Early pregnancy problems	2316	2132	4448 (73%)
Postpartum problems	32	33	65 (1%)
General gynaecological problems	395	569	964 (16%)
Vulval disorders	83	75	158 (3%)
Postoperative problems	125	112	237 (4%)
Infections	75	52	127 (2%)
Assisted conception problems	35	36	71 (1%)
Unrecorded	10	19	29 (0%)
Total	3071	3028	6099 (100%)

Frequency of referrals

An analysis of new gynaecological emergency attendances over 24 months at a large district teaching hospital is presented in Table 4.3. The analysis was performed according to reasons for referral; it does not represent the picture for attendances at a general practitioner's surgery, or emergency call-out.

FUTURE DIRECTIONS   During the past decade early pregnancy assessment clinics have become established in many gynaecological units to manage women known, or suspected, to be pregnant and complaining of vaginal bleeding or pain. These arrangements have improved the service for such patients, although the ready access that these clinics provide to primary care and patients has led to an increased workload for hospitals. A demand that all attending such clinics should have a positive pregnancy test result prior to attending would rationalize the use of the clinic. There are, however, a large number (25% of the total) of other gynaecological emergencies that need similar and often more urgent attention. With restrictions in working practices and available staff, similar strategies need to be developed to provide efficient management of all types of gynaecological emergencies. In the ideal setting, an emergency operating list is available for those patients requiring surgical attention, allowing for a single hospital attendance for both diagnosis and treatment.

Selected References and Further Reading

Bigrigg MA, Read MD. Management of women referred to early pregnancy assessment unit: care and cost effectiveness. BMJ 1991; 302:577–579.

Bowen LW, Beeson JH. Use of a large Foley catheter balloon to control postpartum haemorrhage resulting from a low placental implantation. J Reprod Med 1985; 30:633–635.

Boyd WD, Charnock FMC. Perineal abscesses. In: Morris PJ, Malt RA, eds. Oxford textbook of surgery, vol 2. London: Oxford University Press; 1994:1456–1458.

Dubbins PA. The first trimester transabdominal ultrasound. In: Dewbury K, Meire H, Cosgrove D, eds. Ultrasound in obstetrics and gynaecology. Edinburgh: Churchill Livingstone; 1993:145–170.

Goswamy RK. The first trimester vaginal ultrasound. In: Dewbury K, et al., eds. Ultrasound in obstetrics and gynaecology. Edinburgh: Churchill Livingstone; 1993:171–186.

MacKenzie IZ. Unintentional trauma during gynaecological surgery. Curr Obstet Gynaecol 2001; 11:100–107.

McElhinney B, McClure N. Ovarian hyperstimulation syndrome. Baillière's Clin Obstet Gynaecol 2000; 14:103–133.

Nielsen S, Hahlin M. Expectant management of first-trimester spontaneous abortion. Lancet 1995; 345:84–86.

Royal College of Obstetricians and Gynaecologists. The management of tubal pregnancies. RCOG guideline 21. London: RCOG; 1999.

Stabile I, Grudzinskas JG. Ectopic pregnancy: a review of incidence, etiology and diagnostic aspects. Obstet Gynecol Surv 1990; 45:335–347.

Stovall TG. Medical management of ectopic pregnancy. Curr Opin Obstet Gynecol 1994; 6:510–515.

Chronic pelvic pain and endometriosis

5.

Jane Moore

> **THIS CHAPTER** This chapter aims to summarize current thinking about the broad range of possible causes of chronic pelvic pain that are now considered relevant. It highlights the concept of the biopsychosocial model as a framework for understanding pelvic pain, acknowledging that there may be more than one factor feeding in to the overall pain experience. An algorithm is suggested for the initial management of chronic pelvic pain. The emphasis is on trying to make an accurate diagnosis in the first place and treating the pain empirically, even if the cause or causes of the pain have not been fully elucidated.

Background

Chronic pelvic pain (CPP) is common, presenting in primary care as frequently as asthma or low back pain. Community surveys suggest that about 1 in 6 women aged 18–50 years is affected.

People who suffer from CPP often comment that nobody seems to believe them or take their pain seriously. There is a lot that is still poorly understood about CPP but we can at least listen and accept that the pain is real.

Since pain is perceived in the mind, the experience of pain will inevitably be affected by factors in the sufferer's environment, both physical and psychological. In the assessment of patients with CPP it is imperative to see the individual as a whole and not to dichotomize pain as either organic or psychological.

Suggested definition of the symptom of chronic pelvic pain

CPP is pain felt in the lower abdomen or pelvis, of at least 6 months' duration, occurring continuously or intermittently, not associated exclusively with menstruation or sexual intercourse, and not associated with pregnancy or malignancy.

POSSIBLE CAUSES OF CHRONIC PELVIC PAIN

CPP may arise from any structure in or related to the pelvis, including the abdominal and pelvic walls. Box 5.1 summarizes our current understanding of the more common causes of CPP in women during their reproductive years.

Box 5.1: Possible contributory factors in the genesis of CPP

Gynaecological causes

- Endometriosis or adenomyosis
- Pelvic inflammatory disease
- Adhesions
- Pelvic venous congestion

Bowel-related pain

- Irritable bowel syndrome
- Constipation

Bladder-related pain

- Interstitial cystitis
- Urethral syndrome

Musculoskeletal pain

- Mechanical pelvic pain
- Muscle pain and trigger points

Neurological pain

- Nerve entrapment
- Moderation by the peripheral and central nervous system

Psychosocial factors

- Psychogenic pain
- Physical and sexual abuse

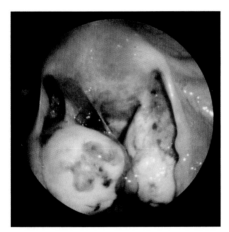

Figure 5.1
Laparoscopic picture of moderate-to-severe endometriosis. Bilateral endometriomas are present with blue–black peritoneal deposits visible on the right. Reproduced from Gordon AG, Lewis BV. Gynaecological endoscopy. London: Chapman & Hall; 1988.

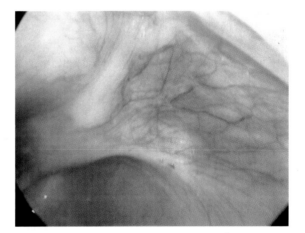

Figure 5.2
A close-up view of peritoneal endometriosis seen at laparoscopy. Abnormal vessel formation is seen with thickening of the peritoneum in the centre of the picture. Red punctate lesions are visible over the uterosacral ligament. Reproduced, with permission, from Howard FM. Baillière's Best Practice & Research Clinical Obstetrics & Gynaecology 14; 2000.

Gynaecological causes

Endometriosis

Endometriosis can occur throughout reproductive life, including the teenage years. It may be asymptomatic, but women with endometriosis are more likely to complain of pain than women with a laparoscopically normal pelvis. Some studies have correlated the degree of pain with features at laparoscopy (see Figs 5.1, 5.2), such as:

- The site of the disease.
- The number of endometriotic implants.
- The degree of infiltration beneath the peritoneal surface.

The pain of endometriosis varies markedly with the menstrual cycle. There is often a peak at the time of ovulation and pain increases again towards the period. In addition to CPP, the cardinal symptoms associated with endometriosis are:

- Dysmenorrhoea (pain with menstruation).
- Dyspareunia (pain with sexual intercourse).

Sufferers frequently experience other symptoms, particularly just before or during menstruation, such as:

- Excruciating pain on defecation.
- Fatigue.
- Malaise.

Adenomyosis

Adenomyosis is a form of endometriosis in which endometrioid tissue is found within the myometrium (Fig. 5.3). Like endometriosis, it causes pain in a cyclical pattern, often associated with dyspareunia and menstrual irregularities.

Pelvic inflammatory disease

The term chronic pelvic inflammatory disease is used to mean either damage from a past upper genital tract infection or episodic pain sometimes thought to be due to recurrent infection. In most cases, the original infection is a sexually transmitted infection (STI) (see Ch. 3). Pelvic infection is common, particularly with chlamydia, and persisting pelvic damage such as adhesions or abscess formation may be identified at laparoscopy (see Ch. 5). It is known that this damage does not always cause pain, but it is not known whether past infection can result in chronic pain in the absence of such damage. Although it is important that STIs are identified and treated, it is equally important that a woman is not incorrectly labelled as having chronic pelvic inflammatory disease. Other more relevant factors may be missed and great damage may be done to her personal relationships by insensitive discussion. The presence of an STI at the cervix does not prove that pelvic pain is due to pelvic inflammatory disease.

Pelvic adhesions

These are common and frequently asymptomatic. They may be caused by:

- Previous surgery.
- Infection.
- Endometriosis.

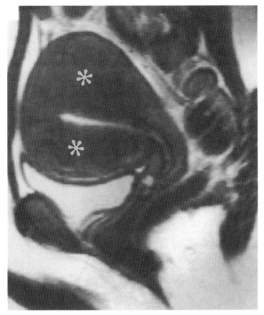

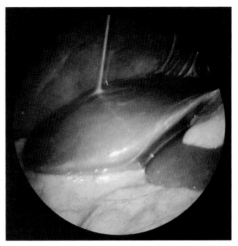

Figure 5.4
Laparoscopic view of the surface of the liver demonstrating 'piano string' adhesions to the peritoneum, in the centre and on the right of the picture. Perihepatic adhesions are pathognomonic of past chlamydial infection (Fitz-Hugh–Curtis syndrome). The liver should always be inspected at diagnostic laparoscopy. Reproduced from Gordon AG, Lewis BV. Gynaecological endoscopy. London: Chapman & Hall; 1988.

Figure 5.3
Magnetic resonance imaging demonstrating the presence of diffuse adenomyosis. The asterisks show the marked widening of the myometrium (specifically the junctional zone) and the characteristic globular shape of the affected uterus. Reproduced from the Journal of Magnetic Resonance Imaging 1999; 9. This material is used by permission of Wiley-Liss, Inc., a subsidiary of John Wiley & Sons, Inc.

It seems likely that some peritoneal adhesions can cause pelvic pain, particularly pain associated with stretching movements or organ distension, and where the adhesions are dense, taut or highly vascular (Fig. 5.4). Division of adhesions may relieve pain.

Two discrete forms of adhesions are recognized:

- Ovarian remnant syndrome: CPP associated with a fragment of ovary left behind following oophorectomy.
- Trapped ovary syndrome: CPP associated with the conservation of one or both ovaries at hysterectomy.

In both conditions, the ovarian tissue continues to function and dense adhesions form around it. The pain is typically cyclical in nature, and may be associated with dyspareunia or a postcoital ache. Suppressing or removing the remnant may relieve symptoms.

Pelvic venous congestion syndrome

This describes a group of symptoms that include:

- Aching or sharp pain in the one or both iliac fossae, made worse by standing and relieved by lying down.
- Dyspareunia.
- Postcoital ache.

The syndrome is associated with dilated pelvic veins, but its existence as a discrete clinical entity is disputed.

Bowel-related pain

Although conditions such as inflammatory bowel disease may present with pelvic pain, there are usually other symptoms present such as bloody diarrhoea.

Constipation

Constipation is very common among women and, although rarely the primary source of pain, may make an important and treatable contribution to the overall pain burden.

Irritable bowel syndrome

This is very common, affecting 10–20% of the general population and 50% of patients with pain symptoms attending the gynaecology clinic. Although essentially a diagnosis of exclusion, it has been shown that irritable bowel syndrome can be diagnosed with confidence from the history alone in the absence of other abnormal symptoms, such as weight loss and rectal bleeding. The agreed features, known as the Rome criteria, are shown in Box 5.2.

Bladder-related pain

The principal urological causes of pelvic pain are:

- Interstitial cystitis.
- Urethral syndrome.

Box 5.2: Diagnostic features of irritable bowel syndrome

Rome II criteria: at least 12 weeks or more, which need not be consecutive, in the previous 12 months, of abdominal pain or discomfort that has two of three of the following features:

- Relief with defecation
- Onset associated with a change in the frequency of the stool
- Onset associated with a change in form (appearance) of the stool

Other features associated with irritable bowel syndrome

- Abdominal distension
- Passage of mucus
- Sensation of incomplete evacuation

These are characterized by irritative bladder symptoms, such as:

- Urgency.
- Frequency.
- Nocturia.

Musculoskeletal pain

Mechanical pelvic pain describes pain due to abnormalities of the joints and ligaments of the pelvis or lower back. Damage may occur as a result of trauma, pregnancy or congenital abnormality but only comes to light years later.

Muscles themselves may be a primary source of pain, perhaps due to chronic muscle imbalance or myofascial trigger points. This is one of many under-researched areas.

Nerve-related pain

Nerve entrapment

This may occur in scar tissue or fascia in the abdominal wall (Fig. 5.5). Pain may be shooting in nature, associated with particular movements, or experienced as an ache locally or in the distribution of the nerve.

Moderation of pain sensation in the peripheral and central nervous systems

The perception of chronic pain is a dynamic process with activity being moderated at many levels, including the peripheral and central nervous systems. Sensation may be increased, decreased or changed, such that previously painless or imperceptible sensations become painful. Pain may be referred to another site from either somatic or visceral

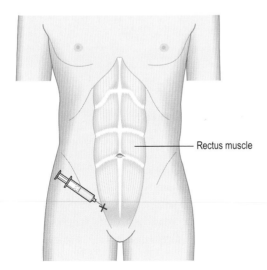

Rectus muscle

Figure 5.5
Line drawing of a typical site for injection of a nerve trapped in the rectus fascia. Tenderness from a nerve trapped in the fascia or scar tissue is usually highly localized and will be exacerbated when the patient tries to do a sit-up (tensing the recti). The injection should be given at the site of maximum tenderness and at the level of the rectus sheath. Injection of local anaesthetic should relieve the pain completely. This can be used as a diagnostic test but may bring long-term relief. It can be repeated.

79

structures. Nerves that have been damaged may themselves become a source of pain. This is termed neuropathic pain.

There is little clinical knowledge of the role of the nervous system in the genesis of CPP, but future research in this area may greatly enhance our understanding.

Psychosocial factors

Personality traits and health beliefs

Research in other chronic pain syndromes suggests that a predisposition to the development of chronic pain and disability may be associated with certain personality traits or health beliefs, such as:

- A tendency to 'catastrophize'.
- Use of negative coping strategies.
- Feeling of no control over the pain.
- A belief that pain represents ongoing tissue damage.

Psychogenic pain

For some women an experience, or sequence of experiences, has been so traumatic or overwhelming that it has become unspeakable. It cannot be processed in the conscious mind and is experienced as physical pain. With help it may be possible to examine the pain of the experience consciously and move on (see Ch. 11).

Physical and sexual abuse

Many women have been or are being abused, but this is not necessarily relevant to their pelvic pain. The link between pain and physical or sexual abuse is complex, but two recent studies have found an increased prevalence of major sexual abuse (meaning unwanted direct genital contact or penetrative sex at any age) in women with CPP compared to women with another pain complaint.

MANAGEMENT OF CHRONIC PELVIC PAIN

Living with chronic pain can be a nightmare, during which many aspects of the woman's life may fall apart, including her job and her relationships. It is important to try to intervene early before patterns of chronic pain behaviour in both the patient and those around her become established. Many women cope very well with remarkable levels of pain and doctors may be able to support a woman's coping strategies (e.g. by helping her to understand and control her pain) (Box 5.3).

Box 5.3: Principles in the management of CPP

- Listen to the patient: allow her to tell her story
- Make sure that the patient knows that you acknowledge the reality of her pain
- Allow or create enough time
- Establish what she wants to achieve
- Involve the patient in decision-making
- Look for contributory factors rather than assigning the pain to a single cause
- Exclude serious pathology, even if a positive diagnosis is not made
- Do something about the pain itself
- Offer access to information and support

Box 5.4: Questions to consider

Careful description of the duration, nature, site and radiation of the pain

- Is there more than one pain? (it may be helpful to note a pain score for each pain at best and at worst)
- Factors that provoke or relieve the pain, particularly movement or posture
- Variation of the pain over time, especially with the menstrual cycle

Gynaecological symptoms, including irregular bleeding and vaginal discharge

- Is there dyspareunia, and what effect is it having?
- Is there dysmenorrhoea, and does the CPP feel any different?

Bladder and bowel symptoms (ask directly for symptoms of irritable bowel syndrome)

Drugs that have been helpful: e.g. combined oral contraceptive or non-steroidal anti-inflammatory drugs

Are there any symptoms suggestive of depression or sleep disorder?

Is there any significant past medical or family history?

What was happening at the time the pain began?

- Is there any experience that the pain reminds her of?
- In what way does the pain affect day-to-day life?
- What does she believe the pain is due to?

What does she want to achieve by coming for help? Why now?

History and examination

Apart from its obvious value as a diagnostic tool, allowing the patient to tell her story and express her thoughts and feelings about the pain may be therapeutic in itself. The initial interview is also a crucial determinant of the doctor–patient relationship. It is important to show the patient that she can trust her doctor to take her pain seriously and not dismiss her. This initial process requires no special skills: respectful listening should be a core skill for all doctors. However, it does require time and it may be appropriate to ask the patient to come back at a later date.

The story told by the patient will usually need to be supplemented with direct questions, ideally covering the points described in Box 5.4. If time is short, or the pattern of the pain is unclear, consider asking her to keep a pain diary for a few months. Be particularly careful when nothing seems to be making sense. The patient may or may not be conscious that there is something more to say but, if she establishes some trust, she will probably come back. It may take two or three visits before she can tell the whole story.

> I just wish someone had thought of looking at my back, then maybe I'd never have had the hysterectomy, but you just trust the advice you're given, don't you. (The words of a patient some months after her chronic pelvic pain had been found to be arising from her lumbar spine and completely cured.)

Vaginal examination

The vaginal examination is not only a physical examination but also an important moment in the doctor–patient relationship – 'a psychodynamic event'. It is an opportunity to demonstrate respect and sympathy. In her vulnerability, a patient may reveal fears or secrets that are crucial to the understanding of her pain. The doctor should be prepared for this and not embark on the examination unless there is time to respond.

In addition to assessing uterine size and tenderness and feeling for adnexal masses and cervical excitation, features should be sought such as vaginal nodules or thickening of the uterosacral ligaments (palpable laterally in the posterior fornix). The exact site of the tenderness should be identified with the patient. If the pain can be recreated, it helps to build the patient's confidence that you believe that the pain is real, even if the explanation is not readily apparent.

Making a diagnosis

Box 5.5 lists signs and symptoms that are suggestive of particular diagnoses. Although it is recognized that each person's complaint cannot readily be boxed into a diagnosis or that features are not always completely consistent, it is an attempt to summarize some clinical pointers to the possible origins of CPP.

Further assessment and investigation

Knowing what the patient wants to achieve may well allow the problem to be managed entirely in primary care. For women in their reproductive years, CPP is rarely a presentation of life-threatening or progressive disease in the absence of other significant symptoms such as rectal bleeding. The algorithm presented in Figure 5.6 (see p. 84) suggests a possible strategy for the investigation of CPP. Decisions about further investigation and treatment should be made in partnership with the patient.

Screening for sexually transmitted infections

This is best performed in a genitourinary medicine unit (see Ch. 3). Not only is the sensitivity of the investigation improved, but contact tracing can readily be arranged. However, if referral to a genitourinary medicine clinic does not seem appropriate, then endocervical swabs for chlamydia and routine culture can be taken at the initial examination, when indicated.

Box 5.5: Signs and symptoms suggestive of particular diagnoses

Diagnosis	Nature of the pain	Associated features	Examination findings
Endometriosis	Marked variation with menstrual cycle	Dyspareunia Dysmenorrhoea Painful defecation Family history	Focal tenderness Thickening of uterosacral ligaments Nodularity
Adenomyosis	Marked variation with menstrual cycle	Menstrual irregularities and menorrhagia	Tender, globular uterus
Pelvic inflammatory disease	Little variation in pain	Vaginal discharge Irregular bleeding Recent change of partner	Cervical excitation Cervical contact bleeding
Adhesions	? variation with movement or organ distension	Previous surgery or infection	Scars
Irritable bowel syndrome	Related to opening of bowels	Constipation or diarrhoea Mucus Bloating	Nothing abnormal per vaginam, but abdomen generally tender
Urological pain	Associated with passing urine	Nocturia Frequency	Tenderness under bladder base
Musculoskeletal pain	Association with movement or posture	History of injury or strain, possibly old	Pain elicited by specific movement Examine the back
Nerve entrapment	Associated with movement		Scars Tenderness highly localized
Psychogenic pain	? history difficult to grasp	? sadness Multiple previous symptoms	? examination traumatic

Ultrasound and magnetic resonance imaging

An ultrasound scan of the pelvis (usually transvaginal) can reliably exclude an ovarian cyst. Hydrosalpinges or tubo-ovarian abscesses may be identified. An MRI scan may be helpful in the diagnosis of adenomyosis.

Diagnostic laparoscopy

The role of diagnostic laparoscopy is controversial. Only two-thirds of diagnostic laparoscopies identify pathology, and its relevance to the pelvic pain is sometimes uncertain. To overcome this, some authorities have advocated the use of laparoscopic conscious pain mapping in which the patient is sedated but conscious, allowing the surgeon to touch abnormal areas and ask the patient about the pain.

Many of the possible causes of pain listed above cannot be seen at laparoscopy. Patients who have had a negative laparoscopy should therefore not be diagnosed as having 'non-organic pain'.

The risks of diagnostic laparoscopy are significant. One in 500 will suffer a significant injury, such as perforation of the bowel or a blood vessel. The patient needs to know the limitations of the test in order to decide whether her symptoms justify the risk and inconvenience incurred. In some units, gynaecologists will, if possible, treat adhesions or endometriosis laparoscopically at the time of diagnosis.

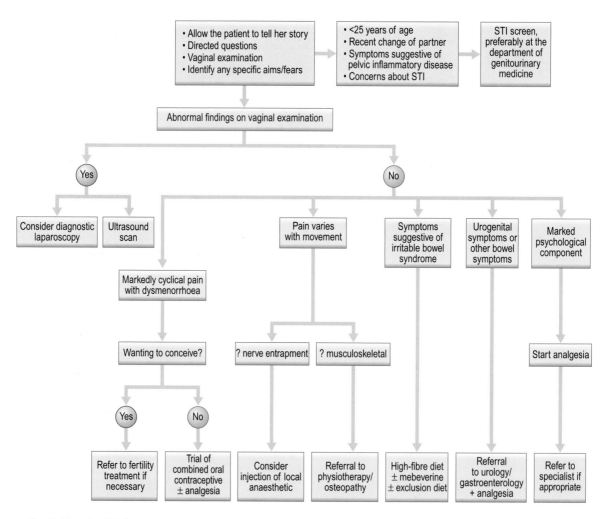

If patient is not satisfied:
- Consider referral to doctor with an interest in chronic pelvic pain, preferably in a multidisciplinary setting
- Consider magnetic resonance imaging/diagnostic laparoscopy
- Consider trial of GnRH analogues
- Consider total abdominal hysterectomy and bilateral oophorectomy if successful
- Offer long-term support as necessary

Figure 5.6
Suggested algorithm for the clinical management of chronic pelvic pain. STI, sexually transmitted infection.

Referral

Referral to other professionals such as physiotherapists, osteopaths or specialist counsellors may be helpful in assessing various components of the pain. Specific investigations such as cystoscopy may be necessary to exclude particular causes.

TREATING THE PAIN

Suggestions for the management of pain on an empirical basis are given in Box 5.6.

Tricyclic antidepressants

Tricyclic antidepressants such as amitriptyline are particularly useful for neuropathic pain. It may take several weeks for the drug to reach its full effect. The anticholinergic side-effects should be explained to the patient. They usually diminish in the first couple of weeks. There is a sedative effect and this can be harnessed to improve sleep pattern. If there is a significant element of depression, it should ideally be discussed openly and consideration given to using a more modern formulation such as an SSRI (selective serotonin re-uptake inhibitor).

> It's not that the pain isn't there, it's just that it doesn't dominate everything anymore.
> (The words of one woman with endometriosis and depression several weeks after starting amitriptyline in combination with an SSRI.)

Combined oral contraceptive pill

It is reasonable to suggest that pain that is strikingly cyclical in nature, particularly when associated with dyspareunia and dysmenorrhoea, may be due to 'an endometriosis-like condition'. If the pelvis is clinically normal and fertility is not desired, a therapeutic trial of the combined oral contraceptive pill (COC) is worthwhile. This is commonly undertaken in primary care. Patients with this type of pain can be reassured that it is perfectly safe to become pregnant if they want to.

Box 5.6: Empirical treatments for pain

Non-steroidal anti-inflammatory drug, preferably used on a regular basis: e.g. diclofenac 50 mg tds or 100 mg per rectum 16-hourly ± paracetamol or stronger analgesic: e.g. co-dydramol

Tricyclic antidepressant: e.g. amitriptyline 25 mg nocte, increasing by 25 mg every 2 weeks until symptoms controlled to maximum of 150 mg (usually 75–125 mg)

Combined oral contraceptive pill taken continuously, conventionally or in the tricyclic regimen

Continuous progesterone: e.g. medroxyprogesterone acetate 10 mg tds

Complementary therapy: e.g. acupuncture, herbal medicine

Conservative measures: e.g. regular exercise, relaxation, stress management

GnRH analogues

In cases where the COC has not been effective, many gynaecologists are now using a therapeutic trial of a gonadotrophin-releasing hormone (GnRH) analogue to treat cyclical pelvic pain, even if the laparoscopy has been negative. Some of these patients probably have a form of endometriosis such as adenomyosis. Such a trial may be helpful in making a decision about surgery in women who have unexplained CPP. If the GnRH analogues do not control the pain, hysterectomy with bilateral oophorectomy is unlikely to be successful.

Psychosocial factors

For some patients, psychosocial factors contribute significantly to the overall problem, often co-existing with physical causes, and should not be overlooked. It may be necessary to address the physical factors first and achieve some improvement before tackling other components. Referral to a specialist may be desirable in both primary and secondary care (see Ch. 11).

Self-help groups

Self-help groups offer an excellent source of support and information (see listing in Box 5.7). It may save a lot of time to put a patient in touch with the relevant organization and ask her to come back to discuss matters further.

Multidisciplinary pain management

In many areas, multidisciplinary pain management services exist and can be very helpful, particularly when the cause of the pain is unknown or untreatable. Pain management teams will generally not investigate the cause of the pain any further and should therefore probably only be involved when a patient has already seen a specialist with a particular interest in pelvic pain.

Ongoing support

Whatever the cause of their pain, CPP sufferers are likely to need ongoing support. This does not necessarily mean that patients should continue to be seen on a regular basis in either primary or secondary care but they should know where to turn for help.

TREATING ENDOMETRIOSIS

Guidelines for the medical and surgical management of endometriosis have recently been published and are outlined in Box 5.8. The hormonal treatments are equally effective and the choice of therapy is based primarily on side-effect profiles and mode of delivery. As a rule of thumb:

Box 5.7: Self-help organizations in the UK and useful web sites

Endometriosis Society	Suite 50 Westminster Palace Gardens 1–7 Artillery Row London SW1P 1RR Tel: 0207 222 2781 (admin); 0808 808 2227 (helpline 7–10 pm)	www.endo.org.uk
Women's Health	52 Featherstone Street London EC1Y 8RT Tel: 0207 251 6333 (admin); 0845 125 5254 (enquiry line)	admin@womenshealthlondon.org.uk
IBS Network	Ms PJ Nunn Northern General Hospital Sheffield S5 7AU Tel: 0114 261 1531	www.ibsnetwork.org.uk
Women's Nutritional Advisory Service (part of Natural Health Advisory Service)	PO Box 268 Lewes BN7 1QN Tel: 01273 487 366 01543 492 1929 (helpline nurse: M–F, 6pm–8pm; Sat, 10am–12noon)	www.naturalhealthas.com
Female Action Against Abuse of Women and Girls	PO Box 124 Bognor Regis PO21 5JT (written correspondence only)	
Cystitis & Overactive Bladder Foundation Support Group	76 High Street Stony Stratford MK11 1AH Tel: 01908 569 169	www.cobfoundation.org info@cobfoundation.org
British DSP Support Group (National Childbirth Trust)	SPD Info National Childbirth Trust Alexandra House Oldham Terrace Acton London W3 6NH Tel: 0870 770 3236; 0870 444 8707 (enquiries services)	www.spd-uk.org information@spd-uk.org
The Miscarriage Association	C/o Clayton Hospital Northgate Wakefield WF1 3JS Tel: 01924 200799	www.miscarriageassociation.org.uk info@miscarriageassociation.org.uk

Other suggested web sites

International Pelvic Pain Society	www.pelvicpain.org
British-based site focusing on endometriosis	www.psiesys.com
American-based wide-ranging site for doctors and patients	www.obgyn.net
Site with excellent links	www.doctorsarah.co.uk/resources.htm

- Progestogens tend to give premenstrual symptoms.
- GnRH analogues tend to give menopausal symptoms.

Patients should be aware of the so-called 'flare effect', in which symptoms may get worse in the first month of treatment with GnRH analogues. Danazol has the worst side-effect profile and can cause irreversible voice changes. Many gynaecologists avoid it altogether.

Box 5.8: Specific treatments for endometriosis

Medical

- Combined oral contraceptive pill taken continuously, or conventionally, or in a 'tricyclic' regimen (three packets together then a break)
- Long-term progestogens: e.g. levonorgestrel intrauterine system; medroxyprogesterone acetate 150 mg (3-monthly injection)
- Progestogens: e.g. medroxyprogesterone acetate 10 mg tds; norethisterone 5 mg tds
- Danazol 200 mg tds
- GnRH analogues: e.g. leuprorelin 3.75 mg monthly i.m. or s.c. injection; nafarelin 200-μg nasal spray bd

Surgical

- Cauterization or laser ablation of endometriotic deposits
- Excision of endometriosis (either peritoneal or deep disease)
- Hysterectomy with bilateral salpingo-oophorectomy

If transvaginal scan or vaginal examination suggests the presence of nodular disease or endometriomas, management is best directed by a gynaecologist with an interest in endometriosis. Typically, these forms of the disease do not respond well to medical treatment and surgical excision may ultimately be required.

Women should understand that they have a chronic disease that treatment is unlikely to cure. Approximately 40% of women with mild disease and 75% of women with severe disease will have a recurrence of symptoms within 5 years of stopping treatment. They need to plan symptom control around the other things they want to achieve, such as having a family.

If symptoms are well-controlled, depot progestogens, the levonorgestrel intrauterine system or the COC (except for smokers over 35 years of age) can be used long term. However, the duration of therapy for all other hormonal treatments has to be limited. GnRH analogues should not be used alone for longer than about 6 months due to bone demineralization, although this can be extended to at least 2 or 3 years by the use of 'add-back therapy', in which a GnRH analogue is given with oestrogen (as continuous combined hormone replacement therapy), norethisterone or tibolone to alleviate the hypo-oestrogenic side-effects.

There is no evidence that a patient's fertility will be progressively impaired. The consensus seems to be that, if the pain is under control (e.g. when on the COC), the disease is probably being controlled as well as possible.

FUTURE DIRECTIONS   As our understanding of CPP develops it is becoming clear that there are many similarities with other chronic pain syndromes. Effective management strategies such as the use of tricyclic antidepressants or pain management programmes that have been applied to other chronic pain syndromes need to be explored with women suffering from CPP.

FUTURE DIRECTIONS—cont'd

The overlap in symptoms between irritable bowel syndrome, interstitial cystitis and cyclical pelvic pain has raised the question of regional dysfunction. The concept of visceral hyperalgesia, in which abnormal visceral function is seen in association with neurological dysfunction, is being explored in the context of irritable bowel syndrome and this work is being extended to CPP. A number of possible factors have been suggested as initiators of dysfunction, the hallmark of which seems to be inflammation. Thus, for example, pelvic infection or endometriosis could be factors that provoke abnormal neurological function.

The place of musculoskeletal factors in the genesis of both primary and secondary pelvic pain has yet to be fully explored. This will best be undertaken by physiotherapists or osteopaths.

Selected References and Further Reading

American College of Gynecology. Chronic pelvic pain. Int J Gynecol Obstet 1996; 54:59–68.

Camilleri M. Management of irritable bowel syndrome. Gastroenterology 2001; 120:652–668.

Chapron C, Querleu D, Bruhat M, et al. Surgical complications of diagnostic and operative gynaecological laparoscopy: a series of 29 966 cases. Hum Reprod 1998; 13:867–872.

Ghaly AF, Chien PW. Chronic pelvic pain: clinical dilemma or clinician's nightmare. Sex Transm Infect 2000; 76(6):419–425.

Grace VM. Mind/body dualism in medicine: the case of chronic pelvic pain without organic pathology. Int J Health Sci 1998; 28:127–151.

Heath I. Following the story: continuity of care in general practice. In: Greenhalgh T, Hurwitz B, eds. Narrative-based medicine. London: BMJ Books; 1998:83–92.

Jansen FW, Kapiteyn K, Trimbos-Kemper T, et al. Complications of laparoscopy: a prospective multicentre observational study. BJOG 1997; 104:595–600.

Moore J, Kennedy S. Causes of chronic pelvic pain. Baillière's Clin Obstet Gynaecol 2000; 14:389–402.

Palter SF. Microlaparoscopy under local anaesthetic and conscious pain mapping for the diagnosis and management of pelvic pain. Curr Opin Obstet Gynecol 1999; 11:387–393.

Reiter RC. Evidence-based management of chronic pelvic pain. Clin Obstet Gynecol 1998; 41:422–435.

Royal College of Obstetricians and Gynaecologists. The investigation and management of endometriosis. RCOG guideline 24. London: RCOG; 2000. Available at: www.rcog.org.uk.

Scialli AR. Evaluating chronic pelvic pain: a consensus recommendation. J Reprod Med 1999; 44:945–952.

Skrine RL. Introduction to psychosexual medicine. Carlisle: Montana Press; 1989.

Wesselmann U, Czakanski PP. Pelvic pain: a chronic visceral pain syndrome. Curr Pain Headache Rep 2001; 5:13–19.

Zondervan K, Barlow DH. Epidemiology of chronic pelvic pain. Baillière's Clin Obstet Gynaecol 2000; 14:403–414.

Gynaecological oncology

6

Brett Winter-Roach, Partha Sengupta and Karina Reynolds

THIS CHAPTER Gynaecological oncology concerns care of women with genital tract cancers. In the UK, breast cancer is managed by specialist surgeons and will not be covered in this chapter. General considerations about the history of the specialty and current service organization are discussed. Management options for the more common gynaecological cancers (of the cervix, ovary, endometrium and vulva) are presented, as well as some new developments in this discipline. Invasive gestational trophoblastic neoplasia is managed at tumour-specific referral centres across the UK. Details of this disease are not examined in this chapter.

Background

Modern gynaecological cancer surgery developed in Vienna towards the end of the 19th century with the work of Wertheim, who devised the technique of radical abdominal hysterectomy for cervical cancer. Schauta, also of Vienna, developed the radical vaginal hysterectomy in 1902. The history of the subspeciality in the UK can be traced to clinicians with an additional interest and training in radical gynaecological surgery, such as Victor Bonney in London and Stanley Way in Gateshead.

Definition

Gynaecological oncology concerns the care of women with genital tract cancers, the most common of which are cancers of the:

- Cervix.
- Ovary.
- Endometrium.
- Vulva.

Occurrence

Table 6.1 summarizes the incidence and mortality of these four cancers for England and Wales, 1950–2002.

Vaginal cancer is the rarest of the common gynaecological malignancies. This and other forms of gynaecological cancer are not dealt with in this chapter.

Rationale for subspecialization and centralization

The initial management of the common gynaecological malignancies is often surgical. Since many gynaecological cancers are uncommon in routine practice, the typical training

Table 6.1: Incidence and mortality of common gynaecological cancers in the UK

Cancer	Incidence (2000) *	Crude rate (per 100 000)	Mortality (2002) *	Crude rate (per 100 000)
Uterine	5624	15.2	1073	2.3
Ovarian	6734	18.2	4687	11.4
Cervical	2991	8.9	1123	2.9
Vulval	996	2.2	364	0.7

Source: Cancer trends in England and Wales, 1950–2002, courtesy of Cancer Research UK website.
*Number of cases as age-standardized rate (ASR), directly standardized to European standard population. Directly standardized rates enable comparisons to be made over time, which are independent of changes in the age structure of the population. In each year, the crude rates in each 5-year age group are multiplied by the European standard population for that age group. These are then summed and divided by the total standard population to give an overall standardized rate.

Box 6.1: The gynaecological oncology multidisciplinary team

The cancer unit

Role
- Diagnosis and initial assessment
- Treatment of early stage disease
- Local audit

Personnel
- Gynaecological oncologists
- Lead gynaecologist
- Pathologist (with interest in gynaecological cancer)
- Radiologist
- Nurse (with interest in gynaecological cancer)

The cancer centre

Role
- Treatment of advanced and rare tumours
- Training of subspecialists
- Audit and research

Personnel
- Clinical oncologist/radiotherapist
- Medical oncologist/chemotherapist
- Histopathologist
- Cytopathologist
- Gynaecological oncology nurse specialist

of gynaecologists is insufficient to develop the level of expertise needed to manage these patients. Radical exenterative surgery and, in particular, the non-surgical oncological expertise required in managing these patients with chemo- and radiotherapy, as well as palliative skills, are not available in most district general hospitals.

Cancer units based at district general hospitals serving a population of up to 1 million people will act as diagnostic and assessment facilities, which would refer confirmed cases of cervical, ovarian, vulval and vaginal cancer to the regional cancer centres for expert management. Selected stage I endometrial cancers and stage Ia1 cervical cancers would be managed locally at the cancer units (see Box 6.1) (Calman–Hine 1995).

A prospective controlled study in Scotland of over 1800 women with ovarian cancer found a survival advantage for those women operated on by subspecialist gynaecological oncologists as opposed to those operated on by either general gynaecologists or general surgeons (Junor & Hole 1999). This finding is supported by retrospective data from the West Midlands.

CERVICAL CANCER

This is the second most common cancer. It is also the leading cause of cancer death in women worldwide (FIGO 2000). Cervical cancer has a bimodal age distribution, mainly affecting women in the age groups 25–35 and 50–60 years.

Histological types

- Squamous cell carcinoma is the most common histological type, accounting for 90% of cases.
- Adenocarcinoma is confirmed in 5–7% of cases, although this subtype is becoming more common.
- Other histological subtypes include adenosquamous, small cell neuroendocrine carcinoma and mesenchymal.
- Mixed histological subtypes also occur.

Secondary cervical cancer is usually adenocarcinoma, spreading directly from an endometrial cancer.

Diagnosis and investigation

The typical presentation of advanced cervical cancer is:

- Abnormal bleeding (intermenstrual, postcoital, postmenopausal).
- Vaginal discharge.
- A hard irregular enlargement of the cervix.

Further features may include:

- Uncontrollable vaginal haemorrhage.
- Uraemia due to bilateral ureteric obstruction.
- Pain from metastatic deposits.

Investigations

Cervical cancer may be detected by screening. The patient with a severely dyskaryotic smear or one suggestive of invasive disease is referred for colposcopy (see Ch. 7).

An abnormal surface contour, ulceration, bizarre vasculature and a densely white reaction upon application of 5% acetic acid solution all suggest invasive disease. At other times the finding of early stromal invasion in a loop or knife cone biopsy done for suspected high-grade intraepithelial disease is unexpected.

The diagnosis of adenocarcinoma of the cervix can be difficult at colposcopy since the lesion may be partially or entirely out of view, high up in the endocervical canal. A barrel-like enlargement of the cervix may be confirmed on examination *per rectum*, even if the ectocervix is apparently normal.

Confirmation of diagnosis

The diagnosis must be confirmed by a biopsy taken either at colposcopy or at the time of an examination under anaesthesia. It is important to stress the need for an adequate-sized biopsy when invasive disease is suspected. This facilitates a rational approach to the options for management (see Fig. 6.1).

Staging

The FIGO (Fédération Internationale Gynécologie et Obstetrique) staging of cervical cancer is clinical (Table 6.2). This is because, worldwide, most cervical cancers are treated with radiotherapy, thus a surgicopathological staging would be impractical. A thorough examination of the patient is necessary, including:

- A chest examination.
- Palpation of the abdomen.
- Palpation of lymph node groups.

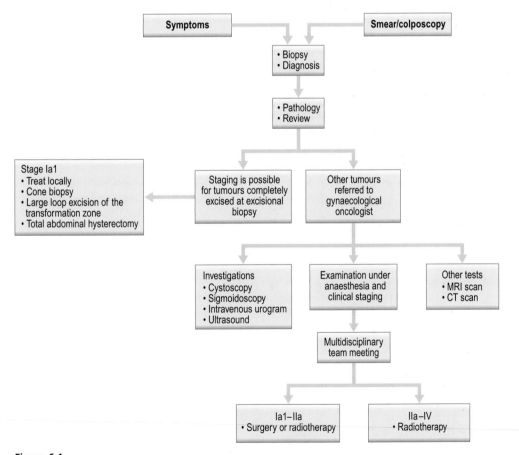

Figure 6.1
Care pathway in the management of cervical cancer. MRI, magnetic resonance imaging; CT, computed tomography.

Table 6.2: FIGO staging and 5-year overall survival for cervical cancer

Stage	Description	5-year survival (%)
Ia	Preclinical/microscopic disease confined to the cervix	
Ia1	Stromal invasion up to 3 mm in depth and 7 mm in horizontal plane	94.6
Ia2	Stromal invasion 3–5 mm deep, but no more than 7 mm wide	92.6
Ib	Macroscopic disease confined to the cervix	
Ib1	Tumour less than 4 cm in size	90.4
Ib2	Tumour more than or equal to 4 cm in size	79.8
II	Extension to upper vagina and paracervix/not pelvic side wall	
IIa	Extension to upper two-thirds of the vagina; no obvious parametrial involvement	76
IIb	Extension to paracervical tissue but not reaching the pelvic side wall	73.3
III	Disease extending to the lower third of the vagina or pelvic side wall	
IIIa	Tumour extends to the lower third of the vagina, with no involvement of pelvic side wall	50.5
IIIb	Pelvic side wall involvement and/or hydronephrosis or non-functioning kidney	46.4
IV	Spread outside pelvis or gross involvement of the bladder or rectal mucosa	
IVa	Spread to either the bladder anteriorly or the rectum posteriorly	29.6
Vb	Distant metastases outside the pelvis	22

Reproduced with kind permission of FIGO.

Box 6.2: Procedure for the staging of cervical cancer: British practice

- Examination under anaesthesia by a gynaecological oncologist and a radiotherapist is often done
- Combined vaginal and rectal examination is done to determine the size and spread of the tumour with special attention to whether it extends into parametrium or is fixed to the pelvic side wall
- Cystoscopy or sigmoidoscopy (if there is any suspicion of bladder or bowel involvement)
- Chest X-ray
- Intravenous pyelogram may be done
- More detailed imaging with computed tomography or magnetic resonance imaging (MRI) do not affect the staging, nor should the results of any surgical pathology
- The extent of parametrial extension of tumour and lymphadenopathy can be assessed by MRI. This is useful in guiding the choice of surgery or radiotherapy for primary treatment. MRI outperforms examination under anaesthesia and transrectal ultrasound in predicting outcome
- The staging directly influences the choice of treatment offered to a woman with a primary cervical cancer

British practice is detailed in Box 6.2.

Treatment

It should be noted that the current trend in the treatment of gynaecological cancer is towards the individualization of care.

Treatment according to cancer stage

All stages of the disease can be treated with radiotherapy, while stages Ia and Ib as well as carefully selected stage IIa tumours may be managed surgically. Randomized trials

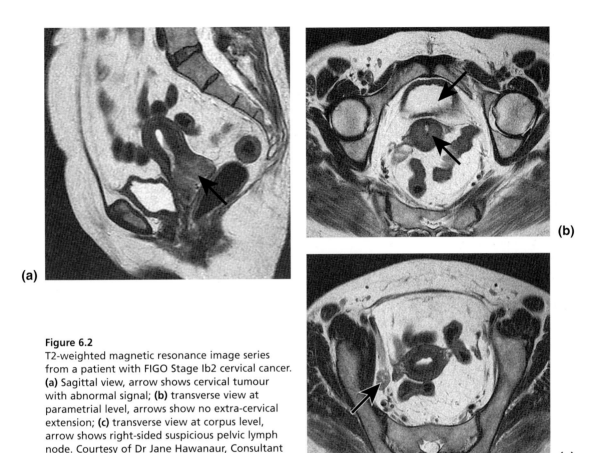

Figure 6.2
T2-weighted magnetic resonance image series from a patient with FIGO Stage Ib2 cervical cancer. **(a)** Sagittal view, arrow shows cervical tumour with abnormal signal; **(b)** transverse view at parametrial level, arrows show no extra-cervical extension; **(c)** transverse view at corpus level, arrow shows right-sided suspicious pelvic lymph node. Courtesy of Dr Jane Hawanaur, Consultant Radiologist, Manchester Royal Infirmary.

comparing surgery and radiotherapy for these early-stage cancers show that survival rates are equally high with either treatment.

Chemoradiation (chemotherapy and radiotherapy administered concurrently) is now considered the ideal primary treatment for advanced-stage cervical cancer (Morris et al 1999). The age, general health and reproductive ambitions of each patient should be weighed carefully in considering the best management, especially in early-stage disease. (See Fig. 6.2 for examples of early-stage disease.)

Assessing the adverse effects

The different patterns of adverse effects of treatments must be considered in determining the preferred management in individual cases. The risk of damage to nearby pelvic organs, particularly the bladder and ureters, with surgery contrasts with the short- and long-term complications of radical pelvic radiotherapy, which may include a deterioration in sexual function. Ovarian failure and vaginal fibrosis after radiotherapy are common problems, which may incline young women with early-stage disease to opt for primary surgical treatment.

Surgery

The surgical options for cervical cancer are presented in Table 6.3.

Stage Ia1 disease is adequately treated by simple local excision (see Fig. 6.3). Cervical conization with confirmation of clear surgical margins is all that is required. More radical treatment is needed in higher stage disease. A simple hysterectomy is adequate for localized disease in stage Ia2 disease, but pelvic lymphadenectomy should be done as well since the risk of nodal involvement approximates 5% in this stage.

Table 6.3: Primary treatment options for cervical cancer by FIGO stage

Treatment option	FIGO stage							
	Ia1	Ia2	Ib1	Ib2	IIa	IIb	III	IV
Cone biopsy	+	–	–	–	–	–	–	–
Simple TAH	+	–	–	–	–	–	–	–
TAH and BPLD	–	+	–	–	–	–	–	–
RAH and BPLD	–	+	+	+	?	–	–	–
Coelio–Schauta and BPLD	–	+	+	+	–	–	–	–
Cone biopsy and BPLD*	–	?	?	–	–	–	–	–
Trachelectomy and BPLD*	–	+	+	–	–	–	–	–
Radical radiotherapy	–	+	+	+	+	+	+	+
Brachytherapy only	–	+	?	–	–	–	–	–
Chemoradiation	–	–	?	?	+	+	+	+

*Fertility-sparing option. TAH, total abdominal hysterectomy; RAH, radical abdominal hysterectomy; BPLD, bilateral pelvic lymph node dissection. +, a recognized treatment option; –, not a treatment option; ?, contentious option.

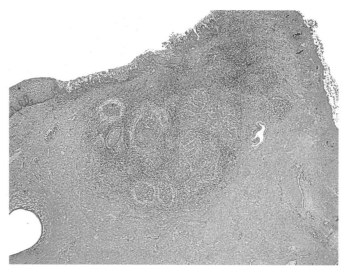

Figure 6.3
Photomicrograph of squamous cell cervical cancer showing early stromal invasion. Courtesy of Dr Rhona McVey, Consultant Histopathologist, St Mary's Hospital, Manchester.

Laparoscopic lymphadenectomy may offer advantages over the open approach and case series have been reported from both Europe and the USA.

Fertility-sparing options are available for carefully selected and counselled patients who may have to accept a greater risk of cancer mortality as a trade-off for their fertility. Radical trachelectomy and pelvic lymphadenectomy may be suitable for stage Ia2–Ib1 (Shepherd et al 1998). It has been suggested that a large knife cone biopsy (with clear surgical margins) coupled with laparoscopic lymphadenectomy may be an even more conservative but adequate approach for similar stage disease, although neither have undergone evaluation in a large prospective clinical trial.

When fertility is not an issue, macroscopic tumours (stage Ib1–IIa) that can be removed surgically with good margins and give the patient a decent chance of single modality treatment may be suited to either a standard abdominal radical hysterectomy with pelvic lymphadenectomy or a radical vaginal hysterectomy with laparoscopic pelvic lymphadenectomy. This latter procedure, the Coelio–Schauta operation, may be considered as an option alongside the traditional abdominal radical hysterectomy. There is no evidence that bilateral salpingo-oophorectomy is routinely indicated in the treatment of cervical carcinoma.

Surgery also retains a role for carefully selected patients with isolated small or large central recurrences of cervical cancer who may be cured or, less commonly, palliated by pelvic exenteration, either anterior (removal of bladder), posterior (removal of rectum) or total (combined anterior and posterior).

OVARIAN CANCER

Types of ovarian cancer

Cancer of the ovary may be primary or secondary (see Box 6.3). Primary ovarian tumours can arise from one of three embryological cell lines represented in the ovary. Epithelial ovarian cancer is the most common type and has several subtypes; serous and mucinous types are those most regularly encountered.

Additionally, tumours with borderline malignant potential may be seen, and early stromal invasion is described. Germ-cell malignancies are more commonly seen in younger women. The sex-cord/stromal tumours are relatively rare and may be functional and secrete hormones.

The further discussion relates mainly to epithelial ovarian cancer, which is the leading cause of gynaecological cancer death in the UK.

Diagnosis and investigation

Ovarian cancer is an insidious disease, which notoriously presents late with vague and often misinterpreted symptoms. The median age at diagnosis is 55 years. Abdominal

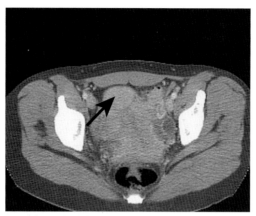

Figure 6.4
Contrast-enhanced computed tomogram image: bilateral complex ovarian masses, arrow shows uterus displaced anteriorly; note minimal abdominal distension despite advanced disease. Courtesy of Dr Jane Hawanaur.

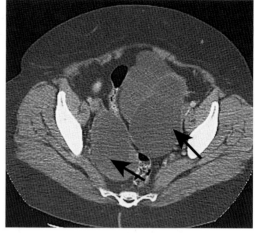

Figure 6.5
Contrast-enhanced computed tomogram image: arrows show bilateral complex (solid and cystic areas) ovarian masses. Courtesy of Dr Jane Hawanaur.

Box 6.3: Differential diagnosis of an ovarian mass

Benign tumours

- Mucinous cystadenoma
- Serous cystadenoma
- Luteal/follicular cyst
- Mature cystic teratoma (dermoid)
- Endometrioma

Borderline tumours

- Serous, mucinous and other subtypes

Malignant tumours

- Epithelial ovarian carcinoma
- Serous adenocarcinoma
- Mucinous adenocarcinoma
- Endometrioid adenocarcinoma
- Clear-cell adenocarcinoma

- Malignant Brenner (transitional cell) tumour
- Germ-cell tumours
- Dysgerminoma
- Choriocarcinoma
- Immature teratoma
- Sex-cord/stromal tumours
- Granulosa cell tumours
- Sertoli–Leydig tumour

Secondary malignancy
Primary sites:
- Stomach
- Breast
- Thyroid
- Endometrium
- Fallopian tube

---

distension or a recognized abdominal mass is a common presenting feature. (See Figs 6.4 and 6.5.)

Gastrointestinal disturbance with nausea and vomiting or a change in bowel habit may relate to compression of hollow organs from a rapidly enlarging pelvic mass or the accumulation of ascites. Pressure on the bladder may give rise to increased urinary frequency or urinary incontinence. Weight loss is uncommon.

The differential diagnosis should include primary ovarian tumours, which may be benign, borderline or malignant (see Box 6.3). Primary bowel cancer may also present similarly,

Table 6.4: FIGO staging and 5-year overall survival of ovarian cancer

Stage	Description	5-year survival (%)
I	Confined to one/both ovaries	
Ia	Limited to a single ovary; no ascites; capsule intact with no surface tumour	89.9
Ib	Limited to both ovaries; no ascites; capsule intact with no surface tumour	84.7
Ic	One or both ovaries have a ruptured capsule or surface tumour; malignant ascites or positive peritoneal washings	80
II	Extension to pelvic structures	
IIa	Extension to uterus or fallopian tubes	69.9
IIb	Extension to other pelvic tissues	63.7
IIc	As for IIa or IIb, but one or both ovaries have ruptured capsule or surface tumour; malignant ascites or positive peritoneal washings	66.5
III	As for stage I/II but also with peritoneal implants outside the pelvis or with positive retroperitoneal lymph nodes	
IIIa	Histologically confirmed microscopic seeding of abdominal peritoneal surfaces and negative retroperitoneal lymph nodes	58.5
IIIb	Histologically confirmed implants of abdominal peritoneal surfaces less than 2 cm and negative retroperitoneal lymph nodes	39.9
IIIc	Histologically confirmed implants of abdominal peritoneal surfaces greater than 2 cm or positive retroperitoneal lymph nodes	28.7
IV	Distant metastases (including liver parenchyma/positive pleural fluid cytology)	16.8

Reproduced with kind permission of FIGO.

as can diverticular disease. Secondary ovarian cancer from a gastrointestinal primary, breast or thyroid cancer should also be considered.

Investigations

Ovarian cancer is staged surgicopathologically at laparotomy using the FIGO system (see Table 6.4). Thorough staging of ovarian cancer is especially important because prognosis depends heavily on the stage. For example, disease apparently confined to a single ovary but with occult retroperitoneal nodal metastasis will make the stage IIIc rather than Ia.

Complete staging can only be achieved by a systematic laparotomy via a midline abdominal incision. This involves:

- Obtaining peritoneal washings.
- Performing a total abdominal hysterectomy and bilateral salpingo-oophorectomy.
- Infracolic omentectomy.
- Peritoneal biopsies.
- Diaphragmatic scrapes for cytology.
- Sampling of pelvic and para-aortic lymph nodes.

The rationale for total abdominal hysterectomy and bilateral salpingo-oophorectomy is the high incidence of bilateral tumours (metastatic or primary) and extension to the uterine cavity. The omentum is removed, as it is the major site of abdominal metastases.

For presumed stage I disease, peritoneal fluid and diaphragmatic scrapings for cytology, peritoneal biopsies, and sampling of pelvic and para-aortic lymph nodes, may exclude occult disease. For advanced disease (stages II–IV), further debulking of disease sites is performed as this may improve chemoresponse and has benefits for quality of life (remove large tumour masses, relieve bowel obstruction).

Conservative surgery (unilateral oophorectomy) can be considered when the disease is presumed to be confined to one intact ovary (stage Ia) and fertility is a consideration. Surgery could then be completed later, after completion of the family, if so desired.

Treatment

The treatment of epithelial ovarian cancer is the joint responsibility of gynaecological cancer surgeons and site-specific non-surgical oncologists in the context of a multi-disciplinary team. The chief modalities of treatment are surgery and chemotherapy (see Fig. 6.6).

Surgery

The therapeutic role of surgery in the management of ovarian cancer may be to cure, extend life or to palliate. Procedures that have been described include:

- Primary debulking surgery.
- Interval debulking.
- Second-look laparotomy.
- Delayed primary surgery.

Primary debulking

The standard primary surgical approach advocates tumour debulking, with the aim to achieve residual tumour of less than 1 cm. Meta-analyses have found that optimal debulking surgery was independently associated with improved prognosis (Hunter et al 1992).

A balance has to be struck between radical surgery and the potential morbidity associated with it: disease involving the spleen, liver parenchyma or root of the small bowel mesentery may be better treated with chemotherapy.

Interval debulking

When the disease is advanced and primary debulking surgery has been suboptimal, some patients may benefit from interval debulking surgery. Following suboptimal surgery, additional cytoreduction may be achieved by commencing preliminary adjuvant chemotherapy (usually three of six cycles), allowing further surgical cytoreduction after this interval, with subsequent completion of chemotherapy. There is evidence from an EORTC randomized controlled trial which suggests improvement in progression-free and overall survival for the group that underwent interval debulking, although this has not been substantiated by a more recent Gynecological Oncology Group (GOG) study.

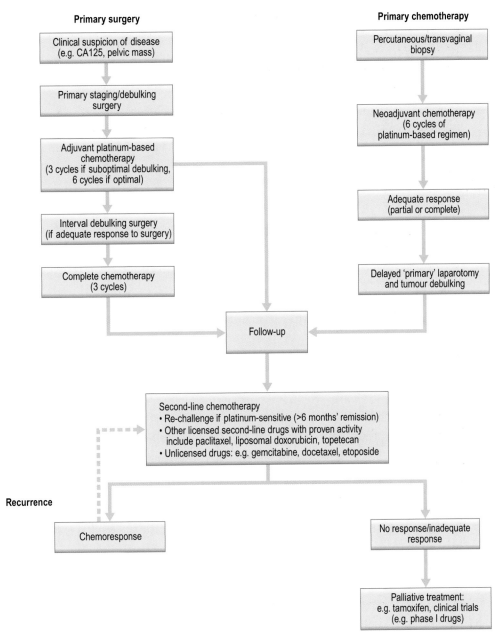

Figure 6.6
Options for treatment of advanced epithelial ovarian cancer.

The determining factor for the success of this type of procedure would appear to be in the identification of those patients, prior to laparotomy, who may be optimally cytoreduced and thereby have a survival advantage. Diagnostic laparoscopy has been put forward as one way to evaluate this, although imaging by contrast-enhanced computed tomography is more conventional.

Delayed primary surgery

This also has a place in the management of women with advanced ovarian cancer. Patients with significant co-morbidity or advanced disease with, for example, massive ascites and pleural effusions, may present unacceptably high anaesthetic risks. Optimal surgical cytoreduction from the outset may not be feasible. For these patients, neoadjuvant chemotherapy with the possibility of delayed primary surgery in carefully selected cases may be the way forward. Some women show dramatic responses (partial or complete) with six completed cycles of primary chemotherapy, making subsequent delayed debulking surgery an option. This approach is currently being assessed in a MRC study, CHORUS.

Chemotherapy

Chemotherapy has been the cornerstone in the treatment of advanced epithelial ovarian cancer. The recently presented results of the ICON1/ACTION trial have established a survival benefit for subgroups of women with stage I disease. Although not usually curative (as it is with the germ-cell malignancies), platinum-based combination regimens can achieve very good results even for high-stage disease.

Complete pathological responses are seen in 60–80% of those women who are optimally cytoreduced at prior surgery. A US Gynecologic Oncology Group phase III clinical trial described a survival advantage with cisplatin–paclitaxel when compared to the combination of cisplatin and cyclophosphamide. The use of carboplatin in place of cisplatin in modern regimens is less nephrotoxic as well as more convenient.

There remains some debate as to whether first-line therapy should be single-agent carboplatin or carboplatin–paclitaxel, although current guidelines from the National Institute of Clinical Excellence (NICE) require that the combination is made available to all women having first-line treatment. This has significant cost implications, although there would appear to be a median survival advantage for at least a subgroup of women having paclitaxel in combination with either carboplatin or cisplatin.

Consolidation chemotherapy (i.e. additional or extra cycles) for ovarian cancer has not yet been proven to have a survival benefit. There are several trials in progress to establish the activity of new agents, routes and dose intensities of chemotherapy. The anti-oestrogen tamoxifen citrate is often used as palliative treatment.

ENDOMETRIAL CANCER

Endometrial cancer is the least frequently referred of the common gynaecological cancers. Early presentation accounts for the relatively low mortality seen.

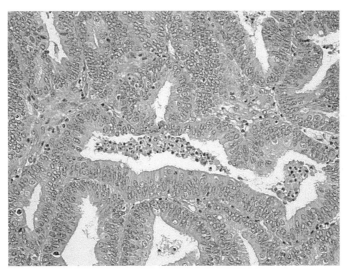

Figure 6.7
Haematoxylin and eosin (H&E) staining of section of endometriod endometrial adenocarcinoma. Courtesy of Dr Rhona McVey.

The perception that the surgery is relatively straightforward and the prognosis good, can induce a false sense of security. The most common histological variant is endometrioid adenocarcinoma, which has the most favourable prognosis (see Fig. 6.7). This variant may co-exist with endometrioid ovarian carcinoma as a separate primary disease or as secondary disease from the ovary, or vice versa. Mucinous and undifferentiated types are also described, while the much less frequent clear cell, papillary serous or carcinosarcoma subtypes are more aggressive tumours. The papillary serous subtype can present with widespread abdominal metastases.

Diagnosis

Endometrial cancer usually presents with postmenopausal bleeding, often in nulliparous women, those with a late menopause or those with hyperoestrogenic states such as in obesity or polycystic ovarian syndrome. Women inappropriately prescribed unopposed oestrogen hormone replacement therapy or those on tamoxifen regimens for breast cancer are at risk. Premenopausal women in their fourth decade present with heavy, irregular vaginal bleeding.

Occasionally, abnormal endometrial cells are detected following cervical cytology. Postmenopausal endometrial thickness greater than 4 mm detected by transvaginal ultrasound is not reassuring. The diagnosis can be confirmed by endometrial sampling using endometrial aspiration in the outpatient setting. If unsuccessful, formal hysteroscopy and endometrial biopsy should be used to confirm the diagnosis.

Magnetic resonance imaging (MRI) of the pelvis may help determine if there is myometrial invasion or cervical involvement of the tumour (see Fig. 6.8).

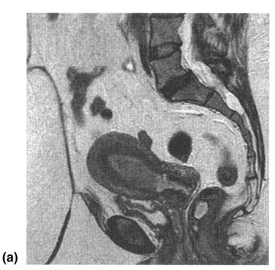
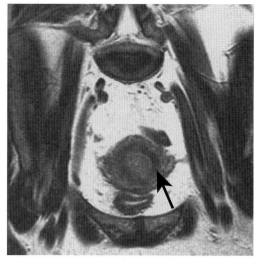

(a)   **(b)**

Figure 6.8
T2-weighted magnetic resonance image series from a patient with FIGO Stage Ib endometrial cancer: **(a)** sagittal view showing endometrial tumour with abnormal signal; **(b)** short axis (uterine) view, arrow shows early myometrial invasion. Courtesy of Dr Jane Hawanaur.

Table 6.5: FIGO staging and 5-year overall survival for endometrial cancer

Stage	Description	5-year survival (%)
I	Tumour confined to uterine corpus	
Ia	Limited to endometrium	88.9
Ib	Invasion of less than half myometrium	90
Ic	Invasion greater than half myometrium	80.7
II	Tumour extends to involve the uterine cervix	
IIa	Endocervical glandular involvement only	79.9
IIb	Cervical stromal invasion	72.3
III	Tumour spread to uterine serosa, ovaries, vagina or retroperitoneal lymph nodes	
IIIa	Invades uterine serosa/adnexa and/or positive peritoneal cytology	63.4
IIIb	Vaginal metastases	38.8
IIIc	Metastases to pelvic and/or para-aortic lymph nodes	51.1

Reproduced with kind permission of FIGO.

Staging

Endometrial carcinoma is staged surgicopathologically and depends on the histological examination of extirpated tissues. Washings from the peritoneal cavity must also be assessed. The FIGO staging is given in Table 6.5.

Box 6.4: Evidence-based treatment for endometrial cancer

Surgery

- Low-risk disease (treated by total abdominal hysterectomy and bilateral salpingo-oophorectomy at cancer unit)
  - FIGO stage Ia or Ib, grade 1 or 2
- Higher-risk disease (treated at cancer centres)
  - FIGO stage Ic, grade 3
  - FIGO stage II and higher
  - Unusual histology

Radiotherapy

- Primary mode of treatment for medically unfit patient or high-stage disease
- Adjuvant therapy for advanced or high-risk disease as advised by MDT (multidisciplinary team)
- Consider for entry into ASTEC trial
- Useful in recurrent disease if patient radiotherapeutically naive

Progestogens

- No proven use as adjuvant therapy
- Can be harmful in some patients

Oestrogen replacement therapy

- Offer if required

MRI, although useful in distinguishing those patients who should not have surgery, cannot be used to formally stage disease.

Treatment

The treatment of endometrial cancer depends largely on the stage of the disease, although the histological subtype of the tumour or patient characteristics are also determining factors. In particular, as the World Health Organization tumour grade increases from low to high (mild differentiation to severe differentiation), the risk of nodal metastases increases (see Box 6.4 for an outline of the evidence-based treatment of endometrial cancer) (Hayward 1999).

Surgery

The primary treatment modality for early-stage disease is usually surgery, unless the patient is medically unfit or is morbidly obese. Since the staging is surgicopathological, the default approach should be a laparotomy via a midline incision, followed by peritoneal washing and thorough exploration of the pelvis and upper abdomen. A simple hysterectomy with bilateral salpingo-oophorectomy is recommended for stage I disease, while disease involving the cervix is often treated by radical hysterectomy removing the paracervical tissue and performing bilateral pelvic lymphadenectomy (see Fig. 6.9).

Infracolic omentectomy is advocated in cases where the histology is known to be the papillary serous subtype since this variant has a propensity for early transcoelomic

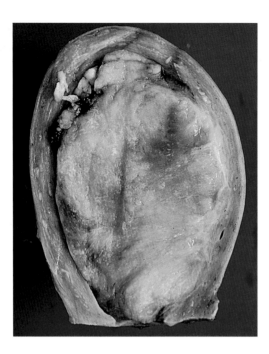

Figure 6.9
Endometrial cancer: gross specimen of transected
uterine corpus with tumour at uterine fundus.
Courtesy of Dr Rhona McVey.

spread. Among the more controversial aspects of the management of endometrial cancer
are the role of lymphadenectomy in stage I disease and the value of the laparoscopic
approach for this procedure. Laparoscopically assisted vaginal hysterectomy and bilateral
salpingo-oophorectomy has proved practical and safe and can be combined with a
laparoscopic lymphadenectomy. The routine practice in the USA and Australia is to
perform pelvic and para-aortic lymph node dissections in stage I endometrial cancer.
Although observational data would suggest a survival advantage for those women who
have systematic lymphadenectomy, this important question will be addressed by ASTEC,
the multicentre international prospective randomized study of the MRC. In this study,
which has both a surgical and a radiotherapy randomization, another question, regarding
the place of adjuvant radiotherapy for stage I disease, is addressed.

Radiotherapy

Management of advanced-stage disease is individualized, usually involving radiotherapy
and/or chemotherapy and possibly up-front surgery.

The place of adjuvant radiotherapy in the management of Stage I endometrial cancer has
been addressed by the PORTEC study (Creutzberg et al 2000). This Dutch multicentre
randomized controlled trial examined adjuvant radiotherapy versus no further treatment
in 715 women with medium-risk stage I endometrial cancer who had total abdominal
hysterectomy and bilateral salpingo-oophorectomy but did not undergo lymphadenectomy.

The results demonstrated a reduction in the risk of pelvic recurrence with adjuvant radiotherapy, but no survival advantage in the treatment group who had a statistically greater incidence of radiotherapy-induced morbidity.

Hormonal treatment

Hormonal treatment has no proven role in the radical or adjuvant treatment of endometrial cancer. Those with recurrent or metastatic disease, or women who at diagnosis are unfit for either surgery or radiotherapy, may benefit from treatment with progestogens or tamoxifen.

Chemotherapy

Chemotherapy for endometrial cancer is limited to those women with recurrent or metastatic disease. Platinum- or paclitaxel-based regimens may provide some response.

VULVAL CANCER

Disease types

- Squamous cell carcinoma is the predominant subtype.
- Primary vulval melanoma, a rare disease with a propensity for early haematogenous dissemination, is the second most frequent malignancy seen at this site.
- Paget's disease of the vulva is another variant, which is often difficult to manage.
- Basal cell cancer of the vulva is sometimes mistaken for a primary squamous lesion, although there are often distinct clinical signs as well as a characteristic histological picture.
- Primary vulval adenocarcinoma is rarely seen, although the Bartholin's gland can be a primary site.
- Sarcomas of the vulva or secondary deposits from another primary have occasionally been reported.

The following discussion relates to squamous cell carcinoma of the vulva.

Diagnosis

Unfortunately, although symptomatic from early on, most women present months after first noticing an abnormality of the vulva. The typical patient is elderly (mostly in the 70–80-year age group) and there will not infrequently be a long history of vulval irritation preceding the appearance of a lump or ulcer that is sore and may bleed. There may be a past history of treatment for vulval intraepithelial neoplasia as about a third of cases are associated with human papilloma virus (HPV) infection; another third have maturation disorders of squamous hyperplasia or lichen sclerosis.

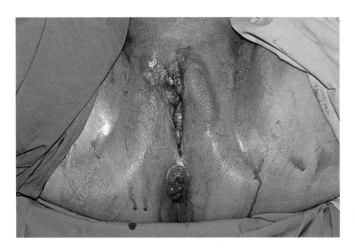

Figure 6.10
Typical presentation of vulval cancer requiring wide excision and groin node dissection.

Table 6.6: FIGO staging and 5-year overall survival of vulval cancer

Stage	Description	5-year survival (%)
I	Disease confined to the vulva or perineum and no more than 2 cm in size; no nodal metastasis	86.5
Ia	Stromal invasion no greater than 1.0 mm	
Ib	Stromal invasion of more than 1.0 mm	
II	Disease confined to the vulva but exceeding 2 cm in size; no nodal metastasis	67.7
III	Tumour of any size with adjacent spread to the lower urethra and/or vagina, or anus, and or unilateral regional lymph node metastasis	40.3
IV	Distant metastasis and/or bilateral inguinal node metastasis	21.7
IVa	Tumour invades upper urethra, bladder mucosa, rectal mucosa, pelvic bone and/or bilateral regional node metastasis	
IVb	Distant metastasis including pelvic lymph nodes	

Reproduced with kind permission of FIGO.

An adequate histological specimen is required for the correct diagnosis and subsequent management of the tumour. For smaller lesions, an excisional biopsy with wide margins of uninvolved tissue may be suitable. A wedge biopsy, including a portion of uninvolved skin, is taken for larger tumours (see Fig. 6.10).

Since the disease is relatively rare, few gynaecologists outside tertiary referral centres will acquire much experience in treating these cancers. Early referral to cancer centres is thus recommended.

Staging

The staging of vulval cancer, as with ovarian and endometrial cancer, is surgicopathological. The stage is determined by the size, depth of stromal invasion and local and distant spread of the tumour (see Table 6.6).

Treatment

The last century saw the development of curative radical vulval surgery for locally advanced disease (Grimshaw et al 1993). This came at the price of considerable cosmetic and psychosexual morbidity. As is the case with cervical cancer, a move towards more conservative surgery with consideration of tumour and patient characteristics has been seen in recent decades. The multidisciplinary interplay possible in gynaecological cancer centres facilitates both multimodality treatment and individualization of patient care.

The chief treatment modalities for vulval carcinoma are:

- Surgery.
- Radiotherapy/chemoradiotherapy.

Surgery

Surgery for vulval cancer involves wide resection of the tumour to achieve local control, and inguinofemoral lymphadenectomy.

Lateral tumours that are at least 1 cm from the midline, and which are sufficiently small, may be removed by wide local excision to preserve the clitoris and therefore sexual function. Ipsilateral inguinofemoral lymphadenectomy is performed as there is a low risk of contralateral lymph node metastases in well lateralized tumours.

For central tumours of the vulva, especially when there is clitoral and distal urethral involvement, bilateral node dissection is required. The butterfly type of incision popularized by earlier surgeons has been nearly universally replaced by the triple incision, wherein the inguinal lymph node dissections are performed via separate incisions. Fears about the risk of skin bridge metastasis may be more theoretical than clinically significant although *en bloc* resection is reserved for large tumours with involved nodes where there is a risk of dividing lymphatics that are permeated by tumour. Joint procedures with plastic surgeons may be indicated when the vulval defect is large.

There is general consensus that stromal invasion of greater than 1 mm depth confers a significant risk of regional inguinal lymph node metastasis. Bilateral inguinal lymph node dissection is therefore customarily performed for central cancers. For lateral tumours at least 1 cm from the midline, it is appropriate to perform ipsilateral inguinal lymph node dissection.

The place of sentinel lymph node detection (i.e. the first node in the chain) and biopsy is not yet unequivocally established for vulval cancer treatment. Early reports indicate that there is a high negative predictive value for this test, which may lead the way to a yet more selective use of systematic groin node dissection. Also experimental is the use of inguinal lymph node ultrasound scanning or magnetic resonance imaging to predict nodal metastasis.

The complications of delayed wound healing or wound breakdown, lymphocyst formation or longer-term problems with lower limb lymphoedema are common with inguinofemoral lymphadenectomy, although preservation of the saphenous vein may be associated with lower short- and long-term morbidity.

FUTURE DIRECTIONS

Human papilloma virus testing HPV testing as an adjunct to cytological screening, or even as an alternative to standard screening, is being developed. More study is needed in this area, but the initial role for HPV testing may be in identifying women who by virtue of their negative results can benefit from reduced surveillance (Cuzick et al 2000).

Liquid-based cytology This is another important development in cervical screening and has already been embraced by the NHS Executive (see Ch. 7, p. 114).

Vaccines The development of vaccines against HPV for either primary prevention or treatment of intraepithelial lesions is an exciting area of research. The early proteins coded by viral DNA serve as epitopes against which antiviral immune reactions can be directed.

Screening for epithelial ovarian cancer The multicentre UKCTOCS trial has the power to determine the place, if any, of pelvic ultrasound and CA125 measurement in screening asymptomatic women for epithelial ovarian cancer.

Radio- and chemotherapy Clinical trials of radiotherapy schedules, sandwich regimens with chemotherapy, novel cytotoxic agents and combinations are ongoing.

Surgery Sentinel node sampling in vulval cancer, laparoscopic staging procedures in cervical and endometrial cancers and delayed primary debulking for ovarian cancers are likely to emerge as standard approaches in years to come.

Selected References and Further Reading

Calman K, Hine D. A policy framework for commissioning cancer services. Department of Health; 1995.

Creutzberg CL, van Putten WL, Koper PC, et al. Surgery and postoperative radiotherapy versus surgery alone for patients with stage-1 endometrial carcinoma: multicentre randomised trial. PORTEC Study Group. Post Operative Radiation Therapy in Endometrial Carcinoma. Lancet 2000; 355:1404–1411.

Cuzick J, Sasieni P, Davies P, et al. A systematic review of the role of human papilloma virus (HPV) testing within a cervical screening programme: summary and conclusions. Br J Cancer 2000; 83:561–565.

FIGO. FIGO annual report on the results of treatment in gynaecological cancer. vol 24. Milan: International Federation of Gynecology and Obstetrics; 2000.

Grimshaw RN, Murdoch JB, Monaghan JM. Radical vulvectomy and bilateral inguinofemoral lymphadenectomy through separate incisions: experience with 100 cases. Int J Gynecol Cancer 1993; 3:18–23.

Hunter RW, Alexander ND, Soutter WP. Meta-analysis of surgery in advanced ovarian carcinoma: is maximum cytoreductive surgery an independent determinant of prognosis? Am J Obstet Gynecol 1992; 166:504–511.

Junor E, Hole D. Specialist gynaecologists and survival outcome in ovarian cancer: a Scottish National Study of 1866 patients. BJOG 1999; 106:1130–1136.

Melville A, Eastwood A, Kleijnen J. Improving outcomes in gynaecological cancer. The manual: the research evidence. NHS Executive; 1999.

Morris M, Eifel PJ, Lu J, et al. Pelvic radiation with concurrent chemotherapy compared with pelvic and para-aortic radiation for high-risk cervical cancer. N Engl J Med 1999; 340:1137–1143.

Shepherd JH, Crawford RAF, Oram DH. Radical trachelectomy: a way to preserve fertility in the treatment of early cervical cancer. BJOG 1998; 105:912–916.

Cervical cytology and colposcopy

7

Cynthia Harper

THIS CHAPTER This chapter describes the normal and abnormal development of cervical epithelium and its identification. It goes on to explain the recommendations of the National Health Service Cervical Screening Programme for cervical screening and colposcopy, together with a description of these procedures. Finally, the management and treatment of women with cervical intraepithelial neoplasia is followed by some discussion of future directions.

Background

There has been interest in the examination of the cervix since the early 20th century, when atypical changes in the epithelium were first observed. In 1925, Hinselmann described his colposcope, which enabled direct observation of the cervix under low-power microscopy. He was able to correlate colposcopic appearances with biopsies and formulate the concept of the development of cervical cancer following a recognizable precancer stage. In the same decade, Papanicolaou demonstrated that, by staining epithelial cells scraped from the surface of the cervix, it was possible to identify premalignant changes. These separate developments were eventually brought together to establish a system for cervical screening and treatment. It is of enormous credit to the National Health Service Cervical Screening Programme (NHSCSP) that, since its introduction in 1988, it has overseen a reduction in the death rate from cervical cancer in England and Wales by more than 40%. In 2002, the death rate fell below 1000 for the first time.

THE NORMAL CERVIX

The cervix opens from the uterus into the vaginal vault. In nulliparae, it is usually less than 25 mm in diameter and has a circular external os. The cervix tends to be larger in multiparae and to have a slit-shaped external os.

Ectocervix

The ectocervix is covered in non-keratinized stratified squamous epithelium (Fig. 7.1). Squamous cells proliferate in the basal layer; they mature, gaining cytoplasm and glycogen, in the middle layer. The cells become flatter as they move towards the surface, where they slough off.

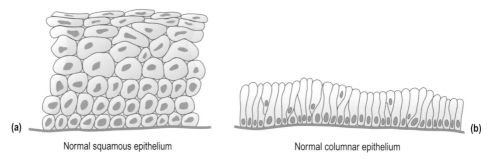

(a) Normal squamous epithelium   (b) Normal columnar epithelium

Figure 7.1
Diagrammatic representation of **(a)** squamous and **(b)** columnar epithelium.

Endocervix

The endocervical canal is lined with simple, mucus-producing columnar epithelium which is convoluted into crypts and mounds that may extend to a depth of up to 0.7 mm into the stroma. The cells are arranged in a single pallisade layer with large oval basal nuclei (Fig. 7.1).

The transformation zone

The squamous epithelium of the ectocervix meets the columnar epithelium of the endocervix at the squamocolumnar junction (SCJ). Under the influence of fluctuating oestrogen and progestogen levels, the SCJ undergoes many changes, starting *in utero* and continuing after the menopause. This area of change is called the transformation zone and it is here that squamous abnormalities may occur. In addition, glandular dysplasia may arise in the columnar epithelium.

Ectropion

Ideally, the SCJ is situated at the external os (Fig. 7.2a). However, under the influence of oestrogen, the cervix tends to evert so that the original SCJ is on the ectocervix (Fig. 7.2b). Because columnar epithelium is only one cell thick, the underlying blood vessels give it a red appearance and it may bleed easily. This is called an ectropion. It should not be called an 'erosion' as no abnormality or ulceration is present.

Squamous metaplasia

The acid pH in the vagina stimulates conversion of the delicate columnar epithelium into thicker, tougher squamous epithelium. This process of transformation is called squamous metaplasia and produces a new physiological SCJ nearer to the external os. The transformation zone may contain gland openings and retention cysts (Nabothian follicles) where the new squamous skin has 'trapped' crypts in the original columnar epithelium (Fig. 7.2c).

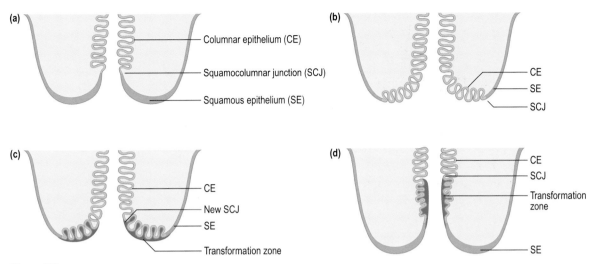

Figure 7.2
Diagrammatic representation of the development of the transformation zone.

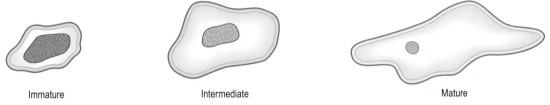

Figure 7.3
Diagrammatic representation of normal immature, intermediate and mature squamous cells.

Inversion

At the menopause, when circulating oestrogen levels fall, the cervix inverts and the new SCJ moves up into the endocervical canal (Fig. 7.2d). This makes sampling of the transformation zone more uncertain.

CERVICAL SCREENING

Cervical screening involves sampling the cells of the transformation zone to detect dyskaryosis of the epithelial cells. In normal squamous skin, the cells mature as they move from the basal layer to the surface of the skin (Fig. 7.3).

Dyskaryosis

Dyskaryosis is the term used for abnormal cellular maturation demonstrated on a cervical smear. The condition may be reported according to the degree of abnormality as:

113

- Mild.
- Moderate.
- Severe.

Dyskaryotic cells typically show the following characteristics:

- Reduced and immature cytoplasm.
- High nuclear/cytoplasmic ratio.
- Dense irregular nuclear staining.
- Poor differentiation of cells at all stages of maturation.

Obtaining a cervical smear

Liquid-based cytology

This new technique (see Box 7.1) is being introduced since 2003. After obtaining a good view of the cervix and transformation zone, the smear must be taken with a plastic sampler (Fig. 7.4) and transferred to a liquid preservative. The cells are later centrifuged and filtered in the laboratory to make a high-quality slide.

Traditional smear-taking

Until the training of smear-takers and laboratory staff for liquid-based cytology is complete, some smears will continue to be taken by the traditional method, normally involving the use of a wooden Aylesbury spatula (Fig. 7.5), although several other similar devices are commercially available.

Box 7.1: Procedure for obtaining a cervical smear

Liquid-based cytology

1. Insert the tip of the soft plastic brush or other sampler into the cervical os. Wooden samplers must not be used as they absorb the material and reduce the number of cells available for the smear.
2. Rotate the sampler five times.
3. Depending on the liquid-based cytology technique employed by the local laboratory, either mash the brush vigorously in the pot of liquid preservative to ensure that all cellular material is removed from the sampler into the liquid, or break off the plastic tip of the sampler into the pot of liquid.
4. The pot must be clearly labelled with the woman's name and date of birth and sent to the laboratory where the slide must be prepared within 3 weeks.

Traditional method

1. Insert the extended tip of the spatula into the cervical os.
2. Rotate the tip through 360° both clockwise and anticlockwise.
3. Remove the spatula carefully.
4. The sample should be thinly spread and fixed with alcohol on a glass slide within 3 seconds to avoid air-drying.
5. The slide must be clearly labelled in pencil with the woman's name and date of birth and sent to the laboratory accompanied by a fully completed request form.

Note: If a large ectropion is present, it may be necessary to repeat the process using the rounded end of the spatula to be certain of sampling the transformation zone.

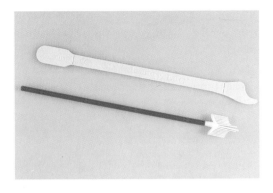

Figure 7.4
Soft plastic brush and plastic spatula used for obtaining samples for liquid-based cytology.

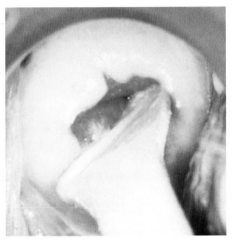

Figure 7.5
Smear-taking using a wooden Aylesbury spatula.

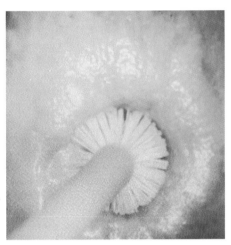

Figure 7.6
Smear-taking using a cyto-brush.

Brush sampler

Where the transformation zone is inside the cervical canal (common in postmenopausal women), it may be necessary to use a brush sampler (Fig. 7.6). The brush is inserted until the last of the bristles are just visible, then rotated. Brush samples should not be taken routinely.

Limitations of cervical cytology

The following limitations of cervical cytology must be noted:

- It is dependent on adequate sampling. This must be the responsibility of the smear-taker who should record any difficulties on the smear request form. Although the presence of endocervical and metaplastic cells indicates that the transformation zone has been sampled, it does not enable the laboratory to comment on the quality of the smear-taking.

- It is only a screening test and is not diagnostic of disease.
- Cervical intraepithelial neoplasia (CIN) can only be diagnosed histologically from a colposcopically directed biopsy.
- Cytology is poor at detecting malignancy. Clinical suspicion of abnormality should always trigger referral for further investigation, even if the cytology is normal.
- The test is poor at detecting glandular abnormalities and is not designed for this purpose.

The National Health Service Cervical Screening Programme

The NHSCSP previously advised cervical screening every 3–5 years for women aged 20–64 years. However, these guidelines have been modified by the Advisory Committee on Cervical Screening in response to recommendations from Cancer Research UK scientists. The changes aim to eliminate variations in service and to ensure adequate screening of those women at highest risk. The new recommendations, made in October 2003, are:

- Age 25 years: first invitation.
- Age 25–49 years: interval 3 years.
- Age 50–64 years: interval 5 years.

Cervical cancer is extremely rare in younger women and screening is no longer recommended for women under 25 years of age. In this age group, the evidence suggests that the risks of unnecessary investigation and treatment outweigh the benefits. This does not preclude the referral of symptomatic younger women for diagnostic tests.

CYTOLOGY RESULTS

Although the large majority of smears are normal, abnormal changes occur in a minority of cases and can vary from borderline to severe. The level of the abnormal changes noted can suggest a diagnosis and will determine subsequent management. The NHSCSP guidelines carry recommendations in this respect. However, it must be borne in mind that the divisions between mild, moderate and severe dyskaryosis are indistinct and subjective. Similarly, correlation between levels of dyskaryosis and CIN can never be exact.

No abnormality

Normal

- Expected for 80–90% of smears.
- No dyskaryotic cells seen.
- Transformation zone cells present.

Repeat in 3–5 years.

Inadequate

- Expected for 5–9% of smears.
- Technically unsatisfactory: a smear cannot be interpreted if it is too thickly spread, too scanty, contains only endocervical cells, is poorly fixed or is air-dried.

- Most occurrences are in younger women, who are more likely to have inflammatory exudate related to infection.
- It may be difficult to obtain good samples from postmenopausal women if the epithelium is atrophic and the transformation zone is not visible.
- The presence of endocervical cells is not essential, except in the follow-up of a previous endocervical abnormality.

Repeat within 3 months. Refer for colposcopy after three inadequate smears or if there is clinical suspicion.

Abnormal reports

Low-grade changes

- Expected for 4–7% of smears.

Borderline nuclear changes

- Usually indicates very low-grade changes that are difficult to interpret.
- The changes may be benign (e.g. due to human papilloma virus; see below) or represent mild dyskaryosis.
- Occasionally, 'borderline' may be used to denote a difficulty in distinguishing benign changes from high-grade dyskaryosis or invasive disease in squamous or endocervical cells.

Repeat in 6–12 months, then annually for three negative smears. Refer for colposcopy after 2–3 borderline smears or if there is clinical suspicion.

Mild dyskaryosis, suggesting CIN 1

- This report is self-explanatory.
- It is vital that borderline and mild dyskaryosis reports are not dismissed.
- Colposcopy is essential if the follow-up smear does not return to normal.

Best practice is to refer for colposcopy after the first mild dyskaryotic smear and certainly after the second, even if there have been intervening normal smears, or if there is clinical suspicion. NHSCSP guidelines recommend colposcopy within 8 weeks of a report recommending referral for a low-grade change.

High-grade changes

- Expected for 1–2% of smears.

Moderate-to-severe dyskaryosis, suggesting CIN 2–3

- This report is self-explanatory.
- Young women with florid wart virus changes and mild-to-moderate dyskaryosis may be recommended a repeat smear in 3 months.

Otherwise, refer for colposcopy. NHSCSP guidelines recommend colposcopy within 4 weeks. See Figures 7.7 and 7.8.

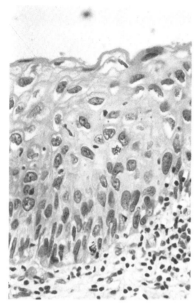

Figure 7.7
Histological appearance of CIN 1–2. From
Anderson M, Jordan J, Morse J, et al. Integrated
colposcopy. 2nd edn. London: Chapman and Hall;
1996. Reproduced by permission of Hodder Arnold.

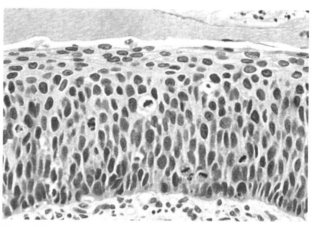

Figure 7.8
Histological appearance of CIN 3. From Anderson M, Jordan J,
Morse J, et al. Integrated colposcopy. 2nd edn. London:
Chapman and Hall; 1996. Reproduced by permission of
Hodder Arnold.

Dyskaryosis in endocervical cells, suggesting glandular intraepithelial neoplasia

- May be reported as high-grade or low-grade and is always an indication for colposcopically directed biopsy.

Refer for colposcopy. NHSCSP guidelines recommend colposcopy within 4 weeks.

Severe dyskaryosis, suggesting invasive disease

Refer for urgent assessment. NHSCSP guidelines recommend assessment within 2 weeks. (See Ch. 6.)

HUMAN PAPILLOMA VIRUS

Understanding of the role of human papilloma virus (HPV) in the aetiology of CIN and cervical carcinoma is still evolving. HPV infection is usually transient and disappears in 18–24 months as immunity develops. Those women whose HPV infection persists may be at higher risk of cervical disease. Co-factors, which include smoking and immune status, also affect risk.

Strains

Only some of the strains of HPV found in the genital tract are thought to be oncogenic. The most common is HPV-16, which is found in 65–80% of UK women with high-grade CIN, but in only 10% of sexually active women with normal smears.

Other oncogenic strains include HPV-18, -31 and -33. The low-risk genital strains (HPV-6, -11 and -42) are more often associated with condylomata and non-progressive CIN 1.

HPV typing

HPV typing is not currently recommended, but in the future it might be useful to identify those women with mildly dyskaryotic smears who are at increased risk of progressive disease. Its usefulness may be limited by the transient and constantly changing infection patterns in individuals.

COLPOSCOPY

Colposcopy is the examination of the cervix by low-power microscopy using a colposcope. It is used to identify areas of squamous CIN, but there are no standard colposcopic appearances for glandular CIN (CGIN).

Cervical intraepithelial neoplasia

CIN is the histological term for abnormal epithelial maturation. It is identified by:

- Delayed differentiation.
- Mitotic activity.
- Nuclear abnormalities.

CIN is graded according to the thickness of epithelium involved (see Box 7.2).

Box 7.2: Grading of CIN

CIN 1	Low-grade change involving up to the lower one-third of the epithelium
CIN 2	Moderate change involving up to the lower two-thirds of the epithelium (Fig. 7.7)
CIN 3	Severe change involving more than two-thirds of the thickness of the epithelium (Fig. 7.8)
Micro-invasive carcinoma	Histologically similar to CIN 3, but with a bud of abnormal cells penetrating less than 5 mm through the basement membrane into the stroma

The colposcopic procedure

Check the vascular patterns

The cervix may be viewed through a green filter to highlight subepithelial vascular capillary patterns. Definition may be enhanced by gently wiping the cervix with normal saline or acetic acid. The following patterns are recognized:

- Mosaic pattern: a coarse crazy-paving-like appearance may indicate high-grade CIN. Fine mosaicism may indicate HPV or low-grade CIN.
- Punctation: hair-pin capillaries giving a coarse stippled appearance may indicate high-grade CIN. Fine punctation may indicate HPV or low-grade CIN.
- Irregularly branching or 'corkscrew' vessels: these are grossly abnormal and may indicate invasive disease.

Check for acetowhite changes

Acetic acid (3–5%) causes whitening of abnormal squamous epithelium (see Fig. 7.9), whereas normal squamous epithelium remains pink. The intensity of the effect increases with the amount of nuclear material in the cells (columnar epithelium whitens even when it is normal):

- Severe changes: dense, opaque, creamy white.
- Minor changes: paler and translucent.
- Low-grade changes: often appear slowly and fade quickly.

Acetowhite change is not always diagnostic of CIN, as a pale translucent 'feathery' effect may be seen in the presence of HPV changes alone. Also, it should be remembered that CIN is always confined to the transformation zone and that satellite lesions do not occur.

Check for staining with Lugol's iodine

Iodine stains the glycogen in normal squamous cells dark brown, whereas iodine uptake is poor or absent in abnormal squamous skin. Iodine does not give any indication of the degree of abnormality; however, as it does not fade, it is useful to define an area for treatment.

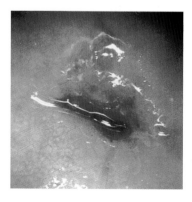

Figure 7.9
Acetowhite changes. Reproduced, with permission, from Rymer J, Fish ANJ, Chapman M. Gynaecology. Colour guide. 2nd edn. Edinburgh: Churchill Livingstone; 1997.

Check for features raising suspicion of early invasive disease

These include:

- Abnormal irregular blood vessels (e.g. corkscrew, bizarre branching or very coarse punctation/mosaic).
- Uneven or ulcerated surface to the cervix.
- Large lesion with a combination of changes.
- Previous high-grade lesion.
- History of irregular bleeding.
- Lack of regular screening in the past.

Glandular lesions

Note that there is no standard colposcopic appearance for CGIN.

Problems that may complicate colposcopy

These are summarized in Box 7.3.

The upper limit of the lesion is not visible

An endocervical speculum may enable viewing of the SCJ within the cervical canal. If the upper limit cannot be demonstrated, colposcopy must be recorded as unsatisfactory.

Wide ectropion

The transformation zone will be far out on the edges of the cervix making visualization and access difficult (Fig. 7.10).

Vaginal extension

Occasionally the transformation zone may be so wide that CIN extends onto the vaginal vault. Confusion may arise if there is a congenital transformation zone that is normal and can only be distinguished by biopsy. Most CIN lesions are confined to the cervix.

Leukoplakia

Thickened white areas of hyperkeratosis on the cervix or vagina are called leukoplakia and are visible without staining. The leukoplakia may not be confined to the transformation zone and can usually be washed away with saline or acetic acid. The area must be biopsied to exclude underlying CIN.

Box 7.3: Conditions that may complicate colposcopy

- The upper limit of the lesion is not visible
- Wide ectropion (see Fig. 7.10)
- Vaginal extension
- Leukoplakia
- Warts
- Flat wart virus (HPV) change
- Hyperaemic cervix and vagina
- Atrophy
- Stenosis
- Pregnancy

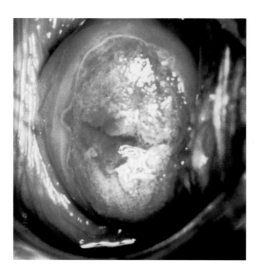

Figure 7.10
Wide ectropion.

Warts

Condylomata acuminata are visible to the naked eye as whitish projections on the cervix, vagina or vulva. Colposcopically, they have frond-like or whorled projections and stain dense acetowhite. Warts must be biopsied to exclude underlying CIN.

Flat wart virus (HPV) change

HPV changes are difficult to identify until acetic acid is added, but they may be pale and shiny with very fine mosaicism and punctation in the capillaries. Acetowhite changes are also subtle, with an irregular feathery outline. They may be very difficult to distinguish from low-grade CIN and so must be biopsied. Satellite lesions may occur.

Hyperaemic cervix/vagina

This may occur postnatally due to oestrogen deficiency, especially in breastfeeding mothers, but could also be due to infection (e.g. *Candida*, bacterial vaginosis or sexually transmitted infection).

Atrophy

Oestrogen-deficient postmenopausal women may have a thin pale epithelium. Underlying capillaries are prominent and may bleed easily.

Stenosis

This may occur in postmenopausal or amenorrhoeic women, or following treatment (especially after a deep cone biopsy). Stenosis may make it impossible to examine the endocervical canal or even to insert a cytobrush. If there is a high index of suspicion for CIN or CGIN, an excision biopsy is warranted.

Pregnancy

Colposcopic assessment may be difficult because the cervix is larger, more vascular and oedematous, with a wider transformation zone and more mucus. Lesions do not progress

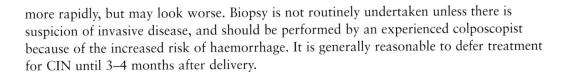

more rapidly, but may look worse. Biopsy is not routinely undertaken unless there is suspicion of invasive disease, and should be performed by an experienced colposcopist because of the increased risk of haemorrhage. It is generally reasonable to defer treatment for CIN until 3–4 months after delivery.

MANAGEMENT OF PATIENTS

Taking the biopsy

Punch forceps may be used to obtain two or more biopsies from areas of densest acetowhite change to:

- Diagnose CIN.
- Identify HPV changes or normal squamous metaplasia.

Local anaesthetic is not required.

A small diathermy loop may be appropriate for diagnosis of CIN if difficulties are encountered with the punch forceps. However, local anaesthetic is required and diathermy artefact may reduce the quality of a small specimen.

Biopsies are mandatory when there is suspicion of invasive disease. A good-sized sample is required.

Who should be treated?

There are two management options:

- Treatment.
- Monitoring.

Low-grade changes

Points to remember

- Up to 30% of low-grade changes may harbour high-grade CIN.
- At least 50% of women with CIN 1 will revert to normal in 12 months.
- Management of low-grade lesions varies from centre to centre and should take account of local and individual circumstances.

Reasons for treating CIN 1

- The woman is unlikely to attend for follow-up/unstable population.
- The woman's preference.
- Older woman, family complete.
- Large abnormal area (increased chance of focus of higher-grade change).
- Persistent CIN 1 or progression 12 months or more after initial diagnosis.

Reasons for monitoring CIN 1

- The woman's preference.
- The woman agrees to attend for follow-up.
- Stable population/low DNA rate.
- Young nulliparous woman.
- Small abnormal area.

Colposcopy and cytology/biopsy should be repeated after 12 months.

HPV without CIN

This can be monitored cytologically in primary care. There is no justification for 'treatment' as the infection will persist until natural immunity is acquired.

High-grade changes

Points to remember

- Probably more than 60% of cases of untreated CIN 3 would progress to invasive disease.
- Treatment should be recommended for CIN 2–3.
- Some centres operate a 'see-and-treat' policy for women if cytology and colposcopy indicate a high-grade lesion (CIN 2–3). Other centres wait for histological confirmation.

Glandular changes

The incidence of adenocarcinoma of the cervix has increased approximately fourfold in the last 10–20 years, but still accounts for only 1 in 5 cervical cancers. Initial management must be guided by the referral smear. Low-grade GCIN may first be further assessed by brush cytology. It may also be appropriate to undertake endometrial sampling.

Treatment of CIN

The whole of the transformation zone must be removed (not just the area that appears abnormal), as microscopic changes might be missed. Success rate is high, with 90–95% of women having no recurrent disease.

Destructive treatment

- Prior biopsy is essential.
- Laser ablation.
- 'Cold' coagulation (burning at about 120°C).
- Cryotherapy and electrodiathermy: rarely used as possibly less effective.

Excision treatment

- Diathermy loop excision (large loop excision of the transformation zone; Fig. 7.11) and laser conization are usually done under local anaesthesia.
- Knife cone biopsy (more likely for glandular lesions) and hysterectomy (especially if there are other indications) require a general anaesthetic.

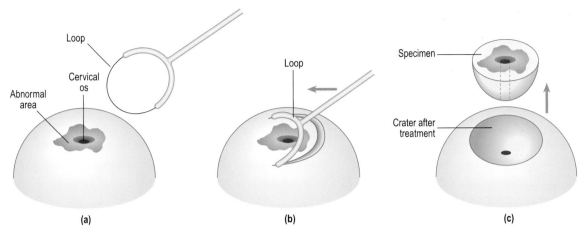

Figure 7.11
Diagrams showing the process of diathermy loop excision of an abnormal area on the cervix. **(a)** Cervix and loop;
(b) loop removing specimen containing abnormal squamous skin; **(c)** crater after excision of the abnormal area.

Excisional treatments are generally preferred because:

- The whole transformation zone is available for histological assessment.
- Excision margins can be examined.
- Unsuspected micro-invasive disease may be identified.

Follow-up

The guidelines for monitoring women after treatment changed in 2004 and are being
implemented as resources permit.

Follow-up after treatment for CIN

At 6 months post-treatment

- Cytology with or without colposcopy.
- Colposcopy is mandatory after micro-invasive disease.
- Colposcopy may be particularly appropriate: after CIN 3; after very large, incomplete
  or difficult treatments; in older women (especially if an SCJ is not seen).

At 12 months post-treatment

- Cytology in primary care.

At 2–10 years post-treatment

- Annually for 10 years if CIN 2–3 and microinvasive disease (ongoing follow-up of
  microinvasive disease should be in consultation with the local gynaecologist. See Ch. 6).
- Three smears in 2 years if CIN 1.
- If smears remain normal, revert to routine 3–5-yearly recall.

Note that an abnormal smear report at any time will generate re-referral for further colposcopic assessment.

Follow-up after treatment for CGIN

Although there are no visual or colposcopic indicators for CGIN, long term colposcopic follow-up is recommended because of the common association with CIN and the need to examine the endocervical canal thoroughly. Smears following glandular changes should contain endocervical cells.

COUNSELLING

At the time of routine cervical screening, information should be given explaining the purpose of the test in the prevention of cancer. If colposcopy is recommended, a simple explanation in the primary care setting before referral can significantly reduce anxiety. Written information from the colposcopy clinic should be sent out with the appointment and should include advice on what to expect. There should be opportunities to ask questions before, during and after colposcopy (Box 7.4).

Box 7.4: Common questions

What causes CIN?
- Some discussion of the role of sexual intercourse and HPV will be necessary.
- Portraying CIN and carcinoma of the cervix as a sexually transmitted disease is misleading and causes inappropriate anxiety.
- CIN can occur in monogamous women and is not a moral judgement.

Where have I caught the wart virus?
- Unfortunately, the reporting of HPV changes on a smear often causes the woman great anxiety, because it is perceived as a sexually transmitted disease.
- It should be explained that HPV is very common and is found in at least 70% of young sexually active women. The partner will already be exposed and is not thought to be at any risk.
- There is no value in recommending changes in sexual behaviour other than giving general advice about the use of barrier contraception for 'safer sex' in a new relationship.

Will CIN affect my fertility?
- The woman can be advised that her fertility should not be affected.
- Statistical evidence suggests that routine treatment for CIN does not affect conception, progress of pregnancy or delivery.
- Some discussion of background subfertility may be appropriate, especially in older or nulliparous women.
- Multiple treatments or knife cone biopsy may compromise fertility because a much larger proportion of the endocervical canal is removed.

Should I change my contraceptive method?
- There is no need to change the method of contraception.
- The exception may be in glandular abnormality, which may be associated with use of combined oral contraceptive pills. It is not clear what advice should be given to such women.

FUTURE DIRECTIONS   Potential new developments include the possible introduction of HPV testing as a triage for referral for colposcopy. The detection of persistent oncogenic strains of HPV may help predict those women at highest risk of cervical cancer or recurrent disease. The results of UK pilot studies may be available in 2004 at the earliest. Additionally, work continues on the development of HPV vaccines as a preventative method against cervical cancer, so there is real potential for the eventual elimination of the disease.

Discussion continues on possible changes in the nomenclature for smear reporting from 'borderline and mild' to 'low-grade' and from 'moderate, severe and possible invasive' to 'high-grade'. This would more clearly reflect the management options of monitoring or treatment. In 2004 the guidelines for referral for colposcopy were altered to include all women with a single abnormal smear, however minor the changes. This will increase the pressure on colposcopy units and needs to be supported by additional staffing.

The major change for women in the next few years will be the alterations in screening interval recommended by the National Institute for Clinical Excellence (NICE) and the NHSCSP. Whilst 5-yearly screening is suitable for older women, research now confirms that there is a clear benefit in more frequent testing of 25–49-year-olds. The new programme will eliminate the current inequalities in service depending on postcode.

In October 2003 the NHSCSP announced the introduction of liquid-based cytology in England to be implemented over the following 5 years. This innovation has been recommended by NICE following the evaluation of pilot studies. The evidence suggest that liquid-based cytology produces clearer samples and will reduce the number of inadequate smears. This should enable more rapid reporting and also reduce the number of repeat smears and therefore the level of anxiety in women awaiting results.

The main change for smear-takers and cyto-screeners will be the introduction of liquid-based cytology over the 5 years 2003–2008. They will need to undergo training in the techniques of obtaining, preparing and reading the samples, as discussed earlier in the chapter. Modern techniques for cervical screening can prevent up to 90% of cancer cases in women who attend for regular smears. In the words of Julietta Patnick, director of the NHSCSP, this new technology 'will mean that English women will have access to the best cervical screening programme in the world'.

Selected References and Further Reading

Anderson M, Jordan J, Morse J, et al. Integrated colposcopy. 2nd edn. London: Chapman and Hall; 1996 (with associated CD-ROM).

Duncan ID. Guidelines for clinical practice and programme management. Oxford: National Health Service Cervical Screening Programme (NHSCSP) National Co-ordinating Network; 1992.

Luesley D, Shafi M, Jordan J. Handbook of colposcopy. London: Chapman and Hall; 1996.

National Health Service Cervical Screening Programme. www.cancerscreening.nhs.uk.

Smith JS, Green J, Berrington de Gonzalez A, et al. Cervical cancer and use of hormonal contraceptives: a systematic review. Lancet 2003; 361:1159–1167.

Control of fertility

8

Annabelle Glasier and Alison Scott

THIS CHAPTER This chapter describes the various methods of contraception that are available, and details for each the action, effectiveness, advantages and disadvantages, indications and mechanism of contraindications, what assessment of the patient is required and side-effects.

Background

Women have sought to regulate the size of their families for thousands of years. Herbal mixtures and various douches were used until the 16th century when condoms became available. Since the 1960s, most methods have been for female use. Family planning services and information about reproductive and sexual health are paramount in improving the health of women and children and are also a human right. It is estimated that, in the UK, some 60% of couples will be using contraception. However, despite its worldwide availability, 50% of pregnancies are unplanned and 1 in 6 pregnancies is terminated.

Choice of contraception

Many different forms of contraception are currently available. The ideal contraceptive should be:

- Safe.
- Effective.
- Affordable.
- Convenient to use.

Women attending for contraceptive advice expect, rightly, to be involved in the decision-making process and to be well-informed about the advantages and disadvantages of each method. Many factors will be involved in the final decision. A contraceptive suitable for women who wish to space their children may not be ideal for a woman for whom pregnancy would be a disaster.

Other factors involved in the decision include:

- The woman's risk of sexually transmitted infection.
- The frequency of sexual intercourse.
- Her medical history.
- The stability of her relationship.

Medical eligibility criteria

A woman's medical history will influence the choice of safe contraceptives available to her. The World Health Organization (WHO) has developed medical eligibility criteria for selecting methods of contraception in various medical conditions. This forms a useful reference text for all those prescribing contraceptives, and uses up-to-date clinical and epidemiological data. The conditions affecting eligibility for the use of each contraceptive method are classified into four categories (Box 8.1).

Age as a factor

During her reproductive career, a woman's choice of contraception is likely to change, not simply because of her age but also because of changes in the intensity of her desire to avoid pregnancy and in her fecundity. Younger women more commonly use oral contraception (including emergency contraception) and condoms, as a combination (Double Dutch method), or as single agents. With increasing age, there is an increase in the use of sterilization and intrauterine devices. Teenagers are the group most likely to use no contraception.

An ideal contraceptive for a teenager needs to:

- Provide protection against sexually transmitted diseases.
- Be extremely effective in preventing pregnancy.
- Be discrete and suitable to be hidden from parents.
- Preserve future fertility.
- Make little demand on compliance.

Effectiveness

Women need to know the effectiveness of the method of contraception. Effectiveness measured in clinical studies is probably an overestimate. Not all women in these studies would have fallen pregnant had they not been using any contraception and not all participants in effectiveness studies will use the method consistently and effectively.

Failure rate

Failure rates will vary according to the age of the women using the method; i.e. younger women are more fertile and therefore tend to have a higher failure rate. They also have intercourse more frequently.

> **Box 8.2: Contraceptive effectiveness**
>
> | | |
> |---|---|
> | Perfect use failure rate | Number of pregnancies occurring with consistent and correct use of the contraceptive all the time |
> | Typical use failure rate | Number of pregnancies occurring when contraceptive is used with a mixture of perfect and imperfect use |
> | Pearl index | Number of pregnancies in a cohort, divided by total number of cycles in which method was used, multiplied by 1300 to give number per 100 woman-years (with each woman contributing 13 cycles) |
> | Cumulative pregnancy rate | Number of pregnancies occurring over time (rather than in first year of use); used for long-acting methods |

Several terms are used to denote the failure rate of any particular method of contraception. For long-acting methods, the cumulative pregnancy rate over time is usually preferred (see Box 8.2).

Legal aspects

The legal age of heterosexual consent in the UK is 16 years, but 1 in 5 women and 1 in 4 men will have broken this law. Concerns about confidentiality and disapproval may deter young people from seeking family planning advice. The legal position regarding the provision of contraceptive services in England was clarified by the Gillick case in 1985. The Law Lords ruled that doctors should encourage young people to inform their parents of their intention to use birth control but could be given contraceptive advice and treatment without parental approval, within the best interests of that minor. Also the minor must be capable of making an informed decision and must not have been coerced. In Scotland, the Fraser guidelines likewise ensure that young people understand the decisions they are making, have thought about informing their parents and are not being coerced.

BARRIER METHODS

A barrier method of contraception acts by blocking the progress of the sperm to the upper part of the female genital tract. Barrier methods may be:

- Mechanical.
- Chemical.
- A combination of both.

The male condom

Also known as French letter, Johnny, sheath, rubber and protective, condoms are widely available from pharmacies, supermarkets, vending machines and by mail order (Fig. 8.1). They can, however, be obtained free of charge from family planning clinics. Some areas have schemes whereby young people carry a card allowing them to obtain free condoms

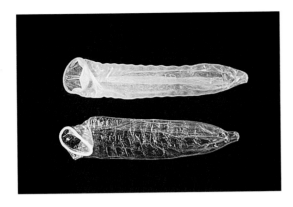

Figure 8.1
Examples of male condoms.

from other outlets. Condoms are extensively promoted as preventing sexually transmitted infection, especially HIV. General practitioners cannot provide free condoms unless as part of an HIV prevention budget.

The majority of condoms are made from latex. Non-spermicidally lubricated condoms are available for those with nonoxyl-9 sensitivity. Condoms made from polyurethane are also available for those with latex hypersensitivity. Polyurethane condoms are associated with less loss of sensation than latex condoms but have a higher breakage rate.

Use and effectiveness

The effectiveness of condoms in preventing pregnancy is variable. It depends on user motivation and proper usage. Adequate instruction prior to using a condom is vital.

Common errors in usage are:

- Damaging the condom while opening the packet or tearing it with fingernails.
- Unrolling it prior to placing it on the penis.
- Re-using the same condom.

Perfect use failure rate is 3 per hundred women-years (HWY); typical use failure rate is 14 per HWY in the first year of use.

Advantages and disadvantages

Box 8.3 summarizes the advantages, disadvantages, indications and contraindications of male condoms.

The female condom

The female condom is a polyurethane sheath 15 cm long by 7 cm in diameter, with its open end attached to a flexible polyurethane ring (Fig. 8.2). A removable polyurethane ring inside the condom acts as an introducer and anchors the device in the vagina. The condom is not spermicidally lubricated, therefore avoiding allergic reactions. It is available for over-the-counter purchase and can be inserted hours in advance of intercourse and left in place for some time afterwards. It transmits heat and therefore has less effect on sensation than the male condom.

Box 8.3: Advantages and disadvantages of male condoms

Advantages	Disadvantages	Indications	Contraindications
■ Readily available ■ Good protection against STIs ■ Effective ■ Simple to use ■ Protects against cancer and premalignancy of the cervix ■ Useful with premature ejaculation	■ Interferes with spontaneity ■ Diminished sensation ■ Reduced tensile strength with oil-based products (e.g. Vaseline) ■ Not biodegradable ■ Erectile difficulty may be exacerbated	■ Reversible contraception ■ Where there is risk of STI ■ While woman is being instructed in the use of cap/diaphragm ■ When additional contraception is needed if woman forgets pill	■ Malformation of the penis ■ Latex allergy of either partner ■ Psychological difficulties

STI, sexually transmitted infection.

Figure 8.2
The female condom.

Use and effectiveness

The female condom has been shown to be as effective as the diaphragm, with failure rates ranging from 5 to 21 per HWY, but it is less effective than the male condom.

Women need to be taught to insert the condom, using a similar technique to inserting a tampon or a diaphragm. It is more expensive than the male condom but research suggests that, if washed appropriately, it can be re-used.

Advantages and disadvantages

Box 8.4 summarizes the advantages, disadvantages, indications and contraindications of the female condom.

Box 8.4: Advantages and disadvantages of female condom

Advantages	Disadvantages	Indications	Contraindications
■ Effective contraception and probably protects against STIs ■ Not affected by oil-based preparations ■ Less change in sensation ■ No disruption of spontaneity ■ Avoids negotiation of male condom use by woman	■ Unattractive appearance ■ Noisy during intercourse ■ May be initial difficulty with insertion ■ May be pushed out or penetration may take place outside it ■ Expensive ■ Not biodegradable	■ Reversible barrier contraception ■ Some protection against STIs	■ Psychologically unacceptable

STI, sexually transmitted infection.

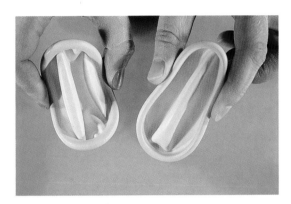

Figure 8.3
Examples of diaphragms.

Diaphragms and caps

Four main types are in current use:

- Diaphragm (Dutch cap).
- Cervical cap.
- Vault cap.
- Vimule.

This is not a popular method of contraception and is probably used by less than 1% of sexually active women. These devices last for approximately 1 year but must be refitted following childbirth or drastic changes in weight.

Diaphragms

A diaphragm consists of a thin latex rubber hemisphere with the rim reinforced by a flexible flat or coiled metal spring (Fig. 8.3). It is available in 55–95-mm sizes.

There are various types of diaphragm:

- The flat spring diaphragm has a firm watch spring and remains in the horizontal plane on compression. It is suitable for the average vagina and is the most commonly used device.

133

- The coil-spring diaphragm has a much softer spiral-coiled spring. It is useful for the woman who has tight pelvic floor musculature and is sensitive to the flat spring.
- The arcing diaphragm combines features of both of the above and exerts strong pressure on the vaginal walls. It is useful when there is laxity of the vaginal walls.

Use

The diaphragm is inserted into the vagina such that it fits between the posterior fornix and the pubic symphysis. The woman is taught to do this and to check that it covers the cervix. It is usually used with a spermicide and must remain in place for 6 h after intercourse to ensure that all the sperm have been killed. Following removal, the device is washed in warm, soapy water.

Effectiveness

Perfect use failure rate is 4–8 per HWY; typical use failure rate is 10–18 per HWY. Additional use of spermicides increases efficacy.

Box 8.5 summarizes the advantages, disadvantages, indications and contraindications of diaphragms.

Caps

These devices are designed to fit closely over the cervix and are held in place by precise fitting and suction. These devices are more commonly used in North America than in the UK. Caps have similar advantages and disadvantages to diaphragms but are suitable for women with uterovaginal prolapse. They can be left *in situ* for several days and are not associated with urinary symptoms.

Box 8.5: Advantages and disadvantages of diaphragms

Advantages	Disadvantages	Indications	Contraindications
▪ No systemic side-effects ▪ Effective when fitted and used correctly ▪ Suitable for breast-feeding mothers ▪ Some reduction in risk of STIs ▪ Reduction in premalignant disease and cancer of cervix	▪ Requires premeditation ▪ Spermicide causes 'mess' ▪ Increased incidence of urinary tract infection (WHO category 2 if history of urinary tract infection or valvular heart disease) ▪ Small risk of toxic shock syndrome (WHO category 3) ▪ Increased incidence of candidal infections ▪ Requires trained personnel to fit correct size and teach insertion technique	▪ Effective barrier contraception ▪ Suitable for women excluded from hormonal contraception ▪ Suitable for couples having infrequent intercourse	▪ Poor vaginal musculature ▪ Psychological aversion ▪ Inability to self-examine or learn insertion ▪ Lack of hygiene or privacy for insertion and care of device

STI, sexually transmitted infection.

Spermicides

These are chemical agents that are capable of destroying sperm. They are commonly non-ionic surfactants (nonoxinol-9) and are available as gels, pessaries and aerosols. Their main role is as an adjunct to other methods and they are not recommended as the sole method of contraception. It has been suggested that frequent use of nonoxinol-9 may increase the risk of HIV transmission.

Vaginal sponge

This is a reservoir for spermicide and has recently been re-introduced in the UK. It is made of polyurethane and requires to be positioned over the cervix. Failure rates are high and it is not recommended as a contraceptive.

HORMONAL CONTRACEPTION

Combined preparations

Oral contraception

In the UK, 35% of women currently use oral contraception. It is popular because of its efficacy (typical use failure rate is 0.1 pregnancies per 100 HWY), ease of use and additional health benefits. The combined pill contains oestrogen (usually ethinylestradiol) and a progestogen (a synthetic form of progesterone). The dosage of oestrogen is currently 20–35 µg, to minimize cardiovascular risks whilst maintaining efficacy.

The progestogens currently available are:

- First-generation progestogens: e.g. norethindrone.
- Second-generation norgestrel derivatives: e.g. levonorgestrel, norethisterone.
- Third-generation progestogens: e.g. gestodene, desogestrel, norgestimate.

The combined pill inhibits ovulation. The oestrogen inhibits secretion of follicle-stimulating hormone; the progestogen inhibits the luteinizing hormone surge. In some women, the pill-free interval can be long enough to allow follicle growth to occur. Thus, if the pill-free interval is prolonged, ovulation and pregnancy may follow.

Prior to prescribing, the following should be done:

- History: to exclude personal and familial risk factors for use of the combined pill.
- Examination: weight may be useful and blood pressure must be measured; routine pelvic examination is not necessary.
- Information: new users should be instructed about taking the pill, what to do when pills are forgotten (see Box 8.6) and about the availability of emergency contraception.

Box 8.6: Missed pill rules

Specific situation	**Recommendations**
Missed any 1 active (hormonal) pill (days 1–21)	■ Take missed pill as soon as possible ■ Take next pill at usual time (even if this means taking 2 pills close together) ■ Continue taking pills as usual *No additional contraception needed*
Started a pack 2 or more days late	■ Start the new pack that day ■ Continue taking the pills as usual ■ Abstain from sex or use additional contraception for 7 days *Consider emergency contraception if appropriate*
Missed any 2–4 of the first 7 active (hormonal) pills (days 1–7)	■ Take the first missed pill as soon as possible ■ Take the next pill at the usual time (even if this means taking 2 pills close together ■ Continue taking the pills as usual ■ Abstain from sex or use additional contraception for 7 days *Consider emergency contraception if appropriate*
Missed any 2–4 of the middle 7 active (hormonal) pills (days 8–14)	■ Take the first missed pill as soon as possible ■ Take the next pill at the usual time even if this means taking 2 pills close together ■ Continue taking the active pills as usual one each day *No additional contraception needed*
Missed any 2–4 of the last 7 active (hormonal) pills	■ Take the first missed pill as soon as possible ■ Take the next pill at the usual time ■ Continue taking the active pills as usual ■ Discard any inactive pills and go straight to the next pack *No additional contraception needed*
Missed 5 or more active pills in a row in any week (days 1–21)	■ Take the first missed pill as soon as possible ■ Take the next pill at the usual time ■ Continue taking the active pills as usual ■ Discard any inactive pills and go straight to the next pack ■ Abstain from sex or use additional contraception for the next 7 days *Consider emergency contraception if appropriate*
Missed 1 or more inactive (non-hormonal) pills (days 22–28 in 28-day pill pack)	■ Discard missed inactive pill ■ Continue taking the pills as usual ■ Start a new pack as usual *No additional contraception needed*

Use and effectiveness

Monophasic pills contain the same dose of hormones in each tablet and are taken for 21 days, with a 7-day break when withdrawal bleeding usually occurs. A few women will be amenorrhoeic, however. Biphasic and triphasic pills reduce the total dose of progestogens in an attempt to mimic the normal cycle and improve cycle control. They are not more effective than monophasic pills and there is no evidence that there are fewer side-effects with triphasics.

Advantages and disadvantages

The main advantages and disadvantages of combined oral contraception are summarized in Box 8.7.

The main concerns in prescribing the combined pill are its effects on:

- Venous and arterial circulatory disease.
- Breast cancer.
- Cervical cancer.

Venous thromboembolism   There is a threefold increase in the risk of venous thromboembolism with the combined pill, independent of factors such as smoking and duration of use (see Table 8.1). Combined pills containing the third-generation progestogens gestodene or desogestrel have a twofold increased risk of venous thromboembolism compared to pills containing levonorgestrel. However, the difference in risk is very small, with the absolute risk for second-generation combined oral contraceptive being 15/100 HWY (significantly less than that associated with pregnancy).

Arterial disease   Arterial disease is less common. There is no increased risk of myocardial infarction in non-smoking, normotensive, non-diabetic users. There is a small relative

---

Box 8.7: Advantages and disadvantages of combined oral contraception

Advantages

- Easy to take
- Highly effective
- Reduced menstrual loss and dysmenorrhoea
- Protection against ovarian and endometrial cancer
- Reduced incidence of benign breast disease, functional ovarian cysts and endometriosis

Disadvantages

- No protection from STIs
- Minor side-effects such as nausea
- Not indicated for women with contraindications to oestrogen

STI, sexually transmitted infection.

Table 8.1: Use of medical eligibility criteria for selecting hormonal contraception in conditions of risk of venous thromboembolism

Condition	COC	POP	Medical eligibility criteria category Progestogen-only injectables	Levonorgestrel-releasing implant system
History of DVT/PE	4	2	2	2
Current DVT/PE	4	3	3	3
Family history of DVT/PE (first-degree relatives)	2	1	1	1
Major surgery with prolonged immobilization	4	2	2	2
Major surgery without prolonged immobilization	2	1	1	1
Major surgery without immobilization	1	1	1	1

COC, combined oral contraceptive; POP, progesterone-only pill; DVT, deep vein thrombosis; PE, pulmonary embolism.

increase in the risk of stroke (RR 1.5), although this is a rare event in women of reproductive age. Smoking and hypertension significantly increase the risk of myocardial infarction and cerebrovascular accident; the risk of the latter is increased naturally over the age of 35 years.

Breast cancer   Breast cancer is a concern to many women, and its association with the combined pill is difficult to interpret from the available data. The risk of breast cancer appears to increase soon after exposure to the combined pill (RR 1.24) and is not related to the duration of exposure. It returns to normal after 10 years of no exposure.

Cervical cancer   Cervical cancer may be more common after more than 5 years of use. This is especially pertinent in women with human papilloma virus infection. In the RCGP study, the relative risk of dying from cervical cancer was 2.5.

Combined injectables and patches

Combined injectables are available in some parts of the world but not currently in the UK.

Combined hormonal transdermal patches are now available in the UK. They are suitable for the same group of patients as combined oral preparations. One patch is used each week for 3 weeks. A withdrawal bleed occurs in the patch-free week.

Progestogen-only preparations

For women for whom oestrogen is not suitable, progestogen-only preparations offer reliable contraception. The mechanism of action and side-effects depend on the dose, with depot medroxyprogesterone acetate completely inhibiting ovulation. Implants and oral progestogen preparations, however, are lower dose and do not completely inhibit ovarian activity, and irregular bleeding is common.

Advantages and disadvantages

The advantages and disadvantages of progestogen-only contraception are summarized in Box 8.8.

Box 8.8: Advantages and disadvantages of progestogen-only contraception

Advantages	Disadvantages
■ Useful in those not suitable for the combined pill	■ Implants require trained personnel for insertion and removal
■ Depot medroxyprogesterone acetate probably protects against endometrial cancer	■ Menstrual disturbances
■ Reduces dysmenorrhoea, premenstrual syndrome and mastalgia	■ Persistent ovarian follicles/follicular cysts
■ Few metabolic effects on lipid and coagulation factors	■ Acne
■ Useful for diabetic or hypertensive patients and those with sickle cell disease or migraine	■ Weight gain with depot medroxyprogesterone acetate
■ Suitable for breastfeeding mothers	■ Implants expensive if continuation rates poor

Progestogen-only pill (POP)/mini pill

Current POPs contain low doses of levonorgestrel, norethisterone, desogestrel or etynodiol diacetate and are effective contraceptives, especially in women over 35 years of age, with or without medical problems.

The POP acts by inhibiting ovulation in 15–40% of cycles. It also causes changes in the cervical mucus to reduce sperm penetration, and changes in the endometrium that prevent sperm survival and blastocyst implantation.

Use and effectiveness

POPs must be taken at the same time (within 3 h) each day for maximum efficacy and are taken without a pill-free interval. Additional contraception is required for 7 days after a forgotten pill. The POP is a useful contraceptive for breastfeeding women. The typical use failure rate is 1 pregnancy per HWY.

Progestogen-only injectables

Use and effectiveness

The preparation used most commonly is medroxyprogesterone acetate in a 150-mg injection administered every 12 weeks. It inhibits ovulation and has a failure rate of 0.3 pregnancies per HWY.

Disadvantages

It tends to cause amenorrhoea or (much less frequently) irregular vaginal bleeding in long-term users. There may also be a delay in return of fertility of up to 18 months. The theoretical risk of bone loss does not appear to be borne out clinically but would be a concern in those already at risk (e.g. long-term steroid use, heavy smokers).

Implants

Use and effectiveness

In the UK the only available implant is a single-rod implant containing 68 mg of etonogestrel (Fig. 8.4). It is more easily inserted and removed than its predecessor, which had six rods and contained levonorgestrel. The etonorgestrel implant lasts for 3 years and acts by inhibiting ovulation.

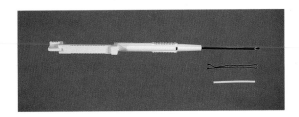

Figure 8.4
Single-rod implant containing etonorgestrel.

Disadvantages

Irregular vaginal bleeding occurs in the majority of users. Amenorrhoea occurs in less than 20%.

EMERGENCY CONTRACEPTION (hormonal)

This is an emergency method for use after unprotected intercourse or failed contraceptive method. It is not for regular use to prevent pregnancy because of its high failure rates.

Indications for emergency contraception are:

- Unprotected intercourse.
- 'Failed' barrier contraception: e.g. burst condom.
- Prolonged pill-free interval (more than 7 days), or more than three forgotten pills in the packet (see Box 8.6).
- More than two forgotten POPs.
- Women who are anxious about the risk of pregnancy, even if it is low.

Use and effectiveness

Available preparations are:

- Progestogen-only: this is the method of choice and available without prescription.
- Levonorgestrel: 1.5 mg as a single dose within 72 h of intercourse.

Efficacy is difficult to quantify but is thought to be at least 75–85%.

Contraindications

There are no contraindications to levonorgestrel, other than pregnancy, when obviously emergency contraception will not have any effect.

Levonorgestrel intrauterine system

This is a T-shaped plastic intrauterine device (Fig. 8.5). It contains 52 mg of levonorgestrel around its vertical stem, releasing a daily dose of around 20 µg. It is highly effective as a contraceptive and is also licensed as a treatment for menorrhagia. The progestogenic component can also be used as part of hormone replacement therapy (although it is not yet licensed for this use in the UK). It acts by thinning the endometrium, suppressing ovulation (in 33% of users) and altering the cervical mucus and uterotubal fluid.

Use and effectiveness

For details of the insertion procedure, see the section on IUDs and Fig. 8.6.

The device lasts for 5 years. Its failure rate is 0.1 per HWY.

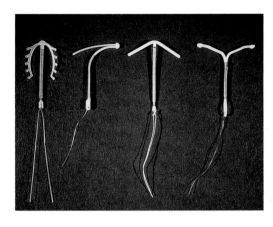

Figure 8.5
The levonorgestrel intrauterine system (right) and other intrauterine devices.

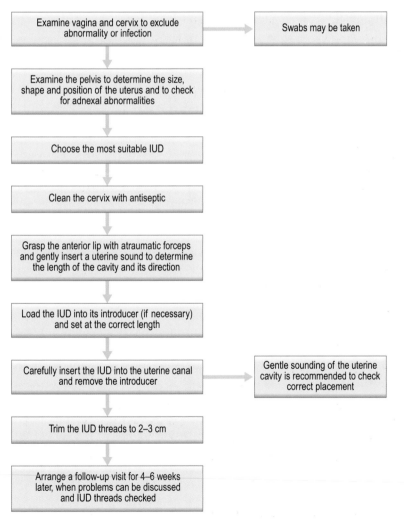

Examine vagina and cervix to exclude abnormality or infection → Swabs may be taken

Examine the pelvis to determine the size, shape and position of the uterus and to check for adnexal abnormalities

Choose the most suitable IUD

Clean the cervix with antiseptic

Grasp the anterior lip with atraumatic forceps and gently insert a uterine sound to determine the length of the cavity and its direction

Load the IUD into its introducer (if necessary) and set at the correct length

Carefully insert the IUD into the uterine canal and remove the introducer → Gentle sounding of the uterine cavity is recommended to check correct placement

Trim the IUD threads to 2–3 cm

Arrange a follow-up visit for 4–6 weeks later, when problems can be discussed and IUD threads checked

Figure 8.6
Protocol for insertion of an IUD.

Box 8.9: Advantages and disadvantages of the levonorgestrel intrauterine system

Advantages

- Immediate, effective contraception
- Reduces menstrual loss
- Suitable for those unable to take oestrogen
- Immediate resumption of fertility on removal
- Coitus-independent
- May be used as the progestin for hormone replacement therapy (NB: not licensed for this use in the UK)

Disadvantages

- Requires trained personnel for insertion
- Insertion may be uncomfortable
- Not suitable with current or recent STI
- Insertion may be difficult in nulliparas
- Irregular vaginal bleeding especially in the months following insertion
- Expensive if discontinued prematurely

STI, sexually transmitted infection.

Advantages and disadvantages

Box 8.9 details the advantages and disadvantages of the intrauterine system.

INTRAUTERINE CONTRACEPTIVE DEVICES

IUDs are the most commonly used reversible method of contraception worldwide. They are safe, effective and convenient. All devices currently used in the UK are copper-bearing and most are based on a plastic frame with copper wire around the stem (Fig. 8.5). There is also a frameless device with six copper beads crimped onto a single thread, which becomes embedded into the myometrium; this is beneficial in reducing the amount of dysmenorrhoea associated with an IUD and is easier to insert in nulliparous patients.

Insertion procedure

The full procedure (see Fig. 8.6) needs to be discussed and the woman's concerns addressed prior to insertion. The optimal time for insertion is during or immediately after menstruation so that pregnancy can be excluded and insertion is easier, although an IUD can be inserted at any time in the cycle if the woman is using a reliable method of contraception or is abstinent.

Use

IUDs can be used as emergency contraception in women not wishing to use hormonal methods or where unprotected intercourse took place more than 72 h but less than 120 h previously. Screening for sexually transmitted diseases should, if possible, take place at the time of insertion and prophylactic antibiotics may be required (see Ch. 3). The IUD can be removed at the next menses or stay *in situ* as a long-term contraceptive. For a woman aged over 40 years, the device may stay *in situ* until she is postmenopausal and no longer requires contraception.

Box 8.10: Advantages and disadvantages of intrauterine devices

Advantages	Disadvantages
▪ Immediate, effective and safe contraception ▪ Coitus-independent and good patient compliance ▪ Reversible ▪ Suitable for those unable to use oestrogen	▪ Menorrhagia and dysmenorrhoea ▪ Small risk of infection at time of insertion. Possible PID if subsequent STI ▪ Expulsion occurs in 3–5% of cases, usually in the first year (leaving the threads 3 cm long allows the woman and doctor to check them) ▪ Uterine perforation (1 per 1000 cases) ▪ Vagal response during insertion ▪ Failure is uncommon but if it occurs there is an increased risk of miscarriage or ectopic pregnancy

PID, pelvic inflammatory disease; STI, sexually transmitted infection.

Effectiveness

Inert devices are not recommended by the WHO as they are less effective. Copper-bearing IUDs are licensed for 5–10 years of use.

Copper-containing IUDs have a failure rate of 0.6 pregnancies per HWY.

Advantages and disadvantages

The advantages and disadvantages of IUDs are given in Box 8.10.

IUDs are best suited to monogamous women (including nulliparas). Those with multiple partners are at increased risk of pelvic infection. Caution should be used in those with valvular heart disease because of the bacteraemia that may occur at insertion and antibiotic prophylaxis needs to be considered (category 4, WHO medical eligibility criteria).

STERILIZATION

Worldwide, more than 150 million women and 50 million men have chosen sterilization as their method of contraception. Sterilization is ideal for those who have completed their families, because:

- It is not user-dependent.
- It does not require repeat clinic attendances.
- There are no ongoing expenses.

Counselling

Correct and adequate counselling is required prior to embarking on the surgical procedure.

143

Points to be discussed:

- Methods of sterilization, including a description of the operations.
- Failure rates (1 in 200) and the importance of seeking a pregnancy test if menses are delayed.
- Risks and side-effects.
- Which partner should be sterilized.
- Alternative long-acting and effective contraception, in particular the lower failure rates with, for example, Mirena (which is reversible).
- Irreversibility.
- Importance of continuing with contraception until the sterilization is complete.

Despite counselling, up to 10% of couples will regret sterilization and 1% of these will request reversal. Factors associated with a high risk of regret include:

- Age (<25 years).
- Sterilization immediately following pregnancy.
- Relationship difficulties.
- Psychiatric illness.
- Couples without children.

Female sterilization (bilateral tubal occlusion)

This involves blocking both fallopian tubes. The procedure is most commonly performed under general anaesthetic by laparoscopic techniques, but a mini-laparotomy may be performed to carry out bilateral salpingectomy or tubal occlusion (Fig. 8.7).

Laparoscopic sterilization

This involves creating a pneumoperitoneum by instilling 2–3 L of carbon dioxide into the peritoneal cavity. The laparoscope is then passed, via a small subumbilical incision, and the pelvic organs are visualized. A second port can then be introduced suprapubically or in the iliac fossa under direct vision. This port allows an instrument to be introduced which will occlude the tubes. The most common means of attaining this is with Filshie clips (titanium lined with silicone rubber) which are applied across the width of the tube. Alternatively, a Falope ring is applied around a loop of tube.

Diathermy

Diathermy is rarely used now since it obliterates large parts of the tube, making reversal almost impossible, and also because of the risks of causing damage to other intra-abdominal organs. These procedures are normally performed as day cases either under general or local anaesthetic.

Complications

The complications of bilateral tubal occlusion are listed in Box 8.11.

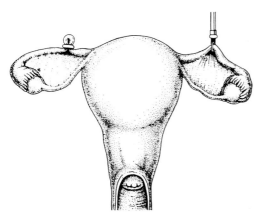

Figure 8.7
Female sterilization by bilateral tubal occlusion.

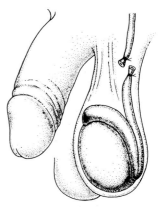

Figure 8.8
Male sterilization by vasectomy.

Box 8.11: Complications of bilateral tubal occlusion

Immediate complications

- Death is very rare (8 per 10 000 procedures)
- Visceral or vascular damage
- Infection of the wound site
- Irreversible

Late complications

- Failure in 1 in 200 cases
- Menstrual bleeding patterns change only in those previously using oral contraception or an IUD
- Bowel obstruction from adhesions is very rare
- Ectopic pregnancy may occur in 50% of failures
  Women must seek a pregnancy test if the menses are late and urgent medical advice if it is positive
- Post-tubal sterilization syndrome: a variety of symptoms, including pain, dyspareunia, premenstrual syndrome and psychosexual problems; may be related to regret

---

Male sterilization (vasectomy)

This prevents delivery of sperm into the ejaculate by occlusion of the vas deferens. It is not effective until the sperm already present in the distal vas have been ejaculated. Couples must be advised of the need to use alternative contraception until two consecutive semen samples demonstrate azoospermia. In the UK, samples are checked at 12 and 16 weeks after vasectomy.

Procedure

Vasectomy is more commonly performed under local anaesthesia. The vas deferens is approached via a small skin incision, the fascia opened longitudinally and the vas ligated and divided or occluded with clips or diathermy (see Fig. 8.8). 'No-scalpel' vasectomy involves two specially designed surgical instruments to deliver the vas through a puncture wound rather than through a surgical incision.

Box 8.12: Complications of vasectomy

Immediate complications

- Bruising is usual. 2% of men develop a haematoma which resolves with support and analgesia; surgery is rarely required
- Infection of the wound occurs in 5%
- Failure occurs in 1 in 2000 cases
- Irreversible

Late complications

- Sperm granulomas; may be painful and require excision
- Chronic intrascrotal pain and discomfort
- Late recanalization can occur up to 10 years after; rare
- Antisperm antibodies develop in most men
- Cancer of prostate and testicle may develop, but there is no causal link with vasectomy

---

Complications

'No-scalpel' vasectomy is said to have a lower complication rate. See Box 8.12 for a summary of the complications of vasectomy.

NATURAL FAMILY PLANNING

A proportion of women (approximately 2% in the UK) wish to avoid using artificial methods of contraception and use awareness of and avoidance of the 'fertile period' to prevent pregnancy. This method requires significant motivation and commitment on the part of the couple and significant time of a health professional to teach the couple about the indicators of ovulation. Many couples use a combination of methods.

Use and effectiveness

Complete abstinence from penetrative intercourse during the fertile period reportedly avoids pregnancy 98% of the time. Typical use effectiveness is around 80%.

Methods

Calendar method (rhythm method, Russian roulette)

After recording at least six cycles, the fertile period is calculated by subtracting 20 days from the shortest cycle and 11 days from the longest cycle. Women with regular cycles will therefore have a shorter period of abstinence. This method should be used in combination with another method.

Standard days method

Intercourse is avoided between day 8 and day 19 of the cycle (provided it is a regular 28-day cycle). A string of coloured beads with a moveable ring is used as a mnemonic device.

Temperature method

Temperature is recorded daily by the same route each day (orally for 5 min, or vaginally/rectally for 3 min). The rise in progesterone associated with ovulation gives a rise in basal body temperature of approximately 0.2–0.4°C. Thus a temperature rise indicates that ovulation has occurred and intercourse should be avoided for 3 days thereafter. To avoid intercourse prior to ovulation requires the use of one of the other methods.

Ovulation (Billings or mucus) method

Cervical mucus changes some days prior to ovulation to become clear, slippery and stretchy. Testing between finger and thumb demonstrates this. If moving the digits apart does not break the mucus (spinnbarkheit), it is considered fertile. Abstinence must be continued from the appearance of fertile mucus until 3 days after its disappearance.

Cervical palpation method

Daily palpation of the cervix is required to identify when it is lower in the vagina, firm and dry (infertile). With approaching ovulation its rises 1–2 cm and becomes moist and soft.

Symptothermal method

This is a combination of temperature and mucus methods in association with symptoms suggestive of ovulation.

Multiple index method

Involves recording and interpreting all of the above.

Lactational amenorrhoea method

Breastfeeding is associated with a delay in the return of fertility. The lactational amenorrhoea method is up to 98% effective for breastfeeding mothers, but only if the following criteria are fulfilled:

- Infant less than 6 months old.
- Infant fully breastfed.
- Infant suckling at least every 6 h.
- Amenorrhoea.

In the developed world, few babies are not having supplementary feeds after 4 months of age and therefore lactational amenorrhoea should not be relied upon.

Figure 8.9
Personal fertility monitor.

Personal fertility monitor

This measures urinary metabolites of oestradiol and luteinizing hormone and uses red lights (fertile: abstinence) and green lights (infertile: may have intercourse) to guide the couple (Fig. 8.9). It is said to be 94% effective if used consistently and correctly but it is expensive.

Coitus interruptus

This is the withdrawal of the penis from the vagina prior to ejaculation. Pre-ejaculatory secretions, however, may contain thousands of sperm and may be sufficient to result in pregnancy. Failure rates range between 5 and 20 per HWY.

THERAPEUTIC ABORTION

Pregnancy may occur because of contraceptive failure, lack of forethought on the part of the couple or lack of access to contraceptive services. Abortion should not be thought of as a contraceptive, but some women may use it as a means of regulating family size.

> **FUTURE DIRECTIONS**   Radically new methods of contraception are unlikely in the near future.
>
> Combined hormonal vaginal rings are likely to become available within a year or so. These avoid the first-pass effect of the liver and are combined preparations.
>
> The male contraceptive 'pill' (a combination of gonadotrophin-releasing hormone antagonist and testosterone replacement) is at an advanced stage of development and is having good results regarding tolerance and return of fertility. Its popularity among the general male population remains to be tested.

Selected References and Further Reading

Arevalo M, Sinai I, Jennings V. A fixed formula to define the fertile window of the menstrual cycle as the basis of a simple method of natural family planning. Contraception 2000; 60:357–360.

Frezieres RG, Walsh TL, Nelson AL, et al. Breakage and acceptability of a polyurethane condom: a randomised controlled study. Fam Plann Perspect 1998; 30:73–78.

Glasier A, Gebbie A, eds. Handbook of family planning and reproductive healthcare. 4th edn. London: Churchill Livingstone; 2000.

Hannaford PC, Kay CR. The risk of serious illness among oral contraceptive users: evidence from the RCGP's oral contraceptive study. Br J Gen Pract 1998; 48:1657–1662.

Oddens BJ, Visser AP, Verner HM, et al. Contraceptive use and attitudes in Great Britain. Contraception 1994; 49:73–86.

Trussell J, Kowal D. The essentials of contraception. In: Hatcher RE, et al., eds. Contraceptive technology. 17th edn. New York: Ardent Media; 1998:216–217.

US Collaborative Review of Sterilization. The risk of pregnancy after tubal sterilisation. Am J Obstet Gynecol 1996; 174:1161–1170.

World Health Organization. Improving access to quality care in family planning. Medical eligibility criteria for contraceptive use. 2nd edn. Geneva: WHO; 2000.

Infertility

9

Gillian Lockwood

> **THIS CHAPTER** The problems of infertility and its psychological toll are discussed, followed by detailed descriptions of the causes and investigation of infertility and the treatment options that are currently available.

Background

The 25 years since *in vitro* fertilization (IVF) was pioneered in the UK have seen over 1 million 'test-tube' babies born worldwide, and IVF is increasingly regarded as an ethically acceptable and technically successful solution to a problem which affects 1 in 6 of all couples.

The apparent 'epidemic' of infertility in women in industrialized countries can best be explained by a trend towards delayed childbearing, and in a 'consumer-orientated' world it can be difficult for women who spent their twenties consciously trying to avoid pregnancy to recognize that, after a woman reaches her mid-thirties, her monthly chance of conceiving drops to 10–15% and by her early forties it is less than 5% a month, *and* she is facing a 40% chance of miscarriage even if she conceives.

The prerequisites for conception, namely regular ovulation, patent fallopian tubes, sperm with fertilizing capacity and a receptive endometrium, can all be readily assessed, and many defects can be corrected with hormonal manipulation (in the case of anovulation), tubal surgery for minor degrees of tubal damage and sperm concentration for mild male factor infertility. More significant defects or cases where multiple subfertility factors are present may be amenable to assisted conception techniques such as IVF and intracytoplasmic sperm injection (ICSI). The challenge of infertility medicine lies with establishing a timely diagnosis and helping the couple to achieve a conception with the least invasive and most cost-effective therapy.

Definition

Infertility is defined as the failure to conceive after 1 year of regular unprotected intercourse.

THE PROBLEM OF INFERTILITY

In the industrialized world, about 1 in 6 couples seek specialist help because of difficulty or delay in conceiving a first or subsequent child, and the problem of infertility seems to be increasing.

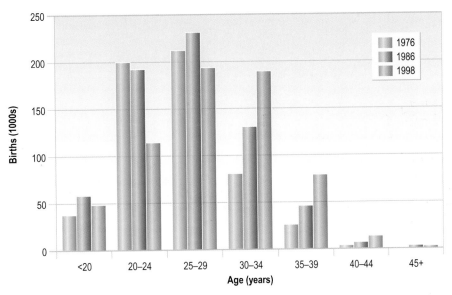

Figure 9.1
Age of women giving birth in the UK, 1976–1998.

Humans are relatively infertile compared with other mammals, and for many women there is only a fairly narrow 'window of opportunity' to have a baby in between their education, establishing a career, finding a husband and becoming menopausal. Current demographic trends towards delayed childbearing due to career or financial pressures, together with a high rate of divorce which results in many women seeking to conceive in a new partnership and at an older age, contribute to this picture. In the UK, 12% of live births are to women aged 35 years or older (Fig. 9.1), and first live births to women 35 years or older account for 7% of all births. Also, the option of adoption, especially adoption of a baby, is no longer available except to a tiny minority of childless couples. Good nutrition, healthy lifestyle and modern medical care mean that many women in their late thirties and early forties look and feel much younger than they actually are, but their chances of successful spontaneous pregnancy are unfortunately quite low. All communities experience a similar and significant fall in fecundity when the female partner reaches her mid-thirties (see Fig. 9.2, p. 152).

THE PSYCHOLOGICAL TOLL OF INFERTILITY

The recognition by a couple that a pregnancy is not 'happening' can cause deep rifts in the relationship, with loss of self-esteem, anger, mutual resentment and guilt adding to the inevitable depression and disappointment. In this classic vicious cycle, stress and anxiety can rapidly lead to sexual dysfunction and disharmony, and it is vital that this psychological burden is recognized during treatment and appropriate support and counselling made available (see Fig. 9.3, p. 153).

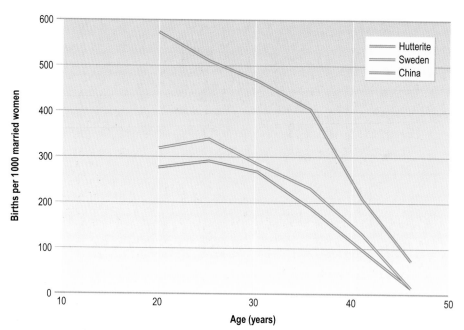

Figure 9.2
Age-specific fecundity rates by race.

Modern infertility treatments are highly effective and it is likely that modern fertility practice can achieve successful pregnancies for about two-thirds of all couples referred for specialist treatment where the woman is less than 40 years of age. Patients' expectations of modern medicine are high, and a culture that places such emphasis on 'success' can make those that 'fail' at something so fundamental as procreation feel alienated and totally despairing. Many couples recognize that they do have other life choices, and can come to accept childlessness and focus on other aspects of their lives. But where there are strong religious or cultural pressures, where a woman is perceived to have failed at her only possible role unless she becomes a mother, then fertility treatment can become a matter of necessity, not choice.

Patients seeking help with a fertility problem are unusual in that the treatment they seek is elective, optional and voluntary. They are not 'ill' by any usual definition of illness (although their infertility may have an underlying pathological cause) and yet a medical solution to their 'problem' is likely to have a greater impact on their lives than almost any other medical intervention. Fertility patients need a high level of information about options for investigation and treatment and are often extremely well informed about their diagnosis and about the therapies that could help them. Achieving successful pregnancy is an 'all-or-none' event and so 'failure' in any given cycle of treatment – which even with a very successful treatment such as IVF occurs in at least 70% of cycles – results in devastating disappointment. It is simply not possible to have infertility 'symptoms' improved by anything other than a baby, unlike the case of a less than totally successful operation, which may nevertheless provide palliation or improved quality of life.

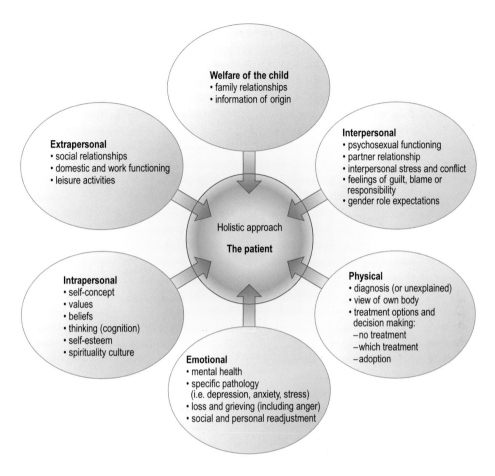

Figure 9.3
The psychosocial model of infertility. Adapted, with permission, from Bulmer C, 2000. Infertility counselling: a pyschosocial model and presenting psychopathology. Post Graduate Centre Series, Infertility 2000. Amsterdam; Excerpta Medica, Elsevier

A further source of stress and anxiety is the inadequate and unequal provision of fertility services within the National Health Service (NHS), which varies enormously from region to region, reflecting a widely held belief that fertility treatment is a low priority within a national health service that is chronically underfunded. Although the NHS Plan clearly sets the abolition of 'postcode prescribing' high on the agenda, the arbitrary and inequitable level of NHS treatment available has led inevitably to the proliferation of private provision of fertility care. The relatively recent development of the new reproductive technologies such as *in vitro* fertilization and embryo transfer (IVF-ET) has accelerated this trend, and nowadays the vast majority of units offering such treatments are private clinics where patients are fee-paying consumers rather than NHS recipients of medical services. More than 70% of IVF cycles in the UK are purchased by couples themselves and, where NHS provision is made, there may be strict eligibility criteria applied, long

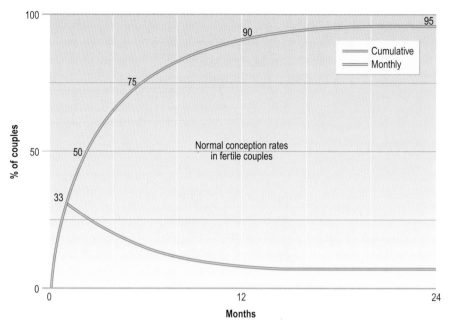

Figure 9.4
Conception rates in a normal population of proven fertility.

waiting lists may develop or certain types of treatment (such as treatment using donor gametes) may be excluded. Notwithstanding the incorporation of the European Human Rights legislation into UK law, many people may feel, or actually be, excluded from fertility treatment because of their age, medical history or sexual orientation.

The National Institute for Clinical Excellence (NICE) has recently recommended increased provision of fertility treatment within the NHS and it is likely that access will increase.

NORMAL FERTILITY

Figures 9.4 and 9.5 show the basic parameters of fertility. Patients often have totally unrealistic expectations of their chance of conceiving spontaneously and, having embarked on fertility treatment, their disappointment is compounded. Whereas 90% of normally fertile couples will have conceived within 1 year of trying to achieve pregnancy with appropriately timed intercourse, the equivalent for infertile couples is 12 cycles of treatment, which is more than most have the financial or emotional resources to complete.

The implication of these data is that the vast majority (90%) of fertile couples where the female partner is aged under 35 will conceive within a year of starting to try. Most other fertile couples will conceive during the following 12 months. Referral for specialist

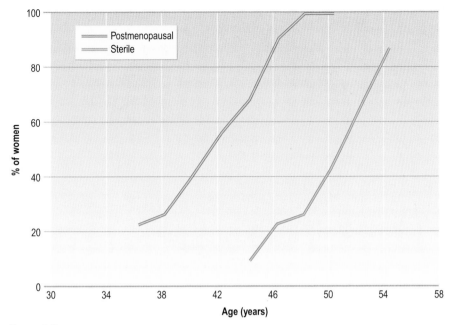

Figure 9.5
Biological infertility and the menopause. The intervening decade represents the 'perimenopausal transition'.

investigation and treatment may therefore be reasonably delayed for many couples until they have been trying for 18 months or so. However, this 'wait and try' approach should not be adopted if failure to conceive is causing psychological stress and anxiety, if the infertility is primary for the couple and the female partner is in her mid-thirties or older, or if there are features in the medical histories of either partner (see below) that are suggestive of underlying reproductive pathology.

CAUSES OF INFERTILITY

The primary causes of infertility in British couples are categorized in Figure 9.6 (p. 156); the various medical diagnoses within these categories are listed in Table 9.1. Male factor infertility, failure to ovulate effectively and tubal disease are by far the most common causes of infertility in British couples. Some specific examples are illustrated in Figure 9.7 (p. 157).

Absolute infertility is relatively rare but subfertility is common, and when two or more factors are present (e.g. oligomenorrhoea in the woman and oligospermia in the man) then the chance of a spontaneous conception occurring becomes very low.

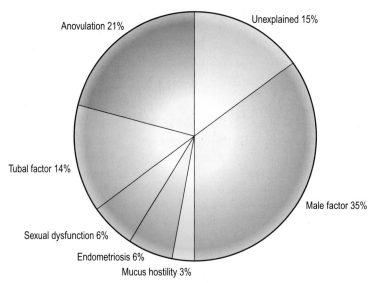

Figure 9.6
Causes of infertility in British couples.

Table 9.1 Causes of primary and secondary infertility

Fertility factor	Causes
Anovulation	Polycystic ovary syndrome Hyperprolactinaemia Hypogonadotrophic hypogonadism Premature ovarian failure Hypopituitarism Weight-related amenorrhoea Exercise-related amenorrhoea
Tubal factor	Infection (chlamydia, pelvic inflammatory disease, appendicitis) Endometriosis Surgical (laparotomy, tubal sterilization)
Sexual dysfunction	Physical (insulin-dependent diabetes mellitus, multiple sclerosis, beta-blockers) Psychological (loss of libido, anxiety, stress)
Mucus hostility	Antisperm antibodies Increased mucus viscosity
Male factor	Obstructive azoospermia Genetic (Kallman's syndrome, XXY) Severe sperm dysfunction Primary testicular failure Congenital abnormality (cryptorchidism) Postchemo-/radiotherapy Endocrine disturbance Antisperm antibodies

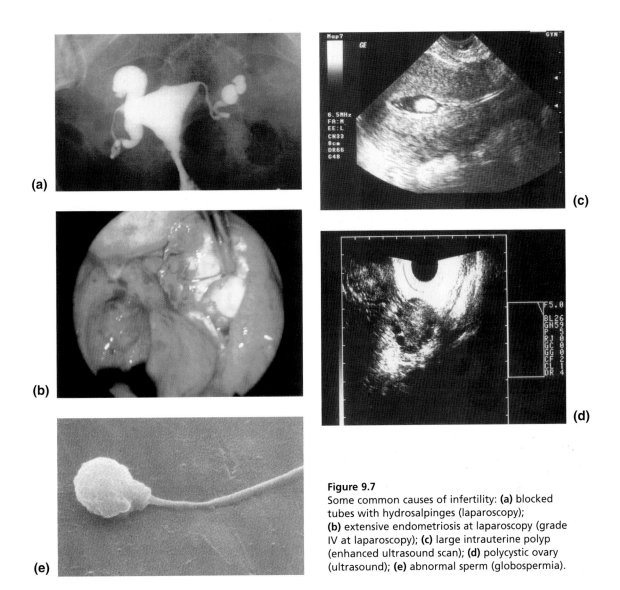

Figure 9.7
Some common causes of infertility: **(a)** blocked tubes with hydrosalpinges (laparoscopy); **(b)** extensive endometriosis at laparoscopy (grade IV at laparoscopy); **(c)** large intrauterine polyp (enhanced ultrasound scan); **(d)** polycystic ovary (ultrasound); **(e)** abnormal sperm (globospermia).

INVESTIGATING INFERTILITY

The Royal College of Obstetricians and Gynaecologists (RCOG) has published guidelines for the investigation and management of the infertile couple at primary, secondary and tertiary levels. The guidelines and further information can be downloaded from the RCOG website (www.rcog.org.uk).

The problem of infertility can frequently be managed at primary care level and, with appropriate investigation, advice and treatment, many couples will achieve a successful pregnancy without recourse to the specialist fertility clinic.

> **Box 9.1: Information required for full medical history**
>
> - Age of both partners
> - Duration of infertility
> - Previous fertility and pregnancy outcome
> - Coital frequency, difficulties and timing in relation to the 'fertile period'
> - Medical disorders such as diabetes, thyroid problems, hypertension, anaemia
> - Previous history of inflammatory disease of the reproductive tract
> - Surgical history of the woman: abdominal, pelvic or cervical surgery
> - Surgical history of the man: groin or genital surgery
> - Drug history for both partners
> - Previous contraceptive use
> - Social history: smoking, alcohol, stress

Investigating infertility at primary care level

The full medical history is vital to accurate diagnosis (see Box 9.1).

Assessment of the menstrual cycle and confirmation of ovulation

It can be assumed that women with regular menstrual cycles in the range 23–35 days ovulate normally most months. Ovulation occurs approximately 14 days prior to the next menstruation and therefore women with particularly short or long cycles need to be aware of their 'fertile period'. Serum progesterone will be elevated to at least 30 nmol/L in the mid-luteal phase (day 21 of a 28-day cycle) if ovulation has occurred. The timing of this test is crucial, but it is only required if the infertility is longstanding in the presence of regular cycles, or if ovulatory therapy is being undertaken. Charting of basal body temperature, to identify the tiny rise in temperature that occurs following ovulation, and the use of urine testing kits, to identify the pre-ovulatory surge in luteinizing hormone, are generally both to be discouraged as they are a source of considerable stress and are prone to mistakes. Most couples can be reassured that they will maximize their chances of conception by having intercourse every 2–3 days between cycle days 8 and 20.

Even when the menstrual cycle is regular and normal, endocrine investigations should include serum follicle-stimulating hormone (FSH), luteinizing hormone (LH), prolactin (PRL) and testosterone and an assessment of oestrogen status. These hormone assessments may be made from one blood sample taken in the early follicular (days 2–5) phase of the cycle. The main purpose of measuring FSH levels is to exclude primary or secondary ovarian failure, in which case the FSH level will be significantly raised (>15 IU/L). If the LH:FSH ratio is >3, and especially if the testosterone is elevated, the diagnosis may be one of polycystic ovary syndrome (PCOS). These endocrine abnormalities are most likely to occur in women with oligomenorrhoea (cycle length >42 days), amenorrhoea (absence of periods >6 months), acne, hirsutism and obesity (see Ch. 2).

The presence of galactorrhoea may suggest hyperprolactinaemia, which is an important cause of secondary amenorrhoea. The interpretation of serum PRL levels that are marginally raised (>800 IU/L) is difficult as PRL is a stress hormone and is often elevated by a physical examination, but infertility patients with hyperprolactinaemia should also be assessed for thyroid function as hypothyroidism is an associated condition. If PRL is consistently elevated (>1000 IU/L), CT or MRI scanning of the pituitary fossa should be requested to exclude a pituitary tumour. If the serum PRL is mildly elevated but the menstrual cycle is regular and ovulatory, there is no need for treatment.

Where a woman complaining of infertility presents with secondary amenorrhoea, a progestogen challenge test will rapidly establish her oestrogen status. The test is based on the principle that an oestrogen-primed endometrium will be shed on progestogen withdrawal. A pregnancy test should be performed first, and, if negative, the patient should take 10 mg of oral medroxyprogesterone daily for 7 days. The majority of patients with ovulatory dysfunction and PCOS will experience withdrawal bleeding at the end of the course of progestogen and they may then proceed to ovulation induction with oral anti-oestrogens such as clomiphene citrate (see later). A negative progestogen challenge test suggests severe hypothalamic–pituitary dysfunction, and this group of women merit early referral to a specialist unit. (See Ch. 2.)

Assessment of the pelvis

Tubal damage and pelvic adhesions are usually due to infection. Sexually transmitted diseases (STDs), including chlamydia, ascending endometritis following childbirth, miscarriage or abortion, complications of intrauterine contraceptive devices, etc. can all cause tubal damage. Infection often causes irreversible functional damage to the tubal-lining ciliated epithelium. Surgical restoration of patency may not be associated with a return of proper tubal function and increases the risk of tubal ectopic implantation. Appendicectomy, ovarian cystectomy and other abdominal surgery can also compromise tubal function. Pelvic examination will reveal unexpected tenderness, immobility of the pelvic organs or swelling in the adnexae. Formal assessment of tubal patency by hysterosalpingogram (HSG), contrast ultrasonography or laparoscopy is required. HSG is an outpatient procedure and is a useful screen for 'low-risk' patients.

Chlamydia serology is a useful screening test of past 'silent' infection indicating likely tubal damage and requiring early laparoscopy. Chlamydial antibodies are quite common in the general population and it is only when the titre is raised (IFT titre >1/512) that there is a strong probability of finding otherwise unexpected tubal or pelvic inflammatory damage and adhesions. If a recent infection is suspected, both partners should be treated with a course of doxycycline and erythromycin or ciprofloxacin. (See Ch. 3.)

Laparoscopy remains the 'gold standard' for the investigation of tubal patency because it offers the opportunity for treatment of a range of pelvic pathologies. Tubal patency is checked by passing methylene blue dye through the cervix and observing its passage through the fallopian tubes. Laparoscopic examination, usually a day-case procedure under general anaesthesia, is ideally combined with diagnostic hysteroscopy to exclude intrauterine pathology such as fibroids, septae, adhesions and polyps.

The diagnosis of endometriosis – the presence of persisting endometrial tissue at sites other than within the uterine cavity – is frequently made during infertility investigations, although there is debate about the relevance of this finding. Clearly significant endometriosis that has caused structural damage to the fallopian tubes and ovaries can lead to infertility, but it is less clear how milder forms of endometriosis contribute to the problem. Epidemiological studies have shown an increased prevalence of endometriosis in infertile women, but these studies do not indicate whether endometriosis predisposes to infertility or vice versa (Mahmood & Templeton 1990). There is no evidence to date that proves that medical treatment is beneficial to women with mild endometriosis in terms of improving their fertility outcome. Thus, many specialists now regard fertility patients with minimal or mild endometriosis as their only diagnostic finding as having 'unexplained' infertility (Thomas & Cooke 1987). However, the Endocan study, a multicentre randomized controlled trial conducted in Canada on over 300 patients with infertility and minimal/mild endometriosis, did show a significantly higher pregnancy rate in patients who had their endometrial implants ablated with electrocautery (Marcoux et al 1997).

Investigation of the male

In a third of infertile couples there is an identifiable defect either in the production or in the functional competence of sperm; moreover, there is evidence of a decline in sperm quality over recent decades (Skakkeback & Keiding 1994). Investigation of the male partner of a couple complaining of infertility in general practice should aim to exclude the relatively few, but sometimes reversible, disorders that may affect sperm and also identify rare but serious associated conditions such as testicular tumours.

The history should include:

- Past STDs.
- Mumps orchitis.
- History of inguinoscrotal, prostatic or bladder neck surgery.
- Testicular injury.

Cryptorchidism (undescended testes) is the most common congenital abnormality associated with male subfertility. Early orchidopexy (before 3 years of age) is recommended, but even with early surgery there may be severe problems with spermatogenesis. The importance of maintaining the testicles at a temperature below body heat by wearing cool, loose-fitting underwear should be stressed, especially to men who drive long distances each year. Frequent hot baths, saunas and cycling are also recognized to reduce sperm function. Enquiry should be made about exposure to toxic agents (e.g. radiation, cytotoxic drugs, chemicals) or drugs affecting spermatogenesis (e.g. medication for Crohn's disease, ulcerative colitis or hypertension). Excessive smoking and alcohol consumption are well recognized as reducing sperm quality.

Physical examination should include:

- Assessment of secondary sexual characteristics.
- An estimation of testicular size and consistency.
- A search for varicocele.
- Assessment of the epididymes and vasa.

Semen analysis is the most important test for the diagnosis of male infertility. It is vital that the sample be produced into a sterile container after the correct period of abstinence (3–4 days) and transported to the laboratory at the correct temperature (a jacket pocket is ideal) within an hour of production.

Table 9.2: WHO criteria for a normal sperm count

Volume	≥2 mL
pH	≥7.2 or more
Count	≥20×10^6 per mL (abnormal: azoospermia [no sperm] or oligozoospermia [reduced numbers])
Motility	≥50% with forward progression, or ≥25% with rapid progression, within 60 min of ejaculation (abnormal: asthenozoospermia)
Morphology	The 1999 edition of the WHO manual does not define normal ranges for morphology, but notes that data from IVF programmes suggest that, as sperm morphology falls below 15% of normal forms (teratozoospermia), the fertilization rate decreases
MAR (mixed antiglobulin reaction) test for antisperm antibodies	Fewer than 50% or motile sperm with adherent particles
Immunobead test for antisperm antibodies	Fewer than 50% of motile sperm with adherent beads

Table 9.2 lists the criteria for a normal (i.e. fertile) semen sample as defined by the World Health Organization (WHO). The laboratory will normally report volume, count, motility and morphology. More detailed analysis, including computer-assisted sperm analysis, which will provide measurements of straight line and curvilinear velocity, linearity and lateral head displacement, can be performed by a specialist andrology service. In the event of low (oligospermic) or absent (azoospermic) sperm counts, endocrine assessment should include FSH, LH, PRL and testosterone. If FSH levels are elevated, this suggests end-organ failure. Male patients who present with azoospermia, normal-sized testes and a normal gonadotrophin profile should be referred for a urological opinion, vasogram and testicular biopsy since some of these patients may have a surgically correctable obstruction. Sperm obtained directly from the testis by fine-needle or open biopsy may be cryopreserved and used in an ICSI-IVF treatment cycle (see later).

Where sperm parameters are persistently poor with low count, low progressive motility and a high proportion of abnormal forms, many specialists would advocate karyotyping and screening the male partner for cystic fibrosis as the incidence of carrier status for cystic fibrosis, congenital bilateral absence of the vas or structural chromosome defects (Y chromosome deletions or translocations) is quite high under these circumstances.

Antisperm antibodies

The MAR (mixed antiglobulin reaction) test may be performed as a routine part of standard semen analysis to screen for antibodies in seminal plasma. It should be requested if the 'sperm count' reports significant 'clumping' or if the proportion of poorly progressive or non-motile sperm is high (asthenozoospermia). This finding is far more significant than a low count (<20×10^6 per mL=oligospermia).

Sperm–mucus interaction

Sperm–mucus interaction can be tested *in vivo* (by the postcoital test) or *in vitro*. The postcoital test is ideally performed 1 or 2 days prior to ovulation (day 12 in a 28-day cycle) as this is when the mucus is well oestrogenized. The patient is instructed to have intercourse the night before attending for the test. A sample of cervical mucus is obtained from the cervical os and inspected under the microscope for the presence of motile sperm. A postcoital test is considered normal if the mucus demonstrates good spinnbarkeit or stretchability, normal ferning pattern and at least 5 sperm per high-power field. Although the postcoital test has become an integral part of fertility investigations, patients find it distressing and intrusive, and a review of the literature suggests that, as an assessment of sperm function, this test is rather inadequate as it has a poor correlation with pregnancy (Kovacs et al 1978).

Specialist fertility treatment

Contemporary fertility treatment is best regarded as a 'ladder of assistance', of which the lowest rungs are perhaps the most important, not least because they offer significant opportunities for early and successful intervention. The 'ladder' (Table 9.3) illustrates the hierarchy of therapies available to the infertile couple, although treatment decisions will be guided both by the clinical diagnosis and by what is acceptable to the couple.

Figure 9.8 shows the cumulative conception rates resulting from the conventional management of couples with a single cause of infertility, compared with conception rates for the normally fertile. It is clear that ovulatory disorders and idiopathic or unexplained

---

Table 9.3: The 'ladder' of assistance

Indication	Therapy
Premature ovarian failure Menopause	Egg donation
Uterine anomaly or absence Very severe male factor or azoospermia Complete azoospermia	Surrogacy ICSI (MESA, TESA, PESA) Donor insemination
Blocked fallopian tubes Cervical hostility Endometriosis Idiopathic infertility	Extracorporeal fertilization (IVF-ET)
Oligo-/asthenozoospermia Antisperm antibodies	Gamete selection (GIFT, ZIFT, IUI)
Oligo-ovulation or anovulation (polycystic ovary syndrome)	Anti-oestrogens Ovulation induction with gonadotrophins

ICSI, intracytoplasmic sperm injection; MESA, micro-epididymal sperm aspiration; TESA, testicular sperm aspiration; PESA, percutaneous epididymal sperm aspiration; IVF-ET, *in vitro* fertilization and embryo transfer; GIFT, gamete intrafallopian transfer; ZIFT, zygote intrafallopian transfer; IUI, intrauterine insemination.

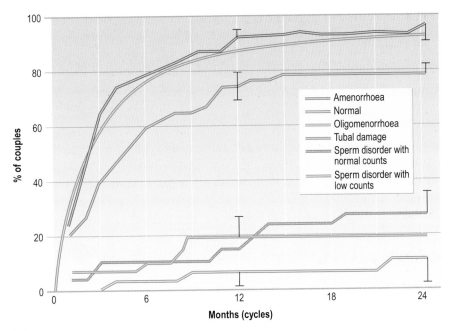

Figure 9.8
Cumulative conception rates resulting from conventional management of couples with a single cause of infertility.

infertility have the best chance of responding to relatively simple procedures such as ovulation induction and intrauterine insemination. However, great progress has been made in IVF in the last 5 years, particularly since the introduction of techniques such as intracytoplasmic sperm injection, and now even patients with irremediably blocked fallopian tubes or very severe sperm dysfunction can be offered a chance of pregnancy that is as good as normal in each cycle of treatment.

TREATMENT OPTIONS FOR INFERTILITY

Anovulation and PCOS

Patients with irregular periods and persistent anovulation may be started on ovulation induction therapy prior to referral to a specialist unit. Clomiphene citrate is the most commonly used anti-oestrogen; it works by boosting endogenous FSH production by interacting with the negative feed-back loop of oestrogen on pituitary FSH production. The treatment is successful in patients who are adequately oestrogenized (i.e. have a positive progestogen challenge test), but is less successful in hypo-oestrogenic states. Approximately 75% of anovular patients respond to clomiphene, with ovulation being monitored by elevation of luteal phase progesterone and the onset of regular menses, but only half of these will conceive on clomiphene alone.

The starting dose of clomiphene citrate is usually 50 mg daily for 5 days, beginning on the second day of a spontaneous or induced bleed. If anovulation persists, the dose may be doubled, but at doses higher than this the deleterious effect of the anti-oestrogen on the cervical mucus becomes significant. The side-effects of clomiphene therapy include multiple gestation (a six-fold increase in twin pregnancies), vasomotor symptoms such as nausea and hot flushes, weight gain and, occasionally, visual disturbance, which is an indication for stopping treatment at once.

Recently, anxieties have been raised about an association between clomiphene and ovarian cancer (Rossing et al 1994), and current guidelines restrict the prescription of clomiphene to a maximum of 6–12 cycles. Clomiphene has been quite widely used empirically in cases of unexplained infertility. There are no good studies showing a benefit over placebo for this indication and it should therefore be discouraged.

Gonadotrophin therapy, with daily injections of FSH or FSH and LH, is indicated for women with PCOS who have been treated with clomiphene and have repeatedly failed to ovulate, show persistent hypersecretion of LH (>10 IU/L) or have a negative postcoital test due to the effect of anti-oestrogens on cervical mucus. Gonadotrophin therapy carries a significant risk of ovarian hyperstimulation syndrome (see later) and multiple pregnancies; in order to minimize these risks, treatment should only be undertaken at specialist units with appropriate monitoring. Monitoring should include ultrasound scanning of the developing follicles and regular assessment of oestradiol levels. Figure 9.9 shows the cumulative conception rates for 103 women with PCOS who did not ovulate with clomiphene.

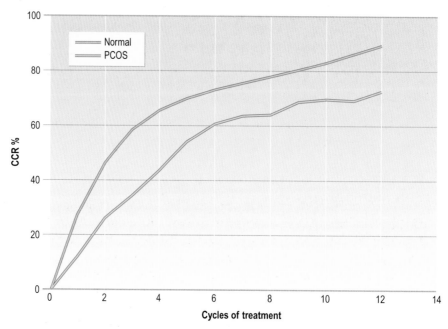

Figure 9.9
Cumulative conception rates (CCR) in 103 women with polycystic ovary syndrome (PCOS). From Balen A, et al. Human Reproduction 1994; 9:1563–1570. Reproduced by permission of Oxford University Press.

Laparoscopic ovarian diathermy has replaced wedge resection for clomiphene-resistant women with PCOS (Armar & Lachelin 1993). It is performed as a day-case procedure and is particularly useful if a laparoscopic assessment of the pelvis is also required and when the patient is not able to attend clinic for the frequent visits required for adequate monitoring of gonadotrophin therapy.

Weight-related amenorrhoea

Anorexia nervosa accounts for 15–35% of patients with amenorrhoea, and for these women it is essential to encourage weight gain as the main therapy, since embarking upon a pregnancy when seriously underweight greatly increases the risk of intrauterine growth retardation. A body mass index (BMI) of at least 20 kg/m^2 should be the goal of amenorrhoeic women who wish to conceive. If amenorrhoea persists, even after a normal BMI has been regained following excessive weight loss, then ovulation may be induced using the GnRH (gonadotrophin-releasing hormone) pump or by injections of HMG (human menopausal gonadotrophin containing FSH and LH).

Premature ovarian failure

The usual definition of premature ovarian failure is raised gonadotrophin levels (FSH >15 IU/L) with cessation of periods before the age of 40. The most common cause is probably genetic, although autoimmune failure, infection, previous surgery, chemotherapy and radiotherapy are also common causes. There appears to be a strong genetic predisposition to early menopause; thus daughters and younger sisters of women who have had early-onset ovarian failure should be appropriately counselled. Ovarian failure before puberty causing primary amenorrhoea is usually due to a chromosomal abnormality such as Turner's syndrome (70%) or a childhood malignancy that required chemotherapy or radiotherapy. Pregnancy is possible by oocyte donation with IVF-ET (see later). Women with ovarian failure should take combined (oestrogen plus progestogen) hormone replacement therapy (HRT) to prevent the cardiovascular and osteoporotic consequences of oestrogen deficiency; women who have been amenorrhoeic for more than 6 months may require 'priming' with cyclic oestrogens and progestogens to restore normal uterine architecture before starting fertility treatment.

Superovulation and intrauterine insemination

Where the diagnosis is one of mild male factor (at least 5 million motile sperm are available for insemination), cervical mucus hostility, unexplained infertility or antisperm antibodies, then intrauterine insemination may offer a fair chance (approx. 10–15% pregnancy rate per cycle) of conception. Since fertilization takes place within the fallopian tube, at least one of the female partner's tubes must be healthy. The treatment usually involves gentle ovulation induction with gonadotrophins to encourage the development of two to three follicles, which are monitored by transvaginal ultrasonography. Ovulation is triggered with an injection of human chorionic gonadotrophin (hCG), and a sperm sample, produced on the morning of ovulation, is prepared and inserted through the cervix into the uterine cavity via a soft plastic catheter.

Box 9.2: Indications for IVF

- Tubal damage (minor degrees of tubal damage may be amenable to tubal surgery such as laparoscopic adhesiolysis or salpingostomy)
- Unexplained infertility (greater than 2 years' duration with no apparent cause identified)
- Endometriosis (moderate and severe disease responds well to IVF, although mild disease should be treated initially as 'unexplained')
- Anovulation (failure to conceive after 6–12 cycles of successful ovulation induction suggests an additional cause for the continuing infertility)
- Male factor (moderate degrees of oligo-/astheno-/teratozoospermia will produce normal fertilization rates of oocytes *in vitro*; men with extremely low numbers of functional sperm or obstructive azoospermia will require micro-assisted fertilization techniques such as ICSI)
- Egg donation (premature ovarian failure, gonadal dysgenesis, iatrogenic, carriers of genetic disease, recurrent miscarriage, failed IVF)
- Failed donor sperm insemination

ASSISTED CONCEPTION AND IVF

The treatment of infertility by assisted conception is one of the great success stories of modern medicine. Since the birth of Louise Brown, the world's first test-tube baby, in 1978, there have been enormous advances both in the success rates for assisted conception techniques and in the range of fertility disorders that they can treat. The original indication for IVF was tubal blockage, but it is now used for a wide range of disorders (see Box 9.2).

The technique of IVF

The IVF procedure involves removing one or more eggs from the ovary, fertilizing them in the laboratory with sperm from the male partner and transferring some of the resulting embryos to the womb for implantation and pregnancy. Box 9.3 shows the steps in an IVF treatment cycle

Embryo cryopreservation

Freezing surplus embryos created in an IVF cycle increases the overall pregnancy per stimulated cycle started by 15–20%. Unfortunately, not all 'spare' embryos are suitable for freezing, as poorer quality ones do not withstand the freeze/thaw process. If the concept of freezing is ethically acceptable to the couple, it should be encouraged because, if the fresh cycle is unsuccessful, the use of frozen embryos permits a 'second chance' without further stimulation and oocyte recovery being required. In addition, if the fresh cycle was successful, then the embryo quality (which often deteriorates markedly with female age) will be frozen at the point that success was achieved. All the evidence available suggests that cryopreservation of embryos is safe for the future child. The frozen embryos must be thawed and transferred at an appropriate stage in the woman's cycle, when the endometrium is receptive to implantation. This can be achieved in either a monitored 'natural' cycle or by creating an artificial cycle using GnRH agonists and HRT.

Box 9.3: The technique of IVF step-by-step

1. Drug treatment, to stimulate the synchronous development of multiple follicles
   - GnRH agonists to suppress all other hormone activity (injections/nasal spray for [usually] 2 weeks before gonadotrophins and then for a further 10–14 days depending on response)
   - Gonadotrophins to stimulate the growth of follicles
2. Monitoring of treatment, to measure the growth of follicles, individualize drug doses and prevent serious side-effects
   - By transvaginal ultrasound scanning (two or three times during a treatment cycle)
   - Sometimes by measuring oestradiol levels in a blood sample
3. Egg collection, usually under local anaesthesia with sedation, lasts between 10 and 20 min
   - Guided by transvaginal ultrasound
   - Collected through the vagina (32–36 h after final hormone injection)
4. Sperm sample, provided on the same day as egg collection
5. Fertilization
   - Eggs and sperm prepared and cultured together overnight
   - Eggs examined next day under the microscope to check for normal fertilization
6. Embryo transfer (usually 2 or 3 days after fertilization)
   - Transvaginal transfer of no more than two embryos (or three in exceptional cases, such as advanced maternal age or multiple previous failures)
   - Embryos placed in the womb
   - Spare embryos usually frozen
7. Pregnancy testing 14 days after embryo transfer
8. Early pregnancy scan at 6 weeks' gestation (2 weeks after positive pregnancy test)

Egg donation

Many women have fertility problems that can only be overcome by the use of donated eggs as part of an IVF programme (Abdalla et al 1989). However, there is a scarcity of egg donors since the treatment requires that the donor (who may be an altruistic volunteer, or a friend or relative of a fertility patient who needs donor eggs) undergoes IVF treatment herself. More recently, 'egg share' schemes have developed whereby an infertile donor is prepared to donate half her oocytes from an IVF cycle to a recipient who pays the cost of both their treatments. The donor undergoes conventional IVF treatment up to the point of oocyte collection; in the meantime, the recipient's cycle is co-ordinated with HRT (for non-functioning ovaries) or GnRH agonist and HRT (for functioning ovaries). The oocytes collected from the donor are then fertilized with sperm from the recipient's partner and the embryos are transferred as normal. If the recipient conceives then HRT needs to be continued till luteoplacental shift has occurred (7–8 weeks' gestation).

Surrogacy

Patients who have no uterus or in whom pregnancy is medically contraindicated can be assisted to have their own genetic offspring through surrogacy. The 'commissioning couple' undergo conventional IVF up to the point of embryo transfer; then their embryos are transferred to the host surrogate whose cycle has been synchronized to that of the 'genetic' mother. Under English law, the birth mother is the legal mother irrespective of the genetic origins of the child, but a 'fast track' adoption process (called a 'parental order') is available to allow the commissioning couple, who must be married, to become the legal parents. Careful counselling of the 'commissioning couple' and the host surrogate (and her partner) are essential, and the couples must seek legal guidance in drawing up appropriate agreements that cover issues such as care of the surrogate's existing children if she becomes ill during the surrogate pregnancy. No money (except allowable expenses) must change hands and the surrogate remains free to change her mind until the 'adoption' process is completed.

Overcoming severe male factor infertility: micro-assisted fertilization and ICSI

Where there is a history of failed fertilization or very low fertilization rates with conventional IVF, then techniques such as ICSI may be employed. In ICSI, a single sperm is injected directly into the cytoplasm of the oocyte (see Fig. 9.10). With this technique, fertilization rates of 60–70% can be expected and the clinical pregnancy rates per cycle started are comparable with those of good conventional IVF. ICSI has also been used to achieve fertilization where sperm have been surgically retrieved from the epididymus or testis of men with obstructive azoospermia.

Other treatments for male factor infertility

If the male partner is azoospermic and no sperm can be obtained by either micro-epididymal sperm aspiration (MESA), percutaneous epididymal sperm aspiration (PESA) or testicular sperm aspiration (TESA) for use in IVF with ICSI, then artificial insemination using donor sperm (AID) may be offered.

If the female partner has normal fertility, the cumulative conception rate in accurately timed AID cycles is close to that for normally fertile couples, and those who are not successful can proceed to IVF using donor sperm.

Donor insemination requires careful consideration, and all couples should be offered counselling to discuss the legal and ethical implications of AID as covered by the Human

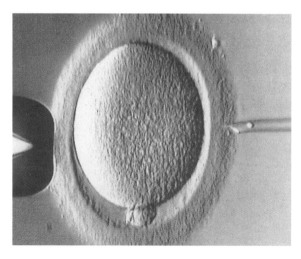

Figure 9.10
ICSI. A single sperm is injected via a micro-needle (14 times thinner than a human hair) directly into the centre (cytoplasm) of the oocyte, which is stabilized with a holding pipette.

Fertilisation and Embryology Authority (HFEA). Any child conceived as a result of AID is the legal offspring of the social father and may be granted access to certain information (but not the identity) of the donor.

SUCCESS RATES FOR IVF

The most important statistic for couples considering IVF is the chance an individual couple has of having a baby following one completed cycle of treatment – the so-called 'take-home baby' rate.

National data for live birth rates after IVF by age of the woman are shown in Figure 9.11. These data are national average figures, and many units, particularly large centres associated with research facilities, report much higher success rates (live birth rates of 25–35% per cycle started). The data in Figure 9.11 were provided by the HFEA, which licenses and inspects all units providing assisted-conception treatments. The HFEA now publishes annual 'league tables' giving the success rates for each unit in a standardized format. However, not all units offer all types of treatments and many centres have upper age limits or other conditions for acceptance onto a programme. The success of IVF should not be measured by one treatment cycle alone. The cumulative conception rates give a better impression of the extent to which IVF compares favourably with spontaneous conception in the natural menstrual cycle.

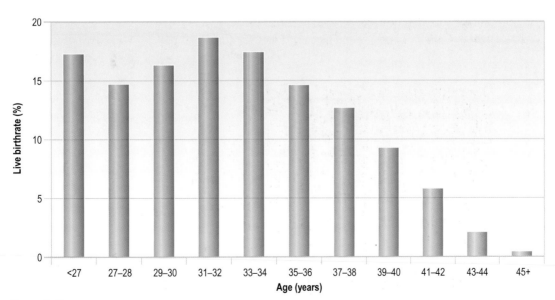

Figure 9.11
IVF success rates by age (HFEA data).

COMPLICATIONS ASSOCIATED WITH IVF TREATMENT

The side-effects of the GnRH agonist treatment include headaches, hot flushes, mood swings, and nasal irritation with the nasal spray. Approximately 15% of patients will develop functional follicular cysts while taking the agonist, especially if they had prior ovulatory dysfunction. These cysts normally disappear if the GnRH agonist administration is continued or they may be aspirated under ultrasound guidance. Bleeding following oocyte retrieval is usually slight and the rate of infection is very low (<1%).

A recent development in IVF treatment is the use of GnRH antagonists, which prevent premature spontaneous ovulation during the stimulation phase of the IVF cycle, thus avoiding the necessity of the prolonged 'down-regulation' phase required with GnRH agonists (see Fig. 9.12).

Ovarian hyperstimulation syndrome

Mild hyperstimulation is a feature of all IVF cycles, but severe ovarian hyperstimulation syndrome (OHSS) occurs in 1–2% of cases and is a medical emergency requiring admission to hospital.

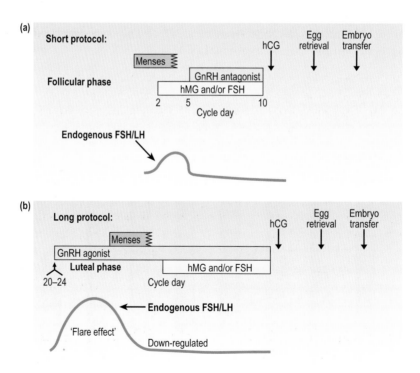

Figure 9.12
Cycles in IVF treatment: **(a)** short protocol (with GnRH antagonist); **(b)** long protocol (with GnRH agonist).
GnRH, gonadotrophin-releasing hormone; FSH, follicle-stimulating hormone; LH, luteinizing hormone;
hCG, human chorionic gonadotrophin; hMG, human menopausal gonadotrophin.

Box 9.4: Features characteristic of OHSS

- Gross ovarian enlargement
- Ascites
- Haemoconcentration
- Electrolyte disorders

- Pleural effusion
- Clotting disorders
- Pericardial effusion

Severe OHSS is characterized by the features listed in Box 9.4. These symptoms are prolonged if conception occurs. Therefore women who appear to be at risk of developing significant OHSS prior to oocyte retrieval should either have their treatment cycle cancelled, or have all their embryos frozen so that no embryo transfer is performed until the symptoms have resolved.

High-order multiple pregnancy

The transfer of two embryos at embryo transfer (where more than four embryos were available) gives a similar pregnancy rate to the transfer of three, but usually avoids triplet pregnancies (spontaneous twinning is a feature of IVF). This is the current recommendation of the HFEA. With a two-embryo transfer, approximately 25% of pregnancies are twins. In 1992, the perinatal mortality rate (PNMR) in the UK for children conceived after assisted conception was 27.4 per 1000 births, compared to a general population figure of 8 per 1000. This difference is largely attributable to the increased PNMR associated with multiple pregnancies.

Multiple pregnancies have significant consequences: not only the risks to the mother and her babies, but also the costs to the community resulting from the distortion these pregnancies produce in the provision of obstetric and neonatal care.

Miscarriage after IVF

Even when the pregnancy test is initially positive, the incidence of 'biochemical' pregnancy or early pregnancy failure (missed abortion) is higher following IVF than in the fertile population. The transfer of more than one embryo can add confusion to the management, as an ongoing pregnancy can persist in spite of very heavy bleeding (from a second implantation site), and ectopic and heterotopic pregnancies can occur, especially where there was pre-existing tubal damage. An early ultrasound scan (6–8 weeks' gestation) is mandatory in all patients with a positive pregnancy test following IVF-ET.

OUTCOME OF CHILDREN BORN FOLLOWING FERTILITY TREATMENT

The perinatal mortality and morbidity rate following treatments such as stimulated intrauterine insemination and IVF is increased and, although this is primarily due to the increased incidence of multiple pregnancies, there remains a higher risk in singletons conceived after IVF compared to spontaneously conceived singletons. It is probable that maternal age, lower parity and cause of infertility are the major reasons and it is reassuring that there is no significant increase in the incidence of congenital or chromosomal abnormalities in children conceived by IVF or intracytoplasmic sperm injection.

GAMETE INTRAFALLOPIAN TRANSFER (GIFT)

GIFT differs from IVF in that the eggs collected from the stimulated ovaries are transferred to the fallopian tubes, together with a small sample of prepared sperm, immediately after collection. Egg collection and transfer of a maximum of three eggs are carried out laparoscopically under general anaesthesia, so, unlike IVF, fertilization takes place in its natural environment in the fallopian tube. GIFT, like IVF, has proved a very successful assisted-conception technique and, because no laboratory fertilization or embryo culture is required, GIFT can be performed in non-specialist units. However, the requirement for general anaesthesia can make GIFT more expensive than IVF (which generally has a better success rate), and its use is restricted to women with totally healthy fallopian tubes and where the sperm has previous proven fertilizing ability.

ZYGOTE INTRAFALLOPIAN TRANSFER

ZIFT is a combination of IVF and GIFT in which stimulation and egg retrieval are carried out as for IVF, with fertilization occurring *in vitro* in the laboratory, but the resulting zygotes are replaced into the fallopian tubes at laparoscopy before cell division to the 4–6-cell pre-embryo stage has occurred. ZIFT is reserved for situations in which it is important to establish that fertilization has taken place, and where cervical transfer of the embryos is difficult.

FUTURE DIRECTIONS

Blastocyst culture   There is increasing evidence that *in vitro* culture of the embryos produced during IVF and ICSI to the blastocyst stage is associated with higher pregnancy rates. Extending the *in vitro* culture period to 5 or 6 days allows the embryologist to select the best embryos for transfer. It also ensures that the embryos reach the uterus at the same stage as would occur in a spontaneous conception, where the newly fertilized oocyte takes 4 or 5 days to travel down the fallopian tube.

Embryo screening and pre-implantation genetic diagnosis   There is a high incidence of chromosomal and genetic abnormalities in human embryos (40–50%) and this contributes to the low implantation rates seen in IVF. Older women (40+ years) produce embryos with a significantly higher rate of aneuploidy, and this explains both their poor pregnancy rates (<10%) and their high miscarriage rates (40%). Also, some individuals carry the risk of passing known genetic problems to their offspring.

It is now possible to screen embryos for genetic abnormalities by removing a single cell (embryo biopsy) for pre-implantation genetic diagnosis (PGD). Common inherited conditions that can be screened for by PGD include

FUTURE DIRECTIONS—cont'd

single gene defects (e.g. Huntington's chorea, cystic fibrosis and Duchenne muscular dystrophy), chromosomal disorders (e.g. translocations) or aneuploidies (e.g. Down's and Edward's syndromes). Embryos that are found to be unaffected can then be transferred to the uterus or frozen for use in subsequent treatment cycles.

Oocyte freezing   Until recently, freezing oocytes was impractical, as the formation of ice crystals within the ooplasm shattered delicate structures such as the mitotic spindle. However, new cryoprotectants permit reliable freezing/thawing of mature oocytes retrieved during an IVF cycle. The thawed oocytes may then be fertilized by ICSI and the resulting embryos transferred or cryopreserved. Although, to date, there have been few live births from frozen eggs, the technique offers the possibility of biological motherhood to young women with Hodgkin's lymphoma or leukaemia whom life-saving chemotherapy or radiotherapy would otherwise render sterile.

Selected References and Further Reading

Abdalla HI, Baber RJ, Kirkland A, et al. Pregnancy in women with premature ovarian failure using tubal and intrauterine transfer of cryopreserved zygotes. BJOG 1989; 96:1071–1075.

Armar NA, Lachelin GCL. Laparoscopic ovarian diathermy: an effective treatment for anti-oestrogen resistant anovulatory infertility in women with polycystic ovaries. BJOG 1993; 100:161–164.

Balen AH, Braat DD, West C, et al. Cumulative conception and live birth rates after the treatment of anovulatory infertility. Hum Reprod 1994; 9:1563–1570.

Botting BJ, Macfarland AJ, Price FV, eds. Three, four and more. A study of triplet and higher order births. London: HMSO; 1990.

Kovacs GT, Newman GB, Henson GL. The postcoital test: what is normal? BMJ 1978; 1:818.

Mahmood TA, Templeton A. Pathophysiology of mild endometriosis: review of literature. Hum Reprod 1990; 5:765–784.

Marcoux S, Maheux R, Berube S. Laparoscopic surgery in infertile women with minimal and mild endometriosis. N Engl J Med 1997; 337:217–222.

Nielsen S, Hahlin, M. Expectant management of first-trimester spontaneous abortion. Lancet 1995; 345:84–85.

Rossing MA, Daling JR, Weiss NS, et al. Ovarian tumours in a cohort of infertile women. N Engl J Med 1994; 331:771–776.

Skakkeback NE, Keiding N. Changes in semen and the testis. BMJ 1994; 309:1316–1317.

Thomas EJ, Cooke I. Successful treatment of asymptomatic endometriosis: does it benefit infertile women? BMJ 1987; 294:1117–1119.

The menopause

Sally Hope

10

> **THIS CHAPTER** This chapter describes the hormonal, physical and psychological changes that occur in the perimenopause, menopause and postmenopausal woman. Causes of a premature menopause are considered. The risks and possible benefits of hormone replacement therapy are discussed. Alternative treatments and lifestyle changes are analysed: the woman must make her evidence-based patient choice on all these options. Her informed choice must be recorded in her notes.

Background

Hippocrates first described the complete cessation of menstruation in an elderly (50-year-old) woman. The age of the menopause has not changed over 2000 years, or across the world in different cultures, although the age of menarche has got earlier. The French physician Brown-Sequard (1817–1894) suggested that testes and ovaries produced 'internal secretions' that were capable of rejuvenating people who took the extracts. Organotherapy caused much notoriety, and it was unscrupulously exploited. Ludwig Fraenkel was the first to try ovarian therapy in Berlin in 1896. In the 20th century, endocrinologists elucidated the functions of hormones for the first time. In 1922, Allen and Doisy extracted a substance from pig ovaries, which was renamed oestrin by Alan Parkes. By 1929, 20 mg of pure estrone had been extracted from 2000 litres of pregnant mares' urine. Four tons of sows' ovaries were required for the first extraction of a mere 12 mg of estradiol.

Follicle-stimulating hormone (FSH) and luteinizing hormone (LH) of the pituitary and their effect on the ovary to mature a follicle and the role of oestrogen and progesterone were then described. By the 1960s, the synthetic production of oestrogen allowed manipulation of the female cycle and hormonal extension beyond the menopause. It was discovered that unopposed oestrogens given to menopausal women caused uterine cancer. The combined preparations of hormone replacement therapy (HRT) have been used extensively for 30 years. The long-term risks from taking HRT are still being monitored in large prospective trials such as the Million Women Study in the UK. There is a billion pound market in vitamins and herbal remedies for women in the menopause and postmenopause but there are few evidence-based papers on their efficacy.

Definitions

Perimenopause

The perimenopause includes the period beginning with the first clinical, biological and endocrinological features of the approaching menopause, such as vasomotor symptoms and menstrual irregularity, and ends 12 months after the last menstrual period.

Menopause

The menopause is the permanent cessation of menstruation resulting from loss of ovarian follicular activity.

Natural menopause is recognized to have occurred after 12 consecutive months of amenorrhoea for which there is no other obvious pathological or physiological cause.

A premature menopause is defined as a true menopause in a woman under 45 years of age.

Postmenopause

Postmenopause should be defined as dating from the final menstrual period, regardless of whether the menopause was induced or spontaneous. However, as noted above, it cannot be determined until after a period of 12 months of spontaneous amenorrhoea.

Problems with the definitions

The definition of the natural menopause can cause confusion for some women who are waiting for their next period but are uncertain as to when the last one was.

In practice, all the definitions have drawbacks for many modern women, which make it difficult to determine their menopausal status, as they may:

- Be taking oral contraception or HRT: both give withdrawal bleeds.
- Have been fitted with a levonorgestrel intrauterine contraceptive system: this causes amenorrhoea.
- Have had a hysterectomy or an endometrial ablation: both cause a cessation of periods.

THE MENOPAUSE

The average life-expectancy at birth of a woman in the UK is now 83 years. She will therefore spend on average 30 years in her postmenopausal state (Fig. 10.1) and must understand the long-term sequelae of oestrogen lack. Most women view the menopause as a natural milestone in their lives, but over the last 15 years women have been wishing to discuss the pros and cons of HRT and the consequences of the menopause with their doctor. Even over a 5-year period this changed radically: in 1994, approximately 50% of women in the UK sought information from any health professional, whereas, by 1998, 75% of perimenopausal women had asked for information. Approximately 20% of women go on to try HRT, which means that 80% choose not to take medication.

Contraception

Many women do not realize that they are still fertile in their late forties and early fifties. There is a very high rate of abortion in this age group for unwanted pregnancies. There is also a high risk of the baby having trisomy 21, and greater risks to the mother if she decides to continue the pregnancy. A women must use contraception for 2 years after her

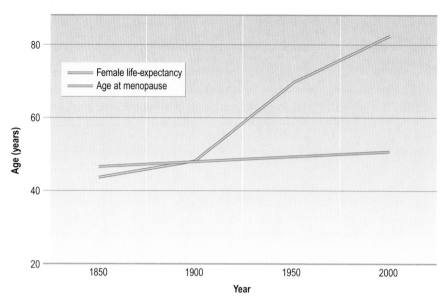

Figure 10.1
Graph showing how life-expectancy in women has changed since 1850.

periods stop if she is under 50 years of age, and 1 year after the menopause if she is over 50, as there may still be the occasional ovular cycle. (See Ch. 8.)

Ovarian failure

The menopause is caused by ovarian failure. The age of menopause may be determined *in utero* since growth restriction in late gestation and low weight gain in infancy may be associated with an earlier menopause. It also occurs earlier in women with Down's syndrome and 2–3 years earlier in smokers.

In premenopausal women, ovarian function is controlled by the two pituitary gonadotrophins follicle-stimulating hormone (FSH) and luteinizing hormone (LH). FSH is itself controlled primarily by the pulsatile secretion of hypothalamic gonadotrophin-releasing hormone (GnRH), and is modulated by the negative feedback of the ovarian steroid hormones estradiol and progesterone and the ovarian peptide inhibin. LH is under the principal control of GnRH, with negative feedback control from estradiol and progesterone for most of the cycle and positive estradiol feedback generating the mid-cycle LH surge, which in turn triggers ovulation (Fig. 10.2).

The ovary has only a limited number of oocytes which is determined *in utero*. The ovary gradually becomes less responsive to gonadotrophins several years before the menopause. FSH and LH gradually rise, with a decrease in estradiol and inhibin levels. This is the perimenopause when women start experiencing intermittent symptoms.

FSH levels fluctuate so wildly during the perimenopause that it is pointless measuring them (Fig. 10.3). As the ovaries fail, anovular cycles occur; estradiol production from the

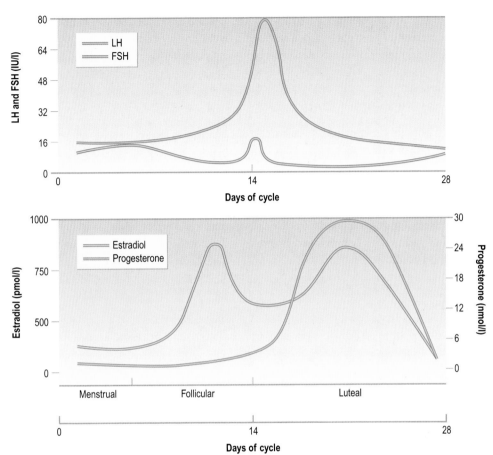

Figure 10.2
Gonadotrophin (LH and FSH), estradiol and progesterone levels during the menstrual cycle.

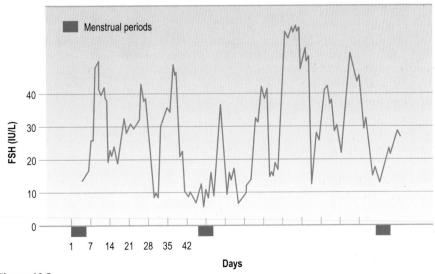

Figure 10.3
FSH levels around the menopause. Reproduced, with permission, from Management of the Menopause. The Handbook of the British Menopause Society 2002 Rees M and Purdie DW (eds).

granulosa and theca cells surrounding the oocyte is no longer sufficient to stimulate the endometrium. Eventually amenorrhoea permanently occurs. FSH levels greater than 30 IU/L are generally considered to be in the postmenopausal range.

Primary premature ovarian failure

This can occur at any age. It can present as primary or secondary amenorrhoea. In the great majority of women no cause can be found. Spontaneous ovarian activity may recur with the resulting fertility implications.

Chromosome abnormalities

X chromosome mosaicisms are the most common abnormality in women with premature ovarian failure. In Turner's syndrome (45,XO) accelerated follicular loss causes ovarian failure. Familial premature ovarian failure has been linked with fragile X permutations. Women with Down's syndrome (trisomy 21) have an early menopause.

Autoimmune disease

Hypothyroidism, Addison's disease and diabetes may be associated with premature ovarian failure.

FSH receptor abnormalities

Mutations of gonadotrophin receptors have been reported.

Disruption of oestrogen synthesis

Specific deficiencies of enzymes such as 17α-hydroxylase can prevent estradiol synthesis leading to primary amenorrhoea and elevated gonadotrophin levels even though developing follicles are present.

Metabolic

Galactosaemia is associated with premature ovarian failure.

Secondary premature ovarian failure

New techniques to conserve ovarian tissue/oocytes must be considered before undertaking toxic treatments and should help with future fertility.

Radiotherapy and chemotherapy

Chemotherapy can cause either temporary or permanent ovarian damage, depending on the cumulative dose received and duration of treatment; long-term treatment with small doses are more toxic than short-term acute therapy. These effects occur at all ages, but especially so in women aged more than 30 years. Radiotherapy is age-, dose- and directed site-dependent in its toxicity.

Bilateral oophorectomy

A surgical menopause results in an immediate menopause. The full extent of the symptoms and risks of increased mortality and morbidity must be discussed with the woman prior to surgery.

Hysterectomy without oophorectomy

This can induce ovarian failure either in the immediate postoperative period (due to surgical disruption of the ovarian artery, where in some cases it may be temporary), or at a later stage where it may occur within 2 years of the surgery. It may depend on ovarian function preceding hysterectomy. The diagnosis can be difficult since not all women suffer acute symptoms, and the lack of a uterus has removed the woman's usual marker for ovarian function. A case can be made for annual FSH estimation in women who have had a hysterectomy before the age of 45 years.

Infection

Tuberculosis and mumps may affect the ovaries. In most cases, normal ovarian function occurs after mumps infection.

Risks of premature menopause

Women with untreated premature menopause are at increased risk of developing osteoporosis and cardiovascular disease, but are at a lower risk of breast malignancy. The cause of premature ovarian failure should always be sought (chromosome analysis, autoantibody screen) and replacement therapy offered unless there is a contraindication.

Acute menopausal symptoms

Around 70% of women in Western cultures will experience vasomotor symptoms such as hot flushes and night sweats. It is interesting to speculate why 30% of women who go through the same hormonal changes seem to have no symptoms whatsoever. Some women also report tiredness, depressed mood, loss of libido and confidence, lethargy, arthralgia and short-term memory loss (Box 10.1).

Box 10.1: Consequences of the menopause

Short-term consequences

- Hot flushes and sweats
- Vaginal dryness
- Mood changes

Long-term consequences

- Osteoporosis
- Pelvic floor dysfunction
- ? Alzheimer's disease
- ? Cardiovascular disease

Vasomotor symptoms

Hot flushes and night sweats can occur in the perimenopause, but are usually most troublesome in the first year post menopause. Sympathetic nervous control of skin blood flow is impaired, with inappropriate heat loss. The mechanism is not understood, but serotonin and its receptors in the central nervous system must be involved as selective serotonin reuptake inhibitors (SSRIs) stop hot flushes.

Sexual dysfunction

Libido declines in both men and women with increasing age, but is more pronounced in postmenopausal women. Female sexual dysfunction has four recognized components:

- Decreased sexual desire.
- Decreased sexual arousal.
- Dyspareunia.
- Inability to achieve orgasm.

Sexual changes can be caused by hormonal and non-hormonal factors. Vaginal dryness from declining oestrogen levels can cause dyspareunia. Reduced oestrogen levels can impair peripheral sensory perception. However, non-hormonal factors, such as conflict between partners, insomnia, inadequate stimulation, life stress or depression, are important contributors to a woman's level of interest in sexual activity. In addition, male sexual problems (e.g. loss of libido or erectile difficulties) should not be overlooked.

Psychological symptoms

Psychological symptoms have been associated with the menopause, including depressed mood, anxiety, irritability, mood swings, lethargy and lack of energy.

Oestrogen receptors in the brain imply a biochemical basis for some psychological symptoms of the menopause as well as postpuerpural psychosis and premenstrual syndrome (see Chapter 11).

Prospective epidemiological studies suggest that psychological problems reported during the menopause are more likely to be associated with past problems and current life stresses (Box 10.2) than stage of the menopause. Treatments may include counselling, psychological therapy, HRT, or antidepressants, depending on the concerns and expectations of each individual woman.

Long-term complications of the menopause

The long-term complications of the menopause (Box 10.1) may have greater bearing on a woman's quality and quantity of life than the acute short-term symptoms. Most women do not appreciate that these long-term sequelae of cardiovascular disease (Fig. 10.4), osteoporosis and pelvic floor laxity are linked to the menopause she experienced 30 years previously.

Box 10.2: Stress factors around the menopause

- Ageing parents and their possible increasing dependency
- Death of a parent, relative or friend
- Loss of partner through death, separation or divorce
- Lack of social support
- Educational or marital difficulties of teenage/adult offspring
- Personal ill-health
- Career
- Economic problems
- Coming to terms with ageing in a culture that values youth and fertility
- Vasomotor instability leading to sleep problems and tiredness

Courtesy of the Editor of the Handbook of the British Menopause Society.

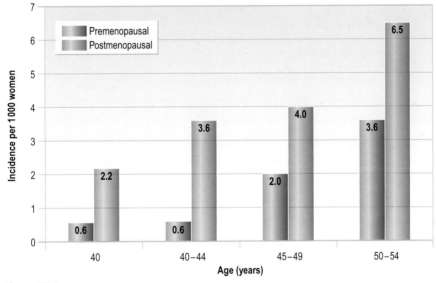

Figure 10.4
Annual incidence of cardiovascular disease per 1000 women by menopausal status. Adapted, with permission, from Kanel WB, et al. Annals of Internal Medicine 1978; 85:447–452.

The main causes of death in women over the age of 50 years in England and Wales in 2000 were heart disease and stroke (Fig. 10.5), as in other Western countries. The number of deaths attributable to osteoporosis and Alzheimer's disease are probably underestimates because these are often not accurately reported on death certificates, especially where 'old age' is given as the cause of death.

Osteoporosis

Osteoporosis is the silent plague of the 21st century Women who have a premature menopause will be at risk of early osteoporosis. A normal 50-year-old woman has a 40%

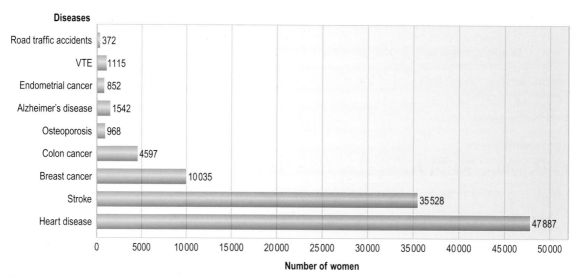

Figure 10.5
Total mortality statistics of UK women by death certificates. Office of National Statistics 2001 Series DH2 no. 27 (total deaths 268 300). VTE, venous thromboembolism.

lifetime risk of fragility fracture, usually in the femoral neck, vertebrae or distal forearm. This has a huge economic effect in the UK, where hip fractures account for 20% of orthopaedic bed occupancy with a 20% mortality in the first year. It has been estimated that direct hospital costs of fractures in England and Wales are over £220 million, of which 90% is accounted for by hip fracture. One in three women will have osteoporosis by the time they are 80 years of age.

HRT can have a bone-sparing effect (see Box 10.3). However, despite the effectiveness of HRT in preventing osteoporosis, the Committee on Safety of Medicines (2003) has concluded that HRT should no longer be recommended as first-line therapy for preventing osteoporosis, due to the increased breast cancer risk on the very long-term treatment required to have a lasting effect on bone metabolism.

Box 10.3: Minimum bone-sparing doses of HRT (daily dose unless otherwise stated)

Conjugated equine oestrogen: 0.3–0.625 mg

Estradiol, tablet: 1–2 mg

Estradiol, patch: 25–50 mcg

Estradiol, gel: 1–5 g, depending on preparation

Estradiol, implant: 50 mg (6-monthly)

Norethisterone: 5–15 mg

Tibolone: 2.5 mg

Note: these are the accepted bone-sparing doses for the average perimenopausal woman in her early fifties. There is increasing evidence that even lower doses have a significant bone-sparing effect in women in their seventies, eighties and nineties.

There are effective non-hormonal treatments for osteoporosis, such as bisphosphonates and calcium plus vitamin D. Bisphosphonates can cause indigestion, and the calcium and vitamin D tablets are difficult to chew if you have false teeth.

It is uncertain how long bisphosphonates should be continued, and there are no long-term safety data.

HORMONE-REPLACEMENT THERAPY

Putting HRT into perspective: evidence-based patient choice

Only 17–25% of British women take HRT and up to 51% of them stop HRT within a year. The lapsed users are often unaware of other possible HRT treatments that might have suited them better, and 38% of the lapsed users stop all medication without ever going back to see their doctor to discuss other options.

A survey of 393 women aged 45–65 years found that women took HRT for symptomatic relief of menopausal symptoms. They were not interested in the possible long-term prophylactic benefit against osteoporosis.

In a consultation, it is essential that women understand both the pros and the cons of whichever decision they make. This is known as evidence-based patient choice. The woman must make up her own mind and understand her decision in terms of risks and benefits. This is important for concordance in a consultation and for medicolegal reasons. The issues discussed, the risks and benefits of taking, or not taking, HRT and the woman's decision must be recorded in her notes.

The different forms of HRT

There is a wide range of different methods of providing the body with oestrogens and progestogens (Box 10.4).

Box 10.4: Forms of hormone replacement therapy

Oestrogens

- Tablets
- Patch
- Transdermal gel
- Implants
- Nasal spray
- Vaginal ring for systemic use
- Local vaginal pessaries, local vaginal creams, pessaries, rings, tablets

Progestogens

- Tablets
- Patch
- Levonorgestrel intrauterine system

Tablets

In the main, women who take HRT seem to prefer the simplicity of taking a tablet.

Various preparations of oral estradiol, estriol and conjugated equine oestrogens are available in tablet form, either on their own or with various doses of progestogen. Hormone is absorbed through the gut into the hepatic portal circulation where 30% is metabolized by the first-past effect.

Oral preparations cause nausea, and the hormonal blood levels achieved depend on each woman's individual metabolism. Moreover, oral preparations should be avoided in women:

- With active liver disease.
- Who are taking other hepatic enzyme-inducing drugs.
- Who may have malabsorption.

Transdermal preparations

Patches

The advantage of patches is that they provide a more constant absorption of hormone than when given by mouth. Different patches use different adhesives; thus one patch may suit one woman and a different manufacturer's patch on the same woman will drop off or give her an allergic reaction. Similarly, care should be taken when prescribing for women who have very thin fragile skin (e.g. from long-term diabetes, old age or steroid use). It is a good idea to use placebo patches for women to try out.

Patches should be applied below the waistline, usually to alternate buttocks. Some women find the black marks remaining after the patch is removed embarrassing, and they can be difficult to erase. Some patches need to be replaced every 3–4 days, which is not always easy to remember; others last up to 7 days. There is also a wide variety of hormone strengths; in general, young women need a larger dose than very old women do.

Gels

There are two different formulations of oestrogen gel that can be rubbed onto the skin of the forearms or legs and allowed to dry. The advantage of a gel is that it is easier to titrate a dose that is precisely suited to a particular woman at a particular time in her life. Some women take readily to rubbing in a gel as part of their daily routine; others find it irksome. It therefore needs to be discussed with the woman whether this method of application will suit her.

Implants

Estradiol implants (25, 50 or 100 mg) can be inserted into the subcutaneous fat. Some gynaecologists also recommend small doses of testosterone to alleviate fatigue and improve libido. The advantage of an implant is that the woman does not have to remember to take daily medication.

The disadvantage of implants is tachyphylaxis. They can supply supraphysiological levels of oestrogen and, as these levels decline, the woman experiences the return of hot flushes even when the hormone level is still well above the physiological norm, leading the woman to request further implants at increasingly shorter intervals. Each implant also causes a small scar which cannot easily be removed. There are no data on whether women with supraphysiological oestrogen levels have a higher risk of breast cancer or venous thromboembolism (VTE).

Nasal preparations

There is a new oestrogen nasal spray that is used once in the morning. It gives a high oestrogen peak, which then drops. In the trials published so far, this preparation appears to be effective in reducing menopausal symptoms; further data are awaited.

Vaginal preparations

Local

Not all women who seek help for vaginal dryness, dyspareunia or increased incidence of urinary tract infections wish to take systemic HRT. Several trials have shown that intravaginal estriol creams significantly reduce the number of recurrent urinary tract infections in postmenopausal women. There are low-dose estradiol or estriol preparations that are not systemically absorbed and can be given long term, either as cream, pessary or a vaginal ring.

There is significant systemic absorption of synthetic and conjugated equine oestrogens with these preparations, so their use cannot be advocated in women with an intact uterus as endometrial hyperplasia can potentially be a problem.

If any postmenopausal bleeding occurs it should be investigated as for any other postmenopausal bleeding.

Systemic

The new vaginal rings, which are specifically designed for systemic use of oestrogen HRT, appear to be useful.

Levonorgestrel-releasing intrauterine system

The levonorgestrel-releasing intrauterine system (IUS) is ideal for women in the perimenopause who have menorrhagia and require contraception (it is licensed for 5 years' contraceptive use). For some women who are unable to tolerate any other sort of progestogen it can be used as the progestogenic part of HRT together with an oestrogen (although it does not currently have a licence for this purpose, it is now widely accepted safe practice to use it in this way). The advantage of this preparation is that it is essentially a true 'no-bleed' regimen, 90% of women experiencing amenorrhoea within a year of insertion of the device. There is no published breast cancer incidence data.

It is extremely effective as a contraceptive with 0.15 pregnancies per 100 woman-years.

The disadvantages of the levonorgestrel IUS are perforation and expulsion. It is sometimes difficult to insert the device in women with a tight cervical canal resulting from previous surgery, nulliparity or atrophy. There is interest in a smaller device, but this is not yet available.

Risks and benefits of HRT

HRT is a controversial area. The randomized Women's Health Initiative (WHI) was designed in the early 1990s to work out ways of preventing and controlling some of the most common causes of morbidity and mortality among healthy postmenopausal women aged 50–79 years. As well as HRT, it also considered calcium and vitamin D supplementation and diets with low fat content. The oestrogen and progestogen part of the trial that has been stopped after 5 years because the risk of invasive breast cancer exceeded the predetermined safety threshold. The oestrogen-alone data has shown no increased breast cancer risk after 5 years. The Million Women Study obtained information from women aged 50–64 years attending the NHS breast screening programme (NHSBSP) in the UK. It is essential to assess studies critically and not to extrapolate the results of a single study to all menopausal women. Points to consider include:

- The appropriateness of the dose/regimen for the age group studied.
- The preparation and route of administration of therapy, since these may have different metabolic effects.
- The age and health profile of the population studied.

Breast cancer

Breast cancer is the most common women's cancer, with a 50-year-old having a 1 in 10 chance of developing this form of cancer during her remaining lifetime. The risk of breast cancer appears to be related to the duration of combined hormone treatment, if counted from the age of 50 years when the average natural menopause would occur (Fig. 10.6). Women with a late menopause at 54 years have a much higher risk of breast cancer than those who have a natural menopause at the age of 46 years (Fig. 10.7). Fat women are twice as likely to develop breast cancer than thin women because of the high level of sex steroids produced in adipose tissue.

Although breast cancer is the most common women's cancer, it will kill 3.7% over the age of 50 years, whereas cardiovascular disease is responsible for 31% of female deaths. It has been shown that women worry about breast cancer but are not so concerned about suffering a heart attack or a stroke; it is important, therefore, when discussing the risks of HRT, that a woman understands the relative risks of these two diseases (see Box 10.5 and Table 10.1).

Several studies, including the Million Women Study and WHI, have shown that progestogen addition increases breast cancer risk compared with oestrogen alone. However, this has to

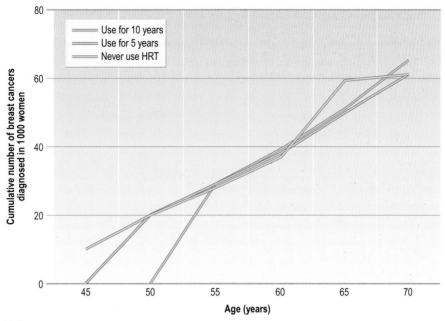

Figure 10.6
Estimated cumulative number of breast cancers diagnosed in 1000 women who never use HRT, 1000 women who use HRT for 5 years and 1000 women who use HRT for 10 years. Reproduced, with permission, from the Collaborative Group on Hormonal Factors in Breast Cancer. Lancet 1997; 350:1047–1059.

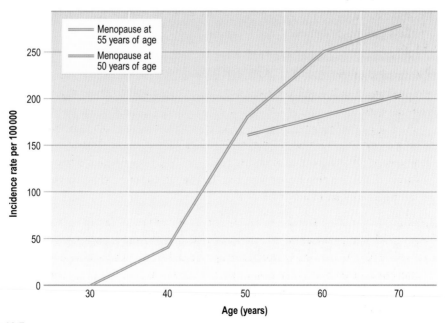

Figure 10.7
Predicted effect of late menopause on breast cancer risk. Reproduced, with permission, from Key TJA, et al. European Journal of Cancer and Clinical Oncology (now European Journal of Cancer) 1988; 24:29–43.

Box 10.5: The increased risk of breast cancer on taking HRT

Taking HRT will increase the incidence of breast cancer occurring after 10 years of use by a relative risk of 1.23. The extra risk per year is:

- 2 in 1000 extra cancers after 5 years of HRT use
- 6 in 1000 extra cancers after 10 years of HRT use
- 12 in 1000 extra cancers after 15 years of HRT use

Table 10.1 Estimated numbers (per 1000 women exposed) of extra breast cancers with unopposed or combined HRT use for 2-, 5- and 10-year treatment

	Duration of HRT exposure		
	2 years	5 years	10 years
Unopposed oestrogen	0.7	2	5
Combined HRT	2	8	22

be balanced against the reduction in risk of endometrial cancer provided by combined therapy. Irrespective of the type of HRT prescribed, breast cancer risk falls after cessation of use, the risk after 5 years from cessation being no greater than that in women who have never been exposed to HRT.

As with previous meta-analyses, in the Million Women Study HRT was shown to increase the relative risk (RR) of breast cancer to 1.66, but what is interesting is that there is a marked difference between HRT types:

- Unopposed oestrogen: RR 1.3, 95% confidence interval (CI) 1.21–1.40.
- Combined HRT: RR 2.0, 95% CI 1.88–2.12.
- Tibolone: RR 1.4, 95% CI 1.25–1.68.

Compared with past HRT users, current use of HRT carried an increase risk of breast cancer mortality: RR 1.22, 95% CI 1.00–1.48.

The degree of risk from the Million Women Study contrasts with the large placebo-controlled WHI study from America. In the WHI study, the hazard ratio for invasive and in situ breast cancer was 1.24 (95% CI 1.02–1.5) after 5.6 years follow-up on continuous combined conjugated equine oestrogens 0.625 mg+medroxyprogesterone acetate 2.5 mg. There was no increased risk in the oestrogen-alone arm of the trial in contrast to the data from the Million Women Study.

It is unlikely that randomized controlled trials will ever be large enough to reliably estimate the effect of HRT on mortality, but observational studies do not show an adverse outcome.

Current sufferers from breast cancer are usually thought to have an absolute contraindication of HRT. A large multicentre trial for breast cancer women and HRT (coordinated by the Royal Marsden Hospital in London) is ongoing; this will not publish its results until about 2005. In small studies, current breast cancer sufferers showed increased mortality or morbidity, but an increase in feelings of well-being on HRT.

Healthcare professionals should encourage women to perform breast self-examination and to commit themselves to mammography under the national screening programme, whatever they choose to do about HRT. Since most breast cancers are discovered in the elderly population and the decision to stop mammography at age 65 years is purely an economic one, it is also up to the medical practitioner to think whether mammograms after the age of 65 years are appropriate for a particular patient and discuss this with her.

Venous thromboembolism

There is an increased risk of deep vein thrombosis and consequent pulmonary thromboembolism, which might be life-threatening, from any additional oestrogens. This is true for the oral contraceptive pill, pregnancy, selective oestrogen receptor modulators (SERMs) and HRT.

HRT increases risk of VTE twofold, with the highest risk occurring in the first year of use. The baseline risk in menopausal women is of the order of 1 in 10 000 per year; the mortality is 1–2%. Advancing age and obesity significantly increase risk. The absolute rate increase is 1.5 VTE events per 10 000 women in 1 year.

A history of VTE is the single biggest risk factor for future VTE and is therefore a strong contraindication to HRT. A clotting screen can be justified in these women as often they had deep vein thrombosis prior to the discovery in 1993 of factor V Leiden. However, it must be remembered that a negative thrombophilia screen should not give false reassurance. Women with a personal history of VTE are at high risk of recurrence even if the screen for known causes is negative, and this must be understood. Not all the genetic problems with the clotting cascade have yet been discovered.

HRT can be prescribed to women who are on long-term warfarin.

The risk of VTE disappears rapidly when HRT is stopped. Thus, if a woman on HRT is having elective surgery, the HRT could be stopped 4 weeks before surgery in discussion with the patient, the anaesthetist and the surgeon. An alternative is to continue HRT and ensure that added prophylaxis is given against VTE.

People who go on long-haul flights (longer than 6 h) appear to be at greater risk of deep vein thrombosis. It would therefore seem sensible when initially doing the consultation on HRT when deep vein thrombosis is mentioned is to add this information and provide an information leaflet on long-haul flights, advising the use of flight socks, possible low-dose aspirin (75 mg/day), avoidance of all alcohol and tranquillizing drugs and to ensure adequate hydration and exercise on the flight.

Endometrial cancer

Women with an intact uterus taking oestrogens without a progestogen are at risk of endometrial cancer. All modern HRT preparations for women with a uterus contain oestrogen and a progestogen in various combinations.

It is important to stress that the progestogenic part of the HRT is there to reduce the risk of endometrial cancer. With some of the older packaged preparations it is possible to intentionally avoid the progestogen tablets and only take the oestrogen. This is dangerous. Similarly, some women take oestrogen plus 'natural' progesterone transdermal cream in the unproven belief that it will protect their endometrium.

There is evidence that women should be changed from a sequential HRT to a continuous combined HRT once they are postmenopausal to reduce the risk of endometrial hyperplasia. If women continue on sequential HRT for many years after the menopause they have an increased risk of endometrial neoplasia which is not found with continuous combined therapy. In the WHI study, the hazard ratio for endometrial cancer with continuous combined HRT was 0.81 (95% CI 0.45–1.36) .

Ovarian cancer

Most data pertain to replacement with oestrogen alone with increasing risk in the very long term (>10 years). However, with continuous combined therapy, this increase does not seem apparent. This was also found in the combined arm of the WHI study, with a relative risk of 1.58 for HRT users (95% CI 0.77–3.24). This issue is unresolved and requires further examination; there is currently insufficient evidence to recommend alterations in HRT prescribing practice.

Weight gain

From many HRT trials, it has been determined that all women put on weight as they go through the menopause, but, in general, those on HRT put on slightly less weight than women who are not taking HRT. In addition, the fat distribution is different, with women on HRT having a gynaecoid fat distribution (increased fat at the breast and hips and a smaller waist). Women after the menopause show significantly greater amounts of intra-abdominal fat (49% more): an android fat distribution.

Osteoporosis

HRT is extremely effective at conserving bone mass. The WHI study has shown a 3.7% increase in total hip bone mineral density after 3 years of treatment with combined HRT, and a reduced risk of hip fracture. Combined HRT reduces the relative risk of hip, spine and total fractures by 33%, 35% and 24%, respectively. However, a woman who takes HRT for about 5 years in her early fifties will have virtually no benefit by the time she is 80. The CSM have advised that HRT cannot be used as a first-line treatment in osteoporosis because the long-term risks outweigh the benefits.

Cardiovascular disease (coronary heart disease and stroke)

Previously thought to be protective, the role of HRT in either primary or secondary prevention remains uncertain and it currently should not be used primarily for this indication. WHI showed an early, albeit transient, increase in coronary events. The excess absolute risk at 50–59 years was 5 cases of non-fatal myocardial infarction and death due to coronary heart disease per 10 000 women per year; at 60–69 years it was 1 case, and at 70–79 years it was 23 cases. Many previous studies failed to differentiate between ischaemic and haemorrhagic stroke: WHI found an increased risk with combined HRT with ischaemic stroke but not with the haemorrhagic stroke. This increased with age. Thus the excess absolute risk at 50–59 years was 4, at 60–69 years 9, and at 70–79 years 13 cases of stroke per 10 000 women per year. However, the timing, dose and possibly the type of HRT may be critical in determining cardiovascular effects. In women with established cardiovascular disease, who are either current or past users, the benefits of HRT to reduce symptoms may be considered in individual cases to outweigh any increased risk of further events.

Alzheimer's disease

Some 10% of women will develop dementia in retirement. Around 20% of all people with Alzheimer's disease are over the age of 80 years. It is more common in thin women than in fat women, and also more common in those who have suffered a previous myocardial infarction or hip fracture, which suggests a link with oestrogen deficiency. From observational data, the age of onset of Alzheimer's disease is later in women who have taken extra oestrogens than in women who have never taken HRT; it is also earlier in women with untreated premature menopause. These observations have led to many studies to determine whether there is a link between HRT and staving off dementia.

While oestrogen may delay or reduce the risk of Alzheimer's disease, it does not seem to improve established disease. It is unclear whether there is a critical age or duration of treatment for exposure to oestrogen to have an effect in prevention, but there may be a window of opportunity in the early postmenopause when the pathological processes that lead to Alzheimer's disease (and cardiovascular disease) are being initiated and when HRT may have a preventive effect. The most recent report from WHI found a twofold increased risk of dementia in women receiving the particular combined oestrogen and progestogen regimen. However, this increased risk was only significant in the group of women over the age of 75 years. It is not clear why these results are the opposite of earlier findings from observational studies. More evidence is required, especially from younger postmenopausal women taking appropriate doses and different regimens.

Colorectal cancer

The WHI study confirmed data from case control and cohort studies that HRT reduces the risk of colorectal cancer by about a third. However, little is known about colorectal cancer risk when treatment is stopped.

It has been argued that this shows that those who accept HRT are better educated and motivated for their own health; also, they have a higher vegetarian to meat ratio in their diet. Other authors have argued that this may be a genuine effect on the lining cells of the colon, but there are no direct data.

> **Box 10.6: Contraindications to HRT**
>
> - Cancer of the breast
> - Pregnancy
> - Undiagnosed abnormal vaginal bleeding
> - Severe active liver disease
> - Presence of deep vein thrombosis or thromboembolic disorders, unless the woman is on long-term warfarin

> **Box 10.7: Contraindications to HRT for which a specialist's advice should be sought**
>
> - Previous thromboembolic disease (or a strong family history)
> - Endometrial hyperplasia
> - Severe endometriosis
> - Fibroids
> - Liver disease or gallstones

CHOOSING THE RIGHT HRT

There are various contraindications to the use of HRT (see Box 10.6); for some indications a specialist's advice should be sought (see Box 10.7).

Hysterectomized women

Women without a uterus need only to take continuous oestrogen in any form. Hysterectomy without oophorectomy can cause a premature menopause; it has been calculated that the mean age of the menopause is advanced by approximately 4 years. The yearly recall of young (<45 years) women who have undergone hysterectomy with ovarian conservation can be done in general practice.

Women with endometriosis

This condition can present a difficult management problem since oestrogen therapy can theoretically re-activate the disease, even where there has been apparent surgical removal of all the endometriotic tissue. The risks, however, appear to be small. Women who have had pelvic clearance for endometriosis might therefore have continuous combined therapy so that the progestogen suppresses any remaining endometriotic tissue. However, this decision has to be balanced against the increased risk of breast cancer with combined HRT. The gynaecologist who performed the pelvic clearance should discuss these issues.

Perimenopausal women with an intact uterus

Women with an intact uterus must take progestogens for endometrial protection. The options available are monthly cyclic or 3-monthly cyclic regimens. While the risk of

Box 10.8: The two main groups of progestogens

Testosterone derivatives

- Norethisterone
- Norgestrel
- Levonorgestrel

Progesterone derivatives

- Hydroxyprogesterone
- Dydrogesterone
- Medroxyprogesterone acetate

Box 10.9: Side-effects of progestogens

- Bloating
- Acne
- Nausea
- Headache

- Tender breasts
- Feeling irritable
- Premenstrual syndrome

Box 10.10: Acceptable daily doses of progestogens for endometrial protection

Sequential

Norethisterone, oral: 1 mg for the last 10–14 days of a 28-day cycle

Norethisterone, patch: 170 μg or 250 μg for the last 14 days of a 28-day cycle

Levonorgestrel, oral: 75–250 μg for the last 10–12 days of a 28-day cycle

Levonorgestrel, patch: 20 μg for the last 14 days of a 28-day cycle

Norgestrel, oral: 150–500 μg for the last 10–12 days of a 28-day cycle

Medroxyprogesterone acetate, oral: 10 mg for the last 14 days of a 28-day cycle; 20 mg for the last 14 days of a 3-month cycle

Dydrogesterone, oral: 10–20 mg for the last 14 days of a 28-day cycle

Continuous

Norethisterone, oral: 0.5–1 mg

Norethisterone, patch: 170 μg

Medroxyprogesterone acetate, oral: 2.5–5.0 mg

Dydrogesterone, oral: 5 mg

Reproduced from Management of the Menopause. The Handbook of the British Menopause Society 2002 Eds Margaret Rees M and David W Purdie with permission.

endometrial cancer is reduced compared to oestrogen alone, it is not completely eliminated. Different formulations contain different progestogens (see Box 10.8) and vary in how long progestogen is included with monthly addition (i.e. during the last 10–14 days of a 28-day cycle).

Progestogens can be a problem as they cause more side-effects than oestrogens alone (see Box 10.9). Acceptable doses of the various progestogens that afford endometrial protection are detailed in Box 10.10. If, after trying a preparation for 16 weeks, the side-effects of progestogen are unacceptable (usually the side-effects settle down), changing to a less androgenic progestogen can sometimes work.

There is a 3-monthly cyclical treatment of 70 days of oestrogen followed by 14 days of combined oestrogen plus medroxyprogesterone acetate 20 mg for the last 14 days of the cycle. Women may have erratic bleeding with this regimen. Some women on the cusp of the menopause prefer four withdrawal bleeds in a year.

Patches, or the levonorgestrel IUS are alternative options that might be acceptable. The levonorgestrel IUS is very useful for the perimenopausal woman who needs contraception but does not want withdrawal bleeds.

Continuous combined regimens are not suitable for perimenopausal women who still have ovarian activity, as they will experience erratic bleeding.

Postmenopausal women with an intact uterus

During the last few years, many different preparations of continuous combined HRT have been introduced. If oestrogen plus progestogen is taken daily without a break in the same dosage, the endometrium becomes atrophied and no bleeding occurs. There is also a lower risk of endometrial hyperplasia and cancer than in the control population. Many women have welcomed these postmenopausal 'no-bleed' regimens. There are now also lower-dose preparations, which appear to have a much better 'no-bleed' profile than the old higher-dose preparations and also seem to have fewer side-effects.

There is controversy about when women should be referred for endometrial assessment if they bleed postmenopausally on a continuous combined preparation. Referral is only necessary if bleeding happens after prolonged (1 year) amenorrhoea.

Women who have had an endometrial resection

Progestogen must be given to women who have undergone endometrial ablative techniques since it cannot be assumed that all the endometrium has been removed, even if prolonged amenorrhoea has been achieved. Whether to give a sequential or a continuous combined regimen depends on whether the woman is menstruating or not.

Tibolone

Tibolone is a synthetic steroid that combines oestrogenic and progestogenic activity with weak androgenic actions. It is the only HRT currently licensed for increasing libido. It does not cause bleeding and is licensed for postmenopausal use. The Million Women Study found an increased risk of breast cancer (RR 1.4).

Older women

Women in their sixties, seventies, eighties and nineties are now asking about HRT. As the relative fear of getting breast cancer reduces and the relative chance of hip fracture increases, older women are more interested in taking effective medication. The newer lower-dose continuous combined regimens are suitable for these older women.

Some older women prefer to have the local vaginal oestrogen preparations for the problems of urogenital ageing, rather than systemic HRT.

Other options for older women

Tamoxifen was the original SERM, but raloxifene is currently the only SERM on the market, although others are being developed. Raloxifene was developed with the idea that it would have the benefits of lowering the risks of breast cancer while preventing bone loss. It reduces the risk of fracture at the spine but not at the hip. Raloxifene can cause hot flushes. It does not cause bleeding. It does, however, have exactly the same increased risk of thromboembolic events as conventional HRT.

Advice on healthy lifestyle, exercise, adequate calcium intake or calcium and vitamin D tablets and options such as bisphosphonates must also be discussed with older women. Alendronate and risedronate reduce the risk of fracture at both the spine and hip and now have the advantage of once-weekly formulations. Parathyroid hormone is to be considered in cases of severe osteoporosis. Strontium will become available in 2005.

ALTERNATIVES TO HRT

Herbal remedies

Many women do not want medication during the menopause and may ask for advice about herbal remedies. These are all over-the-counter preparations that are not on prescription and the evidence of efficacy is poor. Many women are lulled into the belief that, because the product states it is 'natural', it must be safe, effective and beneficial.

Black kohosh   This has been certified by the German Commission E to have a favourable risk/benefit ratio for use in 'climacteric neurovegetative complaints'. It is thought to act like a phytoestrogen.

St John's wort   St John's wort is an antidepressant, and has been tested in randomized controlled trials. A recent study of menopausal women in primary care showed that climacteric complaints diminished or disappeared completely in the majority of women. Sexual well-being also improved after treatment with St John's wort extract. It is a liver enzyme inducer, and could potentially interact with HRT, and does interact with many other medications.

Ginseng   A recent randomized, multicentre, double-blind, parallel group, placebo-controlled trial showed only a slightly better overall symptomatic relief ($P<0.1$) than placebo. Subset analysis reported P-values <0.05 for depression and well-being in favour of ginseng compared with placebo, but no statistically significant effect for vasomotor symptoms.

Phytoestrogens

Phytoestrogens are phenolic compounds found in plants such as soy and red clover that become biologically active when digested in mammalian gut. They are structurally similar to mammalian oestrogens but have a very weak oestrogenic activity (if estradiol has a

195

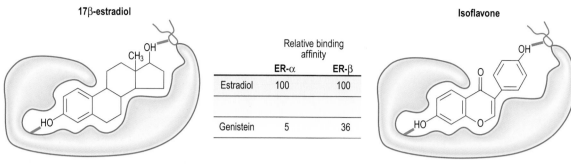

	Relative binding affinity	
	ER-α	ER-β
Estradiol	100	100
Genistein	5	36

Figure 10.8
How phytoestrogens may work on the oestrogen receptor. Courtesy of Novogen.

> **Box 10.11: Why women do not want to take HRT**
>
> - Not wishing to take medication for a natural part of one's life
> - Fear of side-effects, especially weight gain
> - Fear of deep vein thrombosis or pulmonary embolism
> - Fear of breast cancer

potency of 100, genistein has a relative potency of 0.084, equol of 0.0161 and diadzen of 0.013; Fig. 10.8). There is interest in epidemiological data to show that women who have diets high in phytoestrogens such as soya bean or dhal have fewer menopausal symptoms and lower rates of breast and uterine cancer.

GIVING ADVICE ON HRT

It is an interesting challenge to give a woman a consultation about the menopause and the pros and cons of HRT with a calm, evidence-based approach. This is partly because women themselves have very different views about the menopause and whether or not they wish to take medication (see Box 10.11 and Figs 10.9, 10.10), and there are many different cultural views and regional variations. Also much of the evidence that we would want to have at our fingertips is not available at present, and some major prospective trials, for example the WHI and the Million Women Study, will not have their full datasets published for many years. It is difficult to explain within the confines of a short consultation that a lot of the data is poor, or that there are significant design faults with some of the major well-publicized trials.

The most important thing in an HRT consultation is to give women their own evidence-based choice on what they want to do. For some, the choice is finely balanced, so all the advantages and disadvantages of both taking and not taking HRT must be clearly delineated (Fig. 10.11). If a woman chooses HRT, she should be given a clear choice as

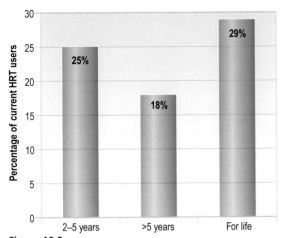

Figure 10.9
Response of current HRT users to the question: 'How long do you expect to take HRT?'

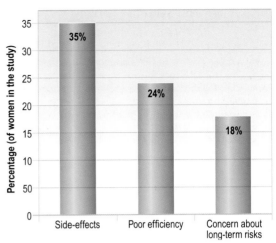

Figure 10.10
Response of previous HRT users to the question: 'Why did you stop using HRT?'

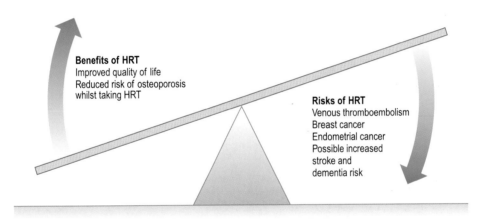

Figure 10.11
Long-term HRT: weighing up the facts.

to which preparation she would feel most comfortable with. This should be recorded in the notes. This is not only good practice, but should prevent litigation at a later date. In the survey of 393 women, 96% believed they should be involved in the decision as to whether they should receive HRT, and 93% wanted to say which formulation was prescribed.

The UK Committee on the Safety of Medicines (CSM, March 2001) advises that clinical breast and pelvic examinations are not routinely necessary in all women taking HRT, but should be performed if clinically indicated. This is because clinical breast and pelvic examinations do not have a sufficiently high sensitivity or specificity to be used for screening in well, asymptomatic women. The CSM advises that breast screening by

---

Box 10.12: Checklist for the consultation

- Woman understands pros and cons of HRT
- Woman has made her evidence-based patient choice
- Check risk factors for osteoporosis, venous thromboembolism, breast cancer
- Check that blood pressure, smear and mammogram are up-to-date
- Weigh patient
- Let patient choose the preparation option
- Arrange follow-up
- Document above in notes

Box 10.13: Some useful addresses

British Menopause Society	4–6 Eton Place Marlow SL7 2QA Tel: 01628 890199	www.the-bms.org
National Osteoporosis Society	Camerton Bath BA2 0PJ Tel: 01761 471771	www.nos.org.uk info@nos.org.uk

---

mammography be encouraged in all women between the ages of 50 and 64 years. Women over the age of 64 years are eligible for 3-yearly mammographic screening on request. However, women must know, understand and accept the extra risk of breast cancer if they take HRT. This must be written down in their medical notes. Women should also be encouraged to participate in the national cervical screening programme between the ages of 25 and 64 years. (See Ch. 7.)

Box 10.12 provides a checklist of points to be covered in the consultation and Box 10.13 gives some useful addresses.

Options for women who do not want to take HRT for hot flushes

Many women want symptomatic relief from hot flushes and do not wish to, or cannot, take HRT. There are many herbal or dietary alternatives (see p. 195). Some women find clonidine 50 µg 1–2 tds helpful, but data on its efficacy are poor.

Selective serotonin reuptake inhibitors   Recent data suggest that some of the SSRI antidepressants (e.g. paroxetine or venlafaxine) may help to reduce hot flush scores significantly. It should be made clear to the patient that this is not related to the antidepressant effect but that there is an interaction between serotonin pathways and the hot flush mechanism. This treatment can be particularly helpful to women who are taking tamoxifen. Often a low dose, such as venlafaxine 37.5 mg at night, is sufficient to relieve symptoms of night flushes within a few days.

FUTURE DIRECTIONS   Over the next few years, more data will be published from the Women's Health Initiative and the Million Women Study to help discussion of risks and benefits of different treatments for the menopause.

The small levonorgestrel intrauterine releasing system for use as the progestogenic part of HRT might be marketed. There are new SERMs that are also going to become available. Intravenous bisphosphonates that would avoid the risk of gastrointestinal irritation are in development.

Selected References and Further Reading

Beral V. Breast cancer and hormone replacement therapy: a collaborative analysis of data from 51 epidemiological studies of 52,705 women with breast cancer and 108,411 women without breast cancer. Lancet 1997; 350:1047–1059.

Cauley JA, Robbins J, Chen Z, et al. Effects of estrogen plus progestin on risk of fracture and bone mineral density: The Women's Health Initiative Randomized Trial. JAMA 2003;290 1729–1738.

Committee on the Safety of Medicines. Further advice on safety of HRT: risk–benefit unfavourable for first-line use in prevention of osteoporosis. CEM/CMO/2003/19.

Hoibraaten E, Qvigstad E, Arnesen H, et al. Increased risk of recurrent venous thromboembolism during hormone replacement therapy: results of the randomized, double-blind, placebo-controlled estrogen in venous thromboembolism trial (EVTET). Thromb Haemost 2000; 84:961–967.

Hope S, Wager E, Rees M. Survey of British women's views on the menopause and HRT. J Br Menopause Soc 1998; 4:33–36.

Loprinzi CL, Kluger JW, Sloane JA, et al. Venlafaxine in the management of hot flushes in survivors of breast cancer. A randomised controlled trial. Lancet 2000; 356:2059–2063.

Marsden J, Sacks N. The national randomised trial of hormone replacement therapy in women with a history of early stage breast cancer: an update. J Br Menopause Soc 2002; 8:129.

Million Women Study Collaborators. Breast cancer and hormone replacement therapy in the Million Women Study. Lancet 2003; 362:419–427.

Nelson HD, Humphrey LL, Nygren P, et al. Postmenopausal hormone replacement therapy: scientific review. JAMA 2002; 288:872–881.

Rapp SR, Espeland MA, Shumaker SA, et al. Effect of estrogen plus progestin on global cognitive function in postmenopausal women: The Women's Health Initiative Memory Study: a randomized controlled trial. JAMA 2003; 289:2663–2672.

Royal College of Physicians. Osteoporosis: clinical guidelines for prevention and treatment. Update on pharmacological interventions and an algorithm for management. London: Royal College of Physicians 2000. Available at: http://www.rcplondon.ac.uk/pubs/wp_osteo_update.htm.

SoRelle R. Second verse of HERS same as the first: no clear benefit or harm for cardiovascular disease. Circulation 2002; 105:9077–9078.

Women's Health Initiative Steering Committee. Effects of conjugated equine estrogen in postmenopausal women with hysterectomy: the WHI randomised controlled trial. JAMA 2004; 1701–1712.

Writing Group for the Women's Health Initiative Investigators. Risks and benefits of estrogen plus progestin in healthy postmenopausal women: principal results from the Women's Health Initiative randomized controlled trial. JAMA 2002; 288:321–333.

Psychological aspects of gynaecology

Fiona Blake

THIS CHAPTER This chapter considers the psychological disturbances that may be present in women seeking gynaecological help. Such problems are common, and failure to recognize and attend to them leads to poorer outcomes, dissatisfaction and increased likelihood of future presentation. Some gynaecological fields are described in which psychological problems most frequently interact with physiological issues; ways of assessing and managing this aspect of care are suggested.

Background

From earliest times, men have written about women's changing moods and behaviour and attributed them to their female anatomy and their menstrual cycle. By the 19th century, the enlightenment brought the rational scientific approach to bodily function. Anatomical dissection revealed new explanations for medical phenomena, and surgery and gynaecology developed to treat abnormality. Into the 21st century, gynaecologists continue to rely on the medical model and attribute much disturbance and distress to pathology of the reproductive system. The mechanism of action of reproductive hormones has also allowed gynaecologists to intervene physiologically.

More recently, as women have steadily fought for more control over their bodies and fertility, a broader understanding of distress is required. It is now clear that, for some gynaecological disorders such as premenstrual syndrome (PMS), psychiatric drugs may be the safest, most-effective treatment. Evidence also emerges that social and psychological factors are important in the experience of infertility, PMS, pelvic pain, menopausal complaints and sexual problems.

Nutritional and complementary treatments are also being explored for gynaecological problems, taking us back to the lore of wise women of the middle ages.

INTRODUCTION

Gynaecological experiences are closely linked with a woman's sense of well-being, and symptoms can disturb her femininity, her self-esteem, her mood and her relationships. Women presenting with gynaecological problems are often tense and anxious and sometimes distressed and tearful. Many find the discussion of intimate issues difficult and the physical examination an ordeal. The examination can remind a woman of previous threatening situations such as rape or childhood sexual abuse. Past examinations may have been painful or carried out in a rough or demeaning way.

Some conditions have overtones of moral judgement, such as termination of pregnancy or sexually transmitted disease. In these cases, anxiety and apprehension may be considerable. In addition, general distress can be presented as gynaecological complaints because there is stigma associated with mental health problems, and social and relationship problems may seem less appropriate to present to the doctor. This chapter aims to tease out some of the issues and find a coherent way to manage emotional problems associated with gynaecological events and complaints.

PRESENTATION

There are several patterns of presentation in the clinic:

- Distress secondary to a gynaecological disorder: e.g. cervical cancer.
- Psychological disorder presenting under the guise of a gynaecological complaint: e.g. depressive illness presenting as PMS.
- Psychological disorder and gynaecological disorder (which may or may not have a common aetiology): e.g. endometriosis and anxiety disorder.
- Intolerance of certain gynaecological events in the setting of particular social and relationship stressors: e.g. complaint of menorrhagia after stopping the oral contraceptive pill following marital breakdown.

GENDER DIFFERENCES IN PSYCHOLOGICAL DISORDER

Women experience more psychological problems than men do, particularly during their reproductive years. The difference in prevalence emerges at adolescence. By adulthood, 8–12% of women at any one time have anxiety or depressive illness, twice the rate in men. Marriage and pregnancy increase the risk of affective (mood) disorder, which is not explained by postnatal depression (see Box 11.1). Three factors may contribute to this excess:

Box 11.1: *Epidemiological pattern of affective (mood) disorder*

- Increase of affective disorder at adolescence to 8–12% of the female population
- Female:male ratio of 2:1
- Higher in parous women
- Pregnancy increases vulnerability
- Rate similar to that of men after 50 years of age
- Not accounted for by postnatal depression

- Psychosocial.
- Hormonal.
- Help-seeking behaviour.

Psychosocial factors

Psychosocial factors contribute to this excess and may predominate. Factors that can often cause stress in women include:

- Low social status.
- Economic dependency.
- Low wages.
- Multiple roles.
- Vulnerability to sexual and domestic violence.
- Being responsible for vulnerable members of society, particularly children and the elderly.

The role of hormones

Psychosocial factors, however, do not fully explain the gender difference in morbidity and it is likely that reproductive hormones make some contribution:

- Gonadal hormones are psychoactive, but it is not clear exactly how they influence women's emotional disorders.
- Oestrogen has antidopaminergic properties and this is most evident in the genesis of puerperal psychosis, where it is thought that a dramatic fall in oestrogen post partum precipitates manic-depressive psychosis in vulnerable women (see Box 11.2 for the role of oestrogen). It also enhances serotonin mechanisms, so it is thought to have a role in mood regulation by increasing serotonin levels and therefore elevating mood or at least enhancing wellbeing. Some randomized controlled trials (RCTs) have shown that oestrogen improved mood in premenstrual syndrome, menopausal low mood and post-oophorectomy menopausal states, but there is little evidence that depressive disorder is relieved by oestrogen.
- Progesterone modulates γ-aminobutyric acid, the neurotransmitter involved in emotional control (see Box 11.3 for the role of progesterone). It may contribute to wellbeing by some degree of anxiolytic action in large doses. Progesterone was advocated for relief of premenstrual syndrome to lift mood and reduce irritability and aggression. PMS was

---

Box 11.2: Oestrogen

- Good evidence for relief of vasomotor symptoms: e.g. hot flushes, sweating
- Some evidence for enhancement of wellbeing, relief of low mood
- Less evidence for relief of depressive illness
- Available as HRT in pills, patches or implants; RCT evidence for efficacy
- Oral contraceptive pill used for PMS; no RCTs
- Used with progestogen to prevent endometrial hyperplasia

Box 11.3: Progesterone

- First widely used as treatment for PMS
- Extraordinary claims of efficacy in early years of use
- No evidence of efficacy in most RCTs
- Unsuitable orally, so progestogens used
- Some evidence that use with oestrogen produces PMS-like symptoms
- Considered safe and natural

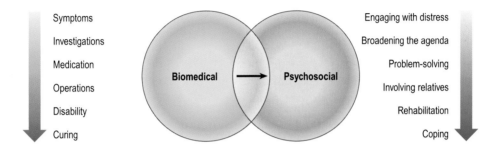

Figure 11.1
Shift from the biomedical to the psychosocial framework of care.

considered to be a progesterone-deficiency condition but no evidence has been found for this pathological mechanism and RCTs largely show placebo to be as effective as progesterone.

Women consult doctors more often

In addition, women present to doctors more readily than men with both physical and psychological problems. Many present psychological problems as physical symptoms and are looking for a physical explanation. This may be in the form of gynaecological complaints. A woman with psychological problems is less able to tolerate PMS, heavy bleeding or menopausal symptoms than usual and therefore presents to the doctor. Attention to both physical and psychological aspects of the problem is likely to offer a greater chance of appropriate management (Fig. 11.1).

PREMENSTRUAL SYNDROME

PMS is a concept that brings a medical slant to an age-old perception that women are unpredictable and emotionally unstable and that this is due to their female biology. Despite much research and media interest over the last 50 years or so, PMS remains a challenging and puzzling syndrome.

> **Box 11.4: Premenstrual syndrome**
>
> - Many symptoms linked to menstrual cycle, none specifically
> - Symptom pattern varies between cycles
> - It is crucial to establish link with menstrual cycle
> - Requires prospective symptom ratings
> - May represent a group of heterogeneous syndromes

Definition

Most women can detect physical and emotional changes that coincide with the phases of the menstrual cycle. These disturbances are very variable. Different women have different symptoms and these may vary from month to month in both type and severity. There are no biochemical or other physical markers for the condition and PMS may represent several heterogeneous syndromes (see Box 11.4).

Definition does not depend on any specific symptoms, but rather on a link with the timing of menstrual cycle events. This requires:

- The regular occurrence of symptoms in the premenstrual (luteal) phase of the cycle.
- Relief with the onset of menstruation.
- Relative lack of symptoms in the postmenstrual (follicular) phase.

Identifying a pattern

External stressors or events (e.g. moving house) may obscure a pattern, and women appear to selectively recall symptoms as associated with the premenstruum and forget or explain away symptoms at other times. This has led to the recommendation that women should keep a prospective daily symptom chart (Fig. 11.2) before the diagnosis can be confirmed. In research, this is mandatory, as it often emerges that other problems better explain the symptoms.

Three patterns emerge (see Fig. 11.3):

- 'Pure' PMS.
- Premenstrual exacerbation of an underlying disorder (such as anxiety).
- Symptoms not linked to the menstrual cycle: e.g. depressive illness or relationship stress.

Identifying anxiety and depressive disorders

In one study of women attending a clinic complaining of PMS, 59% of the subjects fulfilled criteria for anxiety or depressive disorders.

Daily Symptom Diary

Choose the four symptoms that trouble you most (e.g. irritability, depression, tiredness) and list one at the top of each column. Score these symptoms each evening as follows:

None	=	0
Mild	=	1 (present but tolerable)
Moderate	=	2 (interferes with normal activities)
Severe	=	3 (incapacitating)

Add any relevant comments about what is happening in your life in the last column. Note bleeding with an M (for menstruation) in the 'Bleeding' column

Date	Bleeding	Symptom 1	Symptom 2	Symptom 3	Symptom 4	Comments

Figure 11.2
Example of a daily symptom diary.

The strictest criteria are encompassed in the definition in the Diagnostic and Statistical Manual of Mental Disorders IV (DSM-IV) of the American Psychiatric Association. These criteria describe a condition called premenstrual dysphoric disorder (PMDD), with mainly psychological symptoms that are disabling and enduring and must be confirmed by prospective diary evidence (see Box 11.5). PMDD patients are a subset of PMS sufferers; only 3–5% of women meet such criteria.

Aetiology

There have been many hypotheses about the aetiology of PMS, each associated with particular treatments, some contradicting others. The gonadal hormones have always been at the centre of investigations; nutritional deficiencies are also popular. Some interest has been taken in psychopharmacological aetiologies, especially with the advent of fluoxetine and other selective serotonin reuptake inhibitors (SSRIs).

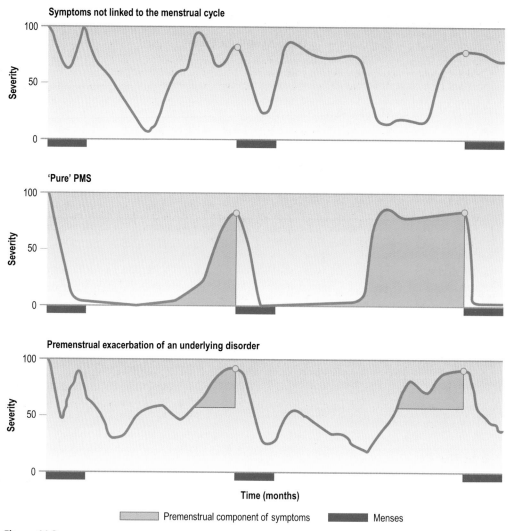

Figure 11.3

PMS symptom patterns. Severity score: 0=least severe/no symptoms; 100=most severe/disabling symptoms. Adapted, with permission, from Sampson GA. Premenstrual syndrome. Baillière's Clin Obstet Gynaecol 1989; 3:687–704.

Link with affective disorder

The link between PMS and affective disorder is strong, especially among those with PMDD (Box 11.6). Many women complaining of PMS:

- Have affective disorder.
- Have a history of affective disorder.
- Have had affective disorders associated with reproduction.
- Have exacerbation of depressive illness premenstrually.

This has lead researchers to consider PMDD as an intermittent affective disorder.

> **Box 11.5: DSM-IV definition of premenstrual dysphoric disorder (PMDD)**
>
> A. In most menstrual cycles during the past year, five (or more) of the following symptoms were present for most of the time during the last week of the luteal phase, began to remit during menses and were absent in the week post menses: low mood, hopelessness, self-deprecating thoughts; anxiety, tension, edginess; lability of mood; anger, irritability, loss of interest; poor concentration; lethargy, fatigue; overeating or cravings; hypersomnia or insomnia; feeling overwhelmed, out of control; physical symptoms e.g. breast tenderness, bloating, headaches, joint aches, weight gain
> B. Markedly disturbs work or school or other activities and relationships
> C. Disturbance is not an exacerbation of another disorder
> D. Criteria A–C must be confirmed by prospective daily symptoms ratings for at least 2 consecutive months

> **Box 11.6: Affective (mood) syndrome: premenstrual dysphoric disorder (PMDD)**
>
> - This is a subset of women with PMS
> - PMDD is a DSM-IV definition used for research
> - Premenstrual dysphoria is similar to depressive disorder
> - Severity is similar to non-menstrually related depressive disorder but is intermittent
> - Sufferers feel less hopeless, more out of control than those with depressive disorder
> - Symptoms are intermittent

Psychosocial factors

Psychosocial factors are also important. This is evident from the response of symptoms to stress, relationship difficulties and the large placebo response associated with PMS treatments.

Management

Many women complaining of PMS are unclear about what they mean by PMS or what doctors mean by it. It is thus important to:

- Take a history of the symptoms, their duration and timing.
- Ask the patient why has she chosen to present now.
- Rule out physical pathology.
- Consider the social and relationship context; often there will have been a crisis, an outburst or other life event.
- What has the patient read about the problem?
- What has she tried so far?

The cornerstones of management are:

- Education.
- Understanding.
- Support.

The woman needs to feel that the doctor has listened, taken her seriously and has shed some light on her distress. Simple explanations and encouragement to problem-solve may be enough to enable her to recover her equilibrium.

Keeping a symptom diary

If further help is required then some effort should be made to persuade her to keep a simple daily symptom diary (Fig. 11.2, p. 205). Some women find diary-keeping difficult and are unable to manage it successfully, but, for those that do, there are benefits beyond establishing the diagnosis.

The diary can:

- Give a woman a sense of control.
- Give her validation for her experiences.
- Assist in clarifying which problems can be solved.
- Be used to demonstrate the effectiveness of any prescribed intervention.

Treatment

Most pharmacological interventions are associated with a large placebo response (up to 94%), and it may take 3–4 months to establish whether a new treatment has been effective. Treatments offered should be:

- As simple as possible.
- Suitable for long-term use.
- Compatible with the woman's other needs.

See Box 11.7 for a summary of treatments used in the management of PMS.

Hormones

RCTs have shown that oestrogen patches at high dose (100 μg twice weekly) relieve PMS. There is less evidence for oral oestrogen preparations. Progesterone has not been shown to be better than placebo in RCTs.

Treatment of severe cases

More potent drugs such as danazol and gonadotrophin-releasing hormone (GnRH) agonists are used when symptoms are severe and unresponsive to other treatments. These establish whether the PMS can be relieved by removing the cycle altogether. This can be a preliminary to the most drastic measure of all: hysterectomy and oophorectomy.

Nutritional supplements

Nutritional supplements are still under review, because evidence so far is inadequate. Such supplements are prescribed readily because they are acceptable and relatively safe.

Box 11.7: Treatment for PMS

- Psychosocial: relaxation training, cognitive behavioural therapy, changes in lifestyle
- Hormones: oestrogens, progesterone, gonadotrophin-releasing hormone (GnRH) agonists
- Treatment given in specialist clinics: bromocriptine, danazol, GnRH agonists
- Symptomatic treatments: diuretics, mefenamic acid, evening primrose oil
- Nutritional supplements: evening primrose oil, vitamin B$_6$, magnesium, zinc, *Vitex agnus castus* fruit, special diets
- Antidepressants: SSRIs (see also Box 11.8)

Box 11.8: SSRIs and PMS/PMDD

- Several RCTs and systematic reviews available
- RCTs have studied sufferers with PMDD
- SSRIs superior to placebo
- Non-SSRI antidepressants are not effective
- Intermittent treatment just as effective as continuous (every day) treatment
- A link between oestrogen and serotonin neurotransmitters is suggested

Mega-dose preparations should be avoided. There is evidence for the effectiveness of evening primrose oil for mastalgia and it may help other symptoms. It is likely that pyridoxine (vitamin B$_6$) helps in mild PMS. A recent RCT found that extract of *Vitex agnus castus* fruit (chasteberry) helps PMS symptoms.

SSRIs and antidepressants

For women with mainly psychological symptoms, antidepressants such as fluoxetine can help (see Box 11.8 for general information). Fluoxetine is an SSRI. It can be used continuously or intermittently on symptomatic days. Other drugs in this group include:

- Citalopram.
- Paroxetine.
- Sertraline.
- Clomipramine.

Other antidepressants are less effective.

Symptomatic treatment

Symptomatic relief can be offered:

- Mefenamic acid helps pain and fatigue.
- Diuretics, particularly spironolactone, relieve bloating.
- Oil of evening primrose helps breast tenderness.

Psychological and behavioural strategies

Psychological strategies can enhance the education and support that are offered to all women. Exercise and improving lifestyle can help. There is evidence to show that cognitive behavioural therapy can be effective in relieving symptoms. Symptoms can be exacerbated by vicious circles of negative thinking that tend to extend and exaggerate low mood, low self-esteem and lack of control that women experience when premenstrual (Fig. 11.4). Teaching a woman to challenge such negative thinking and reappraise herself and her life more realistically and more kindly can be a useful life skill. Cognitive behavioural therapy gives women new perspectives on themselves, their symptoms and others around them. This enhances their ability to identify solvable problems and succeed in managing their lives better. Such a treatment resource is scarce but it may be appropriate for badly affected women who are unable to tolerate, or are keen to avoid, pharmaceutical strategies.

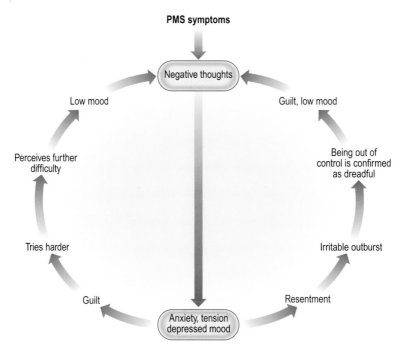

Figure 11.4
Vicious circles of negative thinking in PMS.

HORMONAL CONTRACEPTIVES

Some women cannot tolerate the oral contraceptive pill (OCP) because they feel low in mood while taking it. This is thought to be associated with excess progestogens; thus a preparation higher in oestrogen should improve this symptom. The OCP is not associated with any increase in depressive illness. Women who have had mood disturbance at the menopause are more likely to have a history of similar problems while on the OCP.

INFERTILITY

Most couples expect to be able to enjoy the pleasure and responsibilities of parenthood. They also look for a level of control over their fertility that was unimaginable a hundred years ago. Technological advances are now perceived as allowing a woman to choose when (or indeed whether) to have children. Thus the notion that a pregnancy can simply be 'switched on' can put a couple under pressure to conceive, often with added pressure from friends and family.

As many as one in six couples seek help with conception and this number is likely to grow as couples become less willing to 'wait and see', especially when they have chosen to defer childbearing until late in the woman's reproductive life. Moreover, couples expect more as technology offers more procedures to overcome childlessness. (See Ch. 9.)

Thus, unless the process of investigation and treatment is relatively brief and with a good outcome, the issue becomes a major stress in the lives of some couples. Some assisted reproduction centres recognize this and provide a counsellor to help the most vulnerable couples. This is a legal requirement where *in vitro* fertilization is offered. This acknowledges that fertility treatment can be something of a 'roller coaster' of hope and disappointment, with sexual activity being linked with failure and life plans revolving around treatment cycles.

Deciding to cease treatment is a demanding decision. Even achieving the much-wanted pregnancy can bring unsettling dysphoria when the baby turns out to be exhausting and motherhood overwhelming.

MISCARRIAGE

Many women cope with miscarriage well and go on to have further pregnancies and babies without undue disturbance. If the pregnancy is especially precious or rare, the impact of miscarriage is greater and can be a mourning for the lost possibility of a baby.

Moreover, stress accumulates as miscarriages become more frequent. Multiple miscarriages can seem like cruel pranks, raising hopes and then dashing them. In addition, the physical strain accumulates. This is worse the later the pregnancy ends, with the extra stress of labour and delivery and the fetus appearing more recognizably the baby that was so eagerly sought.

TERMINATION OF PREGNANCY

Pregnancy is not always planned, predicted or welcome. Termination of pregnancy is usually a hurried and pragmatic resolution to a threat to lifestyle, career, relationship or wellbeing. It is loaded with moral importance and is frequently conducted in secret and associated with guilt. Nevertheless, it is not associated with high levels of psychiatric morbidity afterwards and most people come to terms with their decision.

A minority, however, pursue such a course of action with great ambivalence. In such cases it can be helpful for the woman to talk things through with a counsellor who can support her as she makes her decision. Few women have long-term regrets, although these can emerge if there is difficulty conceiving in the future. Counselling can be important to help the woman come to terms with feelings of guilt, anger and remorse and to accept the positive and negative consequences of her choice.

MENOPAUSE

Definition

The menopause is the phase of life in a woman that begins 1 year after her last period and occurs when the ovaries cease to produce sufficient oestrogen to allow ovulation. On average, the menopause occurs at about 50 years of age, but for several years before the cessation of periods there is a decline in the production of reproductive hormones. This period of hormone decline is known as the climacteric and is associated with the development of menopausal symptoms (see Ch. 10) and an increase in psychological symptoms.

Symptoms and their management

About 20% of women will complain of symptoms that they associate with the menopause. Symptoms that are clearly linked to hormone decline are:

• Sweats.
• Flushes.
• Vaginal dryness.

These are the symptoms that respond most consistently to hormone replacement therapy (HRT), which is usually in the form of oestrogen pills, patches or gel. Progesterone has also been found to have some effect on these symptoms.

Side-effects of oestrogen include:

• Nausea.
• Bloating.
• Headaches.

In the long term, oestrogen protects against osteoporosis but is associated with a small excess of thromboembolic events and a small increased risk of breast cancer. For women who have a uterus, progestogens must be given for 7–10 days each month as well because oestrogen can stimulate endometrial hyperplasia. Progestogens can cause psychological symptoms similar to those of PMS.

Other symptoms common at this time include:

• Depressed mood.
• Insomnia.
• Fatigue.

- Anxiety.
- Joint pain.
- Memory problems.
- Difficulty in concentration.

These symptoms are less readily explained by hormonal decline, but may be linked to the secondary effect of insomnia and fatigue due to night sweats, relationship difficulties secondary to dyspareunia or anxiety due to embarrassing flushing.

Psychological aspects

Psychosocial pressures appear to be more significant than hormonal changes in women with these other symptoms, and in many cases it is clear that these women have been under considerable pressure emotionally and physically for years (see Box 11.9) but that as they get older they simply have less resilience to cope. They often come to look for 'a boost' to flagging energy.

Some women feel that the menopause heralds old age and marks the end of their usefulness, their youth and desirability. This may be a result of media coverage that suggests that HRT is the 'elixir of youth'. Oestrogen does improve mood and wellbeing but it does not relieve depressive illness. There will be women who present with menopausal symptoms whose main problem is depressive illness. Depressive illness is not actually more common at the menopause, but it occurs in at least 10% of women at this time and such women may present more readily because they also have menopausal symptoms. Both issues need attention. Affective disorder should always be considered if psychological symptoms are prominent or if HRT is ineffective (Box 11.10). Women with a psychiatric history should be actively treated for their mental disorder but they should not be forgotten for HRT at the menopause.

Box 11.9: Menopause and mood disturbances

Menopause clinic attenders with psychological symptoms have higher rates of past history of:

- Affective disorder
- Oral contraceptive pill dysphoria
- PMS
- Postnatal depression

Box 11.10: Menopause and mood disorder

- No evidence of involutional melancholia
- No excess of depressive disorder
- Higher rate of minor psychological disturbance at age 44–54 years
- Life stresses often more significant than onset of menopausal symptoms
- A subset of women may have menopausal depression triggered by oestrogen decline

CHRONIC PELVIC PAIN

Women frequently experience pelvic pain associated with gynaecological disorders (see Chs 3 and 5). Most cases resolve or can be explained and managed, but a few women have pain that is chronic and difficult to treat. These women have often been evaluated by a gastroenterologist as well as by a gynaecologist. Curiously the degree of endometriosis found in such women is not in proportion to the severity of pain.

Once the main treatment strategies have been tried but the problem continues, it can be frustrating for both patient and doctor. In primary care, it is important to maintain a positive stance, but to resist the temptation (or pressure from the patient) to continue to investigate or try unorthodox treatments, as this tends to foster the hope that someday a 'cure' will be found. It is better to encourage coping, improving general lifestyle and making the most of support and resources already available.

SEXUAL PROBLEMS

Sexual problems may be presented as primary problems but are often revealed in the course of investigating other complaints, usually gynaecological or psychological.

Dyspareunia is a painful and upsetting condition that disturbs a woman's most intimate relationship. Gynaecological disorders such as endometriosis, dermatological disease, sexually transmitted disease and psychological disorder can underlie this problem.

Past sexual abuse can result in vaginismus that causes pain on penetration or may preclude full sexual intercourse altogether. This problem can also follow vaginal examination in medical settings and it is important to be aware that procedures that seem ordinary to a health professional can be potentially traumatic to a patient. This includes procedures associated with childbirth.

Once physical disorders have been ruled out, psychological treatment can prove very effective, usually following behavioural or cognitive behavioural strategies.

Loss of libido

Loss of libido is the other common sexual problem associated with gynaecology. This is mostly associated with relationship difficulties rather than medical disorder. If either partner has psychiatric illness, libido can decline, and some psychotropic drugs cause sexual dysfunction. Hormonal changes can change libido. The oral contraceptive pill can blunt libido.

The menopause can be associated with loss of interest, although it is seldom the only factor. The most striking association is in surgically menopausal women. These women frequently report postoperative loss of libido which may improve with androgen supplements in the form of testosterone implants. These are most often considered for women post hysterectomy and post oophorectomy when there is a sudden removal of natural testosterone production by the ovaries (Box 11.11).

Box 11.11: Testosterone (androgen) treatment for women

- Can improve sexual interest of women, especially at the climacteric
- Frequency of sexual activity depends on relationship with partner, not hormones alone
- Testosterone is usually given as an implant with oestrogen
- It is most effective post oophorectomy

FUTURE DIRECTIONS   Gynaecological events and experiences evoke deep emotions, but underlying links between gynaecological regulation (especially reproductive hormones) and mood regulation are becoming stronger. We believe that it will become clearer in the next few years how oestrogen variations relate to mood and the psycho-pharmacology underpinning this relationship. It will undoubtedly be complex and go beyond the notion that oestrogen is generally an antidepressant.

The complexity of the mechanisms of psychosis will also implicate the role of oestrogens, but this may be further off as, the more we learn, the more subtle the system seems to be.

With the emphasis on choice for patients and the huge amount of information available on the internet, gynaecologists will become more confident and more knowledgeable about psychiatric treatments relevant to their patients. More research and greater experience will clarify the role of herbs and nutritional supplements such as *Agnus castus* fruit, St John's wort and pyridoxine.

Selected References and Further Reading

American Psychiatric Association. Diagnostic and statistical manual of mental disorders. 4th edn. Washington, DC: APA; 1994.

Blake F, Gath D, Salkovskis P, et al. Cognitive therapy for the premenstrual syndrome: a controlled trial. J Psychosom Res 1998; 45:307–318.

Connelly M. Premenstrual syndrome: an update on definitions, diagnosis and management. Adv Psychiatr Treat 2001; 7:469–477.

Dimmock PW, Wyatt KM, Jones PW, et al. Efficacy of selective serotonin reuptake inhibitors in premenstrual syndrome: a systematic review. Lancet 2000; 136:1131–1136.

Pearce J, Hawton K, Blake F. Psychological and sexual symptoms associated with the menopause and the effects of hormone replacement therapy. Br J Psychiatry 1995; 67:163–173.

Pearlstein T, Rosen K, Stone AB. Mood disorders and menopause. Endocrinol Metab Clin North Am 1997; 26:279–294.

Schellenberg GR. Treatment of the premenstrual syndrome with agnus castus fruit extract: a prospective, randomised, placebo controlled study. BMJ 2001; 322:134–138.

Watson NR, Studd JWW, Savvas M, et al. Treatment of severe premenstrual syndrome with oestradiol patches and cyclical norethisterone. Lancet 1989; ii:730–732.

Wyatt KM, Dimmock PW, Jones PW, et al. Progesterone therapy: a systematic review of its efficacy in the premenstrual syndrome. Neuropsychopharmacology 2000; 23:S2.

Index